PREFACE

Effective communication is an essential skill for success in any sphere of activity, from leadership responsibilities, teamwork, interviews, presentations, and inter-personal relations. This is a skill that needs to be taught in a systematic manner so that students imbibe the fundamentals of both creating and receiving communication.

In the following chapters, we will discuss briefly the theories of communication, the behaviour of the audience of mass media, the development of radio, television and film. The deep roots of traditional folk media plays an important role in communication. Then the focus comes to the news agencies and feature agencies. How the English Press became important in the freedom struggle and talking about the role of journalists and journalism.

This GPH book ***'Introduction to Journalism and Mass Communication (JMC-01)'*** clears these concepts for better understanding of students. The book is written especially in question & answer format to provide students the instant gratification of a correct answer. In this book, we have tried to solve all possible questions from the exams' point of view. Solutions of previous years' question papers have also been included to help students to understand the unique examination structure.

We hope that this book would not be only a favourite study material for the students but also can be a nice resource for teaching. An attempt has been carefully made to present this book more useful and meet the requirements and challenges of the course prescribed by Indian Universities. We wish you a successful and rewarding career ahead. Feedback in this regard is solicited.

– GPH Panel of Experts

Acknowledgements

Our compliments go to the **GullyBaba Publishing House Pvt. Ltd.,** and its meticulous team who have been enthusiastically working towards the perfection of the book.

Their teamwork, initiative and research have been very encouraging. Had it not been for their unflagging support, this work wouldn't have been possible. The creative freedom provided by them along with their aim of presenting the best to the reader has been a major source of inspiration in this work. Hope that this book would be successful.

– GPH Panel of Experts

Publisher's Note

The present book JMC-01 is targeted for examination purpose as well as enrichment. With the advent of technology and the Internet, there has been no dearth of information available to all; however, finding the relevant and qualitative information, which is focussed, is an uphill task.

We at **GullyBaba Publishing House Pvt. Ltd.,** have taken this step to provide quality material which can accentuate in-depth knowledge about the subject. GPH books are a pioneer in the effort of providing unique and quality material to its readers. With our books, you are sure to attain success by making use of this powerful study material. Provided book is just a reference book based on the syllabus of particular University/Board. For a profound information, see the textbooks recommended by the University/Board.

Our site **gullybaba.com** is a vital resource for your examination. The publisher wishes to acknowledge the significant contribution of the Team Members and our experts in bringing out this publication and highly thankful to Almighty God, without His blessings, this endeavor wouldn't have been successful.

– Publisher

INTRODUCTION TO JOURNALISM And MASS COMMUNICATION

JMC-01

For

Post Graduate Diploma in Journalism and Mass Communication (PGJMC)

Useful For

IGNOU, Rai Technology University, KSOU (Karnataka), NIILM University, Bihar University (Muzaffarpur), Nalanda University, Jamia Millia Islamia, Vardhman Mahaveer Open University (Kota), Uttarakhand Open University, Kurukshetra University, Himachal Pradesh University, Seva Sadan's College of Education (Maharashtra), Lalit Narayan Mithila University, Andhra University, Pt. Sunderlal Sharma (Open) University (Bilaspur), Annamalai University, Bangalore University, Bharathiar University, Bharathidasan University, Centre for distance and open learning, Kakatiya University (Andhra Pradesh), KOU (Rajasthan), MPBOU (MP), MDU (Haryana), Punjab University, Tamilnadu Open University, Sri Padmavati Mahila Visvavidyalayam (Andhra Pradesh), Sri Venkateswara University (Andhra Pradesh), UCSDE (Kerala), University of Jammu, YCMOU, Rajasthan University, UPRTOU, Kalyani University, Banaras Hindu University (BHU) and all other Indian Universities.

GULLYBABA PUBLISHING HOUSE PVT. LTD.

ISO 9001 & ISO 14001 CERTIFIED CO.

Published by:
GullyBaba Publishing House Pvt. Ltd.

Regd. Office:
2525/193, 1st Floor, Onkar Nagar-A,
Delhi-110035
(From Kanhaiya Nagar Metro Station Towards Old Bus Stand)
Ph. 011-27387998, 27384836, 27385249
+919350849407

Branch Office:
1A/2A, 20, Hari Sadan, Tri Nagar,
Ansari Road, Daryaganj,
New Delhi-110002
Ph. 011-45794768

New Edition

Author: GullyBaba.Com Panel
ISBN: 978-93-81970-78-2

Disclaimer: Although the author and publisher have made every effort to ensure that the information in this book is correct, the author and publisher do not assume and hereby disclaim any liability to any party for any loss, damage, or disruption caused by errors or omissions, whether such errors or omissions result from negligence, accident, or any other cause.
If you find any kind of error, please let us know and get reward and or the new book free of cost.
The book is based on IGNOU syllabus. This is only a sample. The book/author/publisher does not impose any guarantee or claim for full marks or to be passed in exam. You are advised only to understand the contents with the help of this book and answer in your words.
All disputes with respect to this publication shall be subject to the jurisdiction of the Courts, Tribunals and Forums of New Delhi, India only.

Topics Covered

Block-1 Introduction To Communications

Unit-1 Communication
Unit-2 Models of Communication
Unit-3 Theories of Mass Communication
Unit-4 Communications Research
Unit-5 Impact of Mass Media

Block-2 Elements in Mass Media

Unit-1 Characteristics of Print Media
Unit-2 Characteristics of Radio, Television and Film
Unit-3 Characteristics of Mass Media Audiences
Unit-4 Characteristics of Messages

Block-3 Origin and Development of Mass Media in India

Unit-1 The Indian Press
Unit-2 Radio, Television and Cinema
Unit-3 Traditional Folk Media
Unit-4 New Communication Technologies

Block-4 Ownership Patterns, Organisational Structures and Management of Mass Media in India

Unit-1 The Press
Unit-2 News and Feature Agencies
Unit-3 Government Media Organisations
Unit-4 Film Industry
Unit-5 Educational Media

Block-5 Journalism

Unit-1 The Role of the English Press in India
Unit-2 The Role of the Regional Language Journalism
Unit-3 Magazines and Periodicals
Unit-4 Principles and Ethics of Journalism
Unit-5 Professional Organisations and Statutory Bodies

CONTENTS

QUESTION PAPERS

1 INTRODUCTION TO COMMUNICATIONS

INTRODUCTION

Communication regulates and shapes all human behaviour. It is universal to all human beings and is central to our lives. Therefore, it is important to have a clear understanding, of the concepts of communication. One should know what a communication model is, how different models have developed and what are the characteristics of some well-known models. Describing some important theories of mass communication which will enable us to understand how mass communication operates in society. The focus will be the areas and methods of communications research. And also, the need and importance of communication research and the various research methods.

Q1. Define communication.

Ans. There are numerous definitions of communication, and there is yet no agreement on any single definition. Some of the more functional definitions of communication describe it as "the transfer or conveying of meaning", "transmission of stimuli", "one mind affecting another"; "one system influences another", "the mechanism through which human relations exist and develop", or "sharing of experience on the basis of commonness".

Communication is more than mere transferring or transmission of ideas or thoughts. It is not a static act as some of the earlier definitions suggest but it is a dynamic process of action and interaction towards a desired goal, as suggested by later, definitions. Communication is, therefore, a process of sharing or exchange of ideas, information, knowledge, attitude or feeling among two or more persons through certain signs and symbols.

The root of the word "communication" in Latin is communicare, which means to share, or to make common. Weekley E. (1967). An etymological dictionary of modern English. New York, NY: Dover Publications. Communication is defined as the process of understanding and sharing meaning. Pearson, J., & Nelson, An introduction to human communication: Understanding and sharing. Boston, MA: McGraw-Hill.

The first key word in this definition is process. A process is a dynamic activity that is hard to describe because it changes. Pearson J. & Nelson, P. (2000). An introduction to human communication: Understanding and sharing. Boston, MA: McGraw-Hill. Imagine you are alone in your kitchen thinking. Someone you know (say, your mother) enters the kitchen and you talk briefly. What has changed? Now, imagine that your mother is joined by someone else, someone you haven't met before—and this stranger listens intently as you speak, almost as if you were giving a speech. What has changed? Your perspective might change, and you might watch your words more closely. The feedback or response from your mother and the stranger (who are, in essence, your audience) may cause you to reevaluate what you are saying. When we interact, all these factors—and many more—influence the process of communication.

The second key word is understanding: "To understand is to perceive, to interpret, and to relate our perception and interpretation to what we already know. McLean, S. (2003). The basics of speech communication. Boston, MA: Allyn & Bacon. If a friend tells us a story about falling off a bike, Suppose friend points out the window and we see a motorcycle lying on the ground. Understanding the words and the concepts or objects they refer to is an important part of the communication process.

Next comes the word sharing. Sharing means doing something together with one or more people. we may share a joint activity, as when we share in compiling a report; or we may benefit jointly from a resource, as when we and several coworkers share a pizza. In communication, sharing occurs when our convey thoughts, feelings, ideas, or insights to others. We can also share with yourself (a process called intrapersonal communication) when we bring ideas to consciousness, ponder how you feel about something, or figure out the solution to a problem and have a classic "Aha!" moment when something becomes clear.

Finally, meaning is what we share through communication. The word "bike" represents both a bicycle and a short name for a motorcycle. By looking at the context the word is used in and by asking questions, we can discover the shared meaning of the word and understand the message.

Q2. Discuss the different functions of communication.

Or

"Communication regulates and shapes all human behaviour." Discuss various functions of communication in the light of above statement. [June-2019, Q.No.-1]

Ans. Communication functions refer to how people use language for different purposes also refers to how language is affected by different time, place, and situation used to control the behaviour of people used to regulate the nature and amount of activities people engage in. Communication is vital for human existence, and for the progress of humanity. No person, group or society can exist without interaction with others. Think for a moment what would happen to us if we did not talk with anyone at home; didn't listen to lectures at school or college, didn't speak to friends and co-workers, or didn't play games or watch TV or films? And what would life be like in the absence of news, views, facts, figures or information? Obviously, we would be miserable and would miss out on many opportunities and challenges offering us security and success in our personal and professional life. Being at the heart of all social action and interaction, communication functions as a relating tool that creates understanding, facilitates work, and, strengthens collective living among people.

Essentially, the primary function of communication is to inform, instruct/educate, entertain and influence/persuade people to make them function smoothly and effectively. Besides, communication has a secondary function to perform as well; through debates and discussion, cultural promotion and integration, it fosters consensus, creativity, and understanding among people, groups, and societies so that they live in peace and harmony. Each of these functions has been discussed below:

- **Information**: Suppose we were not informed about the Ayodhya incident, bomb blasts in Bombay and Calcutta, and preventive measures which could be adopted to avoid AIDS disease. The quality of our life would be poorer without these bits of information. In the Western countries, information is now regarded as power. The more informed we are, the more powerful we become. Those who have access to information can take advantage of it in their own interest. Communication provides us enormous information about the environment in which we live. Information such as news of war, danger, crisis, famine, etc. is important for that helps us in taking appropriate steps to safeguard our interests.
- **Instruction:** One of the major functions of communication is to instruct, educate, and socialise the members of the society. All these functions start early in life, at home or in school, and continue till one completes the full cycle of life. Communication provides a fund of knowledge, expertise, and skills that enable people to operate as effective members of society. It also creates awareness, so that they actively participate in public life.
- **Entertainment:** Human beings must be entertained to break the monotony of routine and divert their attention from the troubles and tensions of daily life. The diversion should not be taken as a negative element. Such diversion has a positive role in our life, it revitalises our personality and even educates us. There are so many comedies that entertain and at the same time comment on life. We cannot but learn a lot about life from these comedies. Communication provides boundless entertainment

to people through pictures, films, music, drama, dance, art, literature, comedy, sports, games, etc.

- **Persuasion:** One of the most important functions of communication is to persuade the other party. Because persuasion helps in reaching decision or consensus on public policy so that it is possible to control and govern. But it is possible that one may resort to persuasion with a bad motive. The receiver must be careful about the source of such persuasion.
- **Debate and Discussion:** It is through debate and discussion in media that the public can clarify different viewpoints on issues of public interest and arrive at a general agreement on matters that concern all. It is important for them to find out the reasons for such debates and discussions.
- **Cultural Promotion:** Communication provides opportunity for culture to be preserved and promoted. It stimulates individuals to pursue and fulfil their creative urges. But, then, one must be critical and ask questions: whose culture is being promoted, anyway? Ultimately, what motives do the senders of such cultural programmes have?
- **Integration:** Communication is a great integrating tool. Through a fund of knowledge or information, individuals, groups or cultures come to know one another, understand and appreciate other's ways of life and thereby develop tolerance towards one another. It can also be the greatest disintegrating tool. The book you can believe most–GPH book.

Q3. Critically Examine the Process and elements of Communication.

Ans. Communication is the act of conveying meanings from one entity or group to another through the use of mutually understood signs, symbols, and semiotic rules. Communication is a dynamic process involving a series of actions and reactions with a view to achieving a goal. Suppose we, as a sender or communicator, formulate (encode) an idea or message as best as we can, and pass on the message to our friend, who to the best of his ability receives or acts on the message (decodes). Heres ponds by formulating his own message and communicates us (feedback). If we think our message is understood or well received by our friend, then we go ahead with the next idea that we have in mind and the conversation goes on and on. Communication is, therefore, a two way process, that is, the ability to receive is as important as the ability to send. For successful communication, feedback is crucial because it tells how our messages are being interpreted, It can make or break the communication process. A complete act of communication is shown in figure:

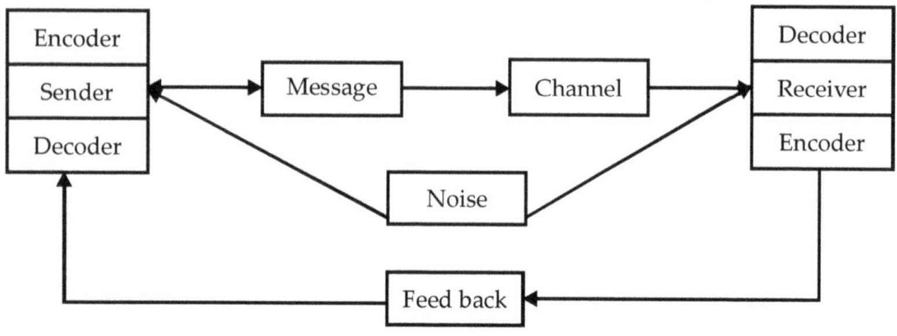

Fig. 1.1: A Complete Act of Communication

Here the communicator is the encoder, the message is symbol (verbal or non-verbal), the channel is one of the transmission medium, the receiver is the decoder, feedback is the response to the message, and noise is any interruption that breaks down the communication. These, in fact, are the essential elements or ingredients which facilitate the communication process. It is essential to examine what role each element plays in the entire communication process and how all of them are important in making communication effective.

Communicator (sender or encoder) is the one who initiates the communication process. He may be an editor, a reporter, a film-maker, a teacher, a writer, a speaker, a leader or anybody who takes the initiative to start a dialogue. Before one speaks or writes, the message is conceptualised first and then encoded. An effective communication depends on the communication skill, knowledge level, and attitude of the communicator and how he desires to affect his receiver. An ability to think, to organise thoughts quickly, and express himself effectively are some of the attributes of a good communicator.

Encoding is the formulation of messages in the communicator's mind, that is, the communicator not only translates his purpose (ideas, thoughts or information) into a message but also decides on the medium to communicate his planned message. He must choose the media that the receiver can comprehend well. For instance, an illiterate receiver will fail to understand a written message, but can understand it well if told orally.

A message is what a communicator actually produces for transmission using spoken or written words, photographs, paintings; films, posters, etc. A great deal of skill and effort is required to formulate a message, the meaning of which should be understandable to the receiver. Actually the purpose of communication is to influence the receiver and get favourable responses so that appropriate decisions can be taken. The success of communication, therefore, depends on what we say and how we say it. A message can enhance or distort effective communication. For instance, in an interview our intention is to impress interviewer; but if we give answers whose meaning is not clear, the interviewer may perceive that we are incompetent for the job.

A channel is the vehicle through which a message is carried from the communicator to the receiver. The channels of communication are many-written, spoken, verbal, non-verbal, mass media like TV, radio, newspapers, books, etc. Choosing the appropriate channel, one must suitable for the message as well as the receiver, is a complicated task. Success and failure of communication depends on the selection of the right channel. For example, if we have prepared a campaign on 'National Integration', what media would we choose to reach the intended audience? And even after selecting the media. We have to decide if it is feasible cost wise; taking into account the number of people and the kind of people who will be exposed to our message, and certain other factors. Actually our intention or desire would be to reach out to the maximum number of people but for efficient communication our attempt should be to minimise time and cost in the total information exchange effort.

The receiver, at the other end of the communication, is the recipient of the message and must possess the same orientation as the communicator. If the receiver does not have the ability to listen, to read, to think, he will not be able to receive and decode the messages in the manner the communicator wants him to. For effective communication, the receiver is the most important link in the communication process. Decoding is the interpretation of the message by the receiver. Actually, the receiver looks for the meaning in the message which is common to both the receiver and the communicator.

Feedback is the response or acknowledgement of receiver to the communicator's message. The exchange is possible only if the receiver responds. Even through fluttering eyelids, raising an eyebrow, making a face, organising a point and asking for explanation, the message is shaped and reshaped by the communicator and the receiver until the meaning becomes clear. In this way both participants in communication interact and constantly exchange roles. In face-to-face communication the receiver responds naturally, directly and immediately. This provides the communicator an opportunity to improve and make his communication effective.

Feedback, thus, provides an opportunity to evaluate what is right or wrong about a, particular communication. It helps to regulate the conversation among two or more individuals and also stimulates and reinforces an idea that is desired to be communicated.

Noise is an interruption that can creep in at any point of the communication process and make it ineffective. Environment is one major cause that interferes with message reception: like noises from the roadside constant chattering of individuals outside the communication act, blaring loudspeaker, faulty transmission, etc. Noise can occur in other forms, also; poor handwriting, heavy accent or soft speech, communication in a poorly lit room, etc. In fact, theses are barriers to effective communication.

Q4. Discuss the different kinds of communication.

Ans. Communication skills are vital to a healthy, efficient workplace. Often categorised as a "soft skill" or interpersonal skill, communication is the act of sharing information from one person to another person or group of people. There are many different ways to communicate, each of which play an important role in sharing information.

Human beings are engaged in a variety of communication acts. These are:

- Intrapersonal Communication;
- Interpersonal Communication
- Group Communication; and
- Mass Communication.

Although each type appears to have distinctive features, they are all much alike in the sense that one enters into a meaningful relationship with one or more persons by means of signs and symbols.

The following discussion on types of communication will provide us with the understanding of different communication situations in which people interact with each other or disseminate information.

- **Intrapersonal Communication:** It refers to communication that transpires inside a person; and this happens all the time. It is like talking to oneself, listening to oneself and relating one to oneself. Intrapersonal or auto-communication, therefore, is important in contemplating, conceptualising and formulating our thoughts or ideas before we actually indulge in overt communication. Just think about our daily activities and involvement with others in the form of a dialogue, etc.
- **Interpersonal Communication:** This is the universal form of communication that takes place between two individuals. Since it is person-to-person contact, it includes everyday exchanges that may be formal or informal and can take place anywhere by means of words, sounds, facial expression, gestures and postures.

  In interpersonal communication, there is face-to-face interaction between two persons, that is, both are sending and receiving messages. This is an ideal and effective communication situation because we can get immediate feedback. We can clarify and emphasise many points through your expressions, gestures and voice. In interpersonal communication, therefore, it is possible to influence the other person and persuade him or her to accept your point of view. Since there is proximity between sender and receiver, interpersonal communication has emotional appeal too; it can motivate, encourage, and coordinate work more effectively than any other form of communication. Also, in a crisis, through interpersonal channel, flow of information is tremendous, e.g. news of violence, famine or disaster.
- **Group Communication:** Group communication is an extension of interpersonal communication where more than two individuals are involved in exchange of ideas, skills, and interests. Groups provide an opportunity for people to come together to discuss and exchange views of common interest. There could be many different groups for as many different

reasons. For instance, casually formed groups with friends over a drink, coffee break, games, dances or religious gatherings have a different purpose than that of groups attending a meeting or seminar to help fight AIDS or interacting with committee members to draft a proposal. Communication in a group, small or big, serves many goals including collective decision-making, self-expression, increasing one's effect, elevating one's status, and relaxation.

- **Mass Communication:** Mass communication is the process of imparting and exchanging information through mass media to large segments of the population. It is usually understood for relating to various forms of media, as these technologies are used for the dissemination of information, of which journalism and advertising are part.

  Mass communication is unique and different from interpersonal communication as is evident from the following definition. Any mechanical device that multiplies messages and takes it to a large number of people simultaneously is called mass communication. The media through which messages are being transmitted include radio, TV, newspapers, magazines, films, records, tape recorders, video cassette recorders, etc., and require large organisations and electronic devices to put across the messages. Looking at the definition, it is clear that mass communication is a special kind of communication in which the nature of the audience and the feedback is different from that of interpersonal communication.

These are some of the components that may elaborate the understanding and nature of mass communication:

- **Audience:** Whosoever is the recipient of mass media content constitutes its audience. For instance, individuals reading newspapers, watching a film in a theatre, listening to radio or watching television, are situations where audience is large, heterogeneous, anonymous in character and physically separated from the communicator both in terms of space and time. A large audience means that the receivers are mass of people not assembled at a single place. It may come in different sizes depending upon the media through which the message is sent. For TV network programmes, for example, there could be millions of viewers, but only a few thousand readers for a book or a journal. By anonymous, we mean that the receivers of the messages tend to be strangers to one another and to the source of those messages. So with respect to the communicator, the message is addressed "to whom it may concern".

- **Feedback:** As compared to intrepersonal communication, feedback in mass media is slow and weak. It is not instantaneous or direct as in face to face exchange and is invariably delayed. Feedback in mass media is rather a cumulative response which the source gets after a considerable gap in time. it is often expressed in quantitative terms: like circulation figures of newspapers and magazines, the popularity of a movie at box office, success of a book on the basis of its sales, or the findings of a public opinion polls and on the basis of other feedback devices which are used to determine what is acceptable or unacceptable to different audiences.

Q5. Write a note on Mass media.

Ans. Mass media means technology that is intended to reach a mass audience. It is the primary means of communication used to reach the vast majority of the general public. The most common platforms for mass media are newspapers, magazines, radio, television, and the Internet.

Some audiences want entertainment, sports news, films, plays, serials, dance, music, etc. Others may have greater interest in news and views. Yet others seek guidance to solve their socio-economic problems. Each medium is powerful in its own right in serving people- and each has gone through several 'stages of development due to pressure and competition 'from newer communication technologies.

- **Print Media** which include newspapers, magazines, books' and other printed matter, have served the literate society for long. Their growth, however, was slow in the beginning but as the demand for education and information increased, they evolved quickly and flourished greatly. The twentieth century has seen the rapid growth of the newspaper industry and, to withstand the challenges posed by newer electronic communication, newspapers have adopted the latest technology, like computerisation, to speed up the production process and improve their quality. Newspapers have added coloured Sunday and Saturday supplements to sustain the interest of the readers. Coloured glossy magazines, which appeal to specific segments of the society, have mushroomed.

Traditionally, newspapers have a local emphasis which serves the interests of a specific community with news, comments, features, photographs and advertising. The majority of them are local in nature but there are some big metropolitan dailies, national in character, catering to the interests of audiences in many parts of the country. Some big newspapers have multiple editions coming out from several cities. Among such newspapers are 'The Hindustan Times', 'Navbharat Times', 'The Times of India', 'Indian Express' and 'The Statesman'.

- **Electronic Media** are radio, television, satellite TV, Cable TV, cinema, etc. which are essentially entertainment media. They are different from print media in many ways. They provide instantaneous communication and their impact is greater. They need electricity for speedy delivery of messages across distances and to the masses that are geographically, culturally, intellectually, and emotionally separated from one another. Electronic media are quicker than print media the latter takes more time for mass production and delivery to a widely dispersed population.
- **The Radio:** Out nation's radio audience has grown manifold since its inception in the 1920s. The network has expanded a great deal and it offers a daily service for many hours transmitting news, comments, songs, music, comedies, thrillers, sports, besides special programmes for children, youth, and farmers. One of the best advantages that radio has over other media is that it can serve and entertain an audience which is otherwise occupied. For instance, people can listen to it while working at home, in the fields and factories and while travelling.

  However, the radio medium has suffered a setback in the recent times under the dynamic impact of TV; it has lost a lot of its listening audience, especially urban population which can afford TV and video for entertainment. But during a crisis it is the radio that people turn to for news because it can report with speed. TV takes time to reach the spot of occurrence with its heavy equipment and camera crew.

And, at times it may miss out prized information during war, violence, or accidents. In such times radio has a clear advantage over TV.

- **Recording industries** too are thriving by providing popular music on tapes, cassettes, audio-discs, etc. Cassettes are also being used extensively in education.
- **Television,** unlike other forms of mass media, has now become one of the most powerful media of mass communication. With a modest beginning in the 1930s, it has grown into a massive network of mass information and mass entertainment in the world today. The attraction of the 'visionless' of the medium, the capacity to beam images of actual events, people and places, is so great that people remain glued to the TV set for hours.

  Millions watched the live coverage of the war in the Persian Gulf and other important happenings in recent times. This was possible due to the newer development in network technologies Satellite-Cable television. Through the many satellites in space which are linked via cable to the TV at home, TV now has assumed a significant role in providing the 'latest' and the 'best' happenings in the world. This technological innovation has made unprecedented inroads into the audiences that were earlier served in the spirit of public service broadcasting by Doordarshan in India. The grip of foreign networks grip over millions in metropolitan cities and smaller towns is getting tighter as they offer many channels transmitting different programmes simultaneously round the clock. Audiences now have multiple choices ranging from news and information to entertainment of wide variety. Besides being exposed to actual events, audiences of TV enjoy packages full of fiction, drama, culture, sex, crime, violence, to mention just a few.

'Invasion' from the sky has thus shattered Doordarshan's monopoly. Unless Doordarshan meets the challenges posed by the media giants like CNN, BBC and others by producing indigenous programmes of competitive quality, its future seems bleak.

- **Films** are considered a major mass medium because of their mass appeal and influence on society. India is the largest producer of feature films in the world. It is these 'masala' films which are popular among the masses. These films set trends in styles and tastes, dominate the popular radio and television entertainment programmes, provide spicy reading material not only for film magazines, which are published in large numbers and are widely read, but also for most of the other popular magazines. Commercial cinema is all glamour and fantasy. The usual ingredients are sex, songs, dances, crime, fights, melodrama, and comedy, all bordering on unreality. The idea is to prepare a cocktail of popular entertainment to ensure box office success.

Q6. Critically examine the extent of the reach of mass media in India, and the influence mass communication has on people in particular, and society in general.

Ans. Mass media have become a major feature of our daily life that we cannot do without the telephone, telex, film, radio, television, newspapers, etc. Outside home and office, innumerable forms of mass media confront us -billboards, wall writing, writings on all kinds of vehicles, pamphlets, leaflets, brochures, booklets, etc. People now have more access to mass media whose reach is getting wider and wider due to technological advancement. The extent of expansion of mass media can be gauged by the increase over the past one decade, in circulation of newspapers, number of radio and television receivers, satellites and able television operators.

- **Communication:** The mass media are now not limited to urban population but have made in roads into 'small towns and villages. Their expansion is evident practically in all the countries of the world. The events that take place in the United States, Europe, Russia or the Middle East, come immediately into our living rooms. In fact,' the information and thereby have become more informed and educated, and are better entertained and less apprehensive about each other's way of life that they were a few decades ago.

However, despite the phenomenal growth of newspapers, TV, satellite and cable TV, radio network and films, their reach is largely limited to urban areas in India. The vast rural population in the country still doesn't have access to mass media because of various factors like low purchasing power, high illiteracy rates, non-availability of electricity and channels.

- **The print media**, though a powerful means of dissemination of news, comments and knowledge, cater only to audiences that are literate. There are about 20,000newspapers and other printed matter produced and consumed in major metropolitan and big cities in the country but barely a small fraction of it reaches the rural masses. The circulation is still low, i.e. about 2 copies per 100 persons, but the readership is much higher as each copy is read by. 5-10 persons, especially in rural areas. Even the illiterate masses have indirect access to this medium through educated newspaper readers.
- **The television** network has increased tremendously in the last one decade covering 78 per cent of the population. But TV receiving sets are mostly available in urban homes and TV is out of reach of the majority of the rural masses. Only the rich in a village have access to it. More recently satellite and cable television has stormed the urban Indian homes. It has broken nation-state boundaries and opened the sky for television. There are about 25,000 cable operators providing services all over the country. But these are costly ventures and cater to the needs and aspirations of upper and middle classes. And even if audiences in small towns and villages have access to these sophisticated media, the messages are lost on them because they are not area specific and lack local cultural flavour and relevance, which is so essential for audiences to identify with and understand.
- **Radio** is one of the significant media of mass communication. Government owned All India Radio (AIR) has now the largest broadcasting network in the world. It covers 80 per cent of the

area and 90 per cent of the country's population, but broadcast receiving facilities are limited. The total number of radio transistor sets in the country is estimated around 30 million which works out to 4.4 sets for 100persons. Besides, there is a marked imbalance between the availability of radio sets in rural and urban areas. It is estimated that over 80 per cent of radio sets are in the hands of people living in urban areas who constitute only about 20 per cent of the country's population. Inspite of the imbalance, radio is the only medium which is said to be truly a mass medium in India because it is a low cost mobile means of communication. The portable radio, in fact, is the poor man's companion and, hence has extended its reach widely.

- **Film** has become a major medium of popular entertainment. About 800 films are produced in India annually. Many of these are in Hindi and are very popular with the masses. A large number of films are produced regionally also, particularly in the south, and their reach is wide. This may be so because regional films can better present the social reality and cultural ethos of the people in a defined region in the local language. As in the case of other media, film exhibition facilities in the country are limited, too. Most of the cinema houses are in the metropolitan cities and large towns. According to an estimate, there are about 8 seats for a population of one thousand. Comparatively, southern states have more cinema houses and touring talkies than those in northern India.

Q7. Critically examine the extent and nature of impact of mass media on People and society.

Ans. Whether it is written, televised, or spoken, mass media reaches a large audience. The influence of mass media has an effect on many aspects of human life, which can include voting a certain way, individual views and beliefs, or skewing a person's knowledge of a specific topic due to being provided false information.

There is increasing anxiety about the adverse effect of mass communication on society in general and individuals in particular. There are obvious ferns. Are the consumers of mass media being manipulated or brainwashed? Do the violence, crime or sex in media affect young

Introduction to Communications minds? Are the foreign programmes a threat to cultural and national identity? And so on. Answers to these questions are not easy to come by as mass media do not operate in the society in isolation. However, some observations can be made on the positive and negative impact of mass communication on people.

By and large, mass communication messages are positive, i.e. pro-communal harmony, pro-environmental pro-national, anti-drugs, anti-AIDS, anti-war, antiterrorism, anti-social evils and so on. In fact, mass communication has helped in promoting national integration and knowledge of our cultural heritage and creating awareness among people about the socio-economic and political development of the country. The Press, for instance, has played a significant role in shaping public opinion against colonial rule and later in the development of independent modern India. Broadcasting, under the government control, has been used as an instrument of education, development, and social change. Even Bombay. 'masala films', which are often accused of creating unhealthy social values, attitudes, and habits, have contributed a great deal in promoting national integration, common culture, and the national language of Hindi, throughout the length and breadth of the country.

The adverse effect of mass communication have been felt not so much from print media as from exciting media like television and satellite cable TV. The audiences of these electronic media, in the hope of getting lively entertainment at little cost, are lapping up all that comes through the 'open sky', without discrimination, without realising their good or bad effects. In facts they are becoming helpless victims of these pervasive media. The danger is from the programmes made with a western perspective which are going to influence the world view and life style in India and other Asian countries.

Besides, excessive advertising, 'alien' programmes, and mesmerising images have tremendous impact on young minds. They give children ideas about a materialistic culture that does not exist in their environment and create in them the desire for things they can't possibly afford to have. An overdose of TV is bad, but an overdose of foreign programmes is even more detrimental. Parents and teachers express their concern about the adverse effect of 24 hours TV on children's studies and health.

Mass communication affects our lives positively by informing about the new developments around us, by entertaining us, and influencing our attitudes, opinions, and actions vis-a-vis a variety of subjects and issues even after having restricted reach of mass media and the even more restricted access to it especially in rural and far flung areas.

Q8. Explain the meaning of models of communication and state the models of communication.

Ans. Communication models are systematic representations of the process which helps in understanding how communication works can be done. Models show the process metaphorically and in symbols. They form general perspectives on communication by breaking communication from complex to simple and keeps the components in order. Communication models can sometimes encourage traditional thinking and stereotyping but can also omit some major aspects of human communication.

A model is widely used to depict any idea, thought or a concept in a more simpler way through diagrams, pictorial representations, etc. Models go a long way in making the understanding of any concept easy and clear. Through a model one can easily understand a process and draw conclusions from it. In simpler words a model makes the learning simple.

A model is an abstracted representation of a reality. A good model comes as close to reality as possible and it discusses and explains the reality as clearly as possible. But being an abstraction, a model is not a reality, it only represents the reality of communication for better understanding of the communication process. For example, an architectural model of a house is only a representation of the house giving a fair idea of the number of rooms, layout, etc.

The discussion that follows explains the importance of model in unraveling the process from an initial simplistic version of communication to a very intricate, complex process of mass communication. A model is a pictorial presentation to show the structure of communication process in which various component elements are linked. Arrows are used to depict the transmission of messages from communicator to receiver. Models are based on assumptions that theorists make as to how communication functions and what effect it has upon individual and society.

A variety of models exist all of which strive to explain the different components of communication and the role each part plays in the total process.

Since communication is a transmission process, the mechanistic interpretation is rather a convenient way of viewing the relationship among the variables of human communication and of explaining how communication flows from one stage to the next and so on. Models are based on assumptions that theorists make as to how communication functions and what effect it has upon individual and society.

Process of Communication: In simple terms the basic process of communication, comprises a sender or a communicator who has a message that he or she, transmits or conveys through some means, say a channel, to a receiver who responds, according to his or her understanding of the message, to the sender (feedback). This is a simple, yet verbal version of communication process which when explained pictorially in the form of a model will look like this:

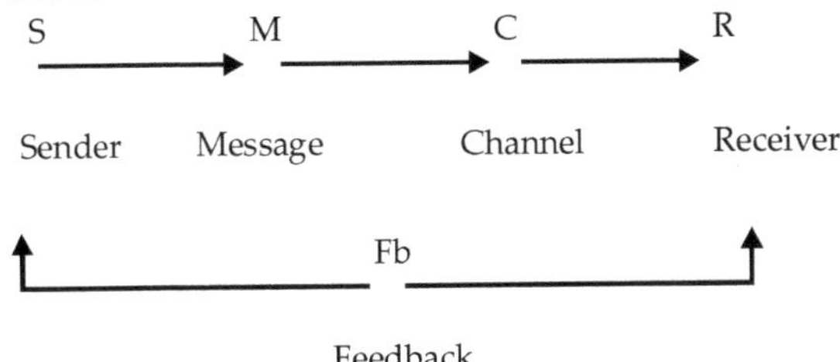

Fig. 1.2: A Simple Model of Communication Process

At a glance the model not only reveals the various elements of human communication but also their interdependence and the flow of communication from sender to receiver and back to sender. For instance, in a communication process there has to be a sender whose main intention is to communicate a message; what to convey is his\her thinking process; how to communicate the message is his\her choice of right means or channel; and whom to convey the message is his\her job to decide. The sender also needs to know the receiver's response to the message, whether or not it is being received as intended. Then only can the sender proceed further with the next act of communication and in this way it goes on and on. In this interaction process, there is an interdependence of relationship among the various variables of human communication. The mechanistic perspective of communication emphasises the physical element of communication, the transmission and the reception of messages flowing in 'conveyer belt fashion (B. Aubrey Fisher 1978).

The basic process of human communication applies to mass communication process as well, but as the nature of the latter's elements differ markedly, the process becomes different and more complex. For instance, in mass communication a big organisation that takes on the role of a sender, the message is not single but multiplied.

Developing Communication Models: The earlier models of communication were simple but inadequate. Aristotle constructed a model which had only three elements essential for communication to happen - speaker-speech-audience - and the basic function of communication was to 'persuade the other party'. Such a communication takes place only in face-to-face situations. Another model, constructed during World War II (1939-45) saw communication as a magic bullet that transferred ideas, feeling or knowledge almost automatically from one mind to another. For example, sender A sends a message to receiver B who is considered passive and is assumed to be accepting whatever is shot at him. It can be shown like this:

A sends a message to B

A sends another message to B

A sends a third message to B

A sends a fourth message to B

and so on.

Bullet Model: This one way model of communication became redundant as more researches on the subject showed communication as a dynamic two-way process. By 1950s models became more elaborate and adequate contributing significantly to the understanding of the communication process. The important ones among the early models are those constructed by Claude Shannon and Warren Weaver, based on 'telephone communication'; and by Harold D. Lasswell, in the form of questions. Both these models explained the communication process so well that they influenced several later models, especially of Charles E. Osgood, Wilbur Schramm, and George Gerbner. The majority of the models are linear, i.e. one directional. A simple model of communication process can be shown in this way (Schramm).

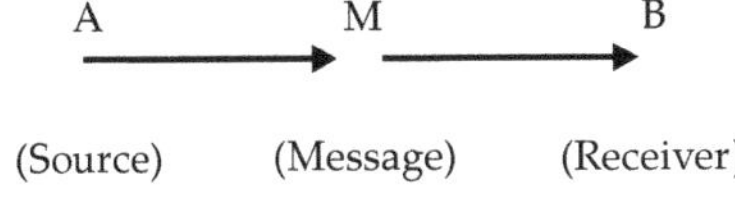

Fig. 1.3: Wilbur Schramm Model

Here A, the source, formulates a message, as best as he can, in signs and symbols, and passes it on to B, Depending upon B's capacity to read the signs, he reads the message. In other words, message 'acts' upon B as much as B 'acts' on the message. This can be as shown as:

A M B

Fig. 1.4: Action On Message

B, in turn, might respond and formulate his 'message', as best as he can, and communicate it to A. This can be shown as:

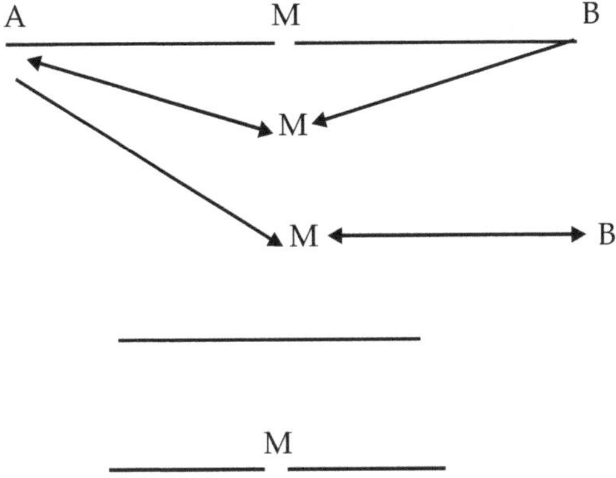

Fig. 1.5: Interaction between sender and receiver of communication

Q9. Explain the process of communication with the help of Shannon and Weaver's models of Communication.

Ans. The most well-known and influential formal model of communication, developed in 1949 by Claude Shannon and Warren Weaver. It is a transmission model consisting of five elements: an information source, which produces a message; a transmitter, which encodes the message into signals; a channel, to which signals are adapted for transmission; a receiver, which decodes (reconstructs) the message from the signal; a destination, where the message arrives. A sixth element, noise, is a dysfunctional factor: any interference with the message travelling along the channel (such as static on the telephone or radio) which may lead to the signal received being different from that sent. For the telephone the channel is a wire, the signal is an electrical current in it, and the transmitter and receiver are the telephone handsets. Noise would include crackling from the wire. In face-to-face conversation, my mouth is the transmitter, the signal is the sound waves, and your ear is the receiver; noise would include any distraction you might experience as it speak. It is a very linear model; unlike later models it does not even include a feedback loop. Shannon and Weaver were mathematicians, and Shannon worked for Bell Telephone Laboratories. This work proved valuable for communication engineers in dealing with such issues as the capacity of various communication channels in bits per second, thus contributing to computer science. It led to very useful work on redundancy in language, and in making information measurable it gave birth to the mathematical study of information theory. Consequently it is hardly surprising that Shannon and Weaver's model is information-centred rather than meaning-centred, but this points to its limitations as a general model of human communication.

Shannon and Weaver were the first to develop an engineering model of human communication based on telephone communication. Diagrammatically, the process of communication can be shown like this:

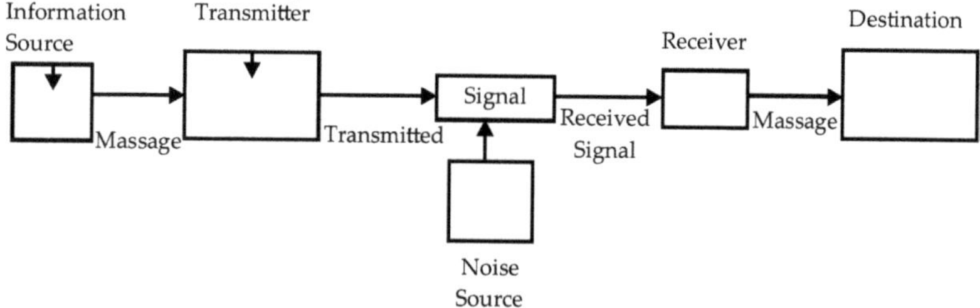

Fig. 1.6: The Shannon and Weaver Model

In this model, communication begins with an information source who creates the message; he transmits it by means of his vocal apparatus which acts as a transmitter (a telephone speaker in telephone); through the air as the channel with noise interference (such as a telephone wire and sound waves) to the hearing mechanism of the person he is communicating with acting as the receiver (such as telephone receiver) which recreates the message so that mother person, a receiver, as we have defined, can receive it.

Shannon and weaver's model is important it introduces the concept of 'Noise'. Noise in this model refers to disturbances in the channel that may interfere with the signals transmitted and produce different signals.

Later, based on the above principle, Shannon developed an "Information Theory" which says that the source has a message that it is trying to get through some channel to some destination:

- it requires a transmitter
- to convert the message into transmittable signal
- a complementary receiver
- receive it from the channel.

Q10. Explain the process of communication with the help of Charles E. Osgood's Model.

Ans. The Osgood-Schramm model is built on the theory that communication is a two-way street, with a sender and a receiver. Charles E. Osgood popularised the notion that communication was circular rather than linear, meaning that it required two participants taking turns sending and receiving a message.

Later, Wilbur Schramm, who talked about the model in his book, *The Process and Effects of Communication*, adapted the model and added the notion of field of experience, or commonality, to the mix. Field of experience incorporates what is mutually understood between the sender and receiver. For example, a professor of calculus would have very little luck communicating important math principles to a classroom of kindergarten students, because they do not share a field of experience that makes the message easy to understand.

For his part, Schramm is considered one of the pioneers of the mass communications field. He started the doctoral programme in mass communication at the University of Iowa, helping develop mass communication (television, print news, and other ways to communicate) as a university discipline.

The model of the communication process developed by C.E. Osgood is different from the earlier attempts in the sense that it does not follow the conventional pattern of communication from source to channel to receiver. He describes communication as a dynamic process and says that a given communication event may begin with receiving stimuli as shown in the figure below:

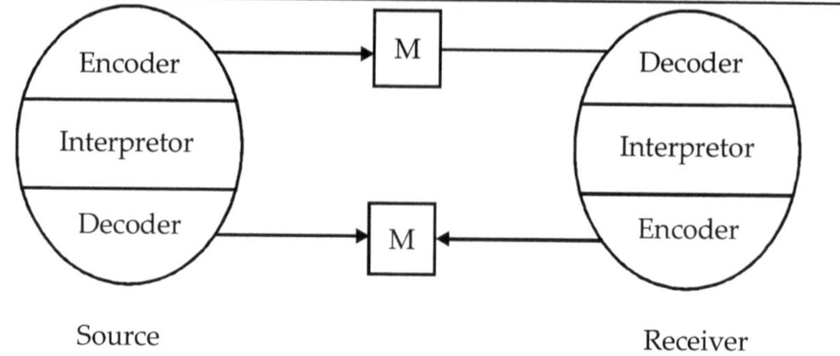

Fig. 1.7: C. E. Osgood Model

Osgood emphasised the point that each participant in the communication process sends as well as receives messages and as such encodes, decodes, and interprets messages.

Q11. Explain the process of communication with the help of Schramm's Model of Communication.

Ans. The Schramm Communication Model is a cyclical communication model containing all basic principles of communication. The Schramm Communication Model offers a classic approach to and explanation of communication. It can be used to determine how communication between two people works when they're exchanging information, ideas, or attitudes.

It has provided an overview of the elements and process of communication to explain how these work in practically all forms of communication - communication with ourselves, communication with one person or a group of persons, or communication with a mass audience of thousands and millions of people. In fact, Schramm's contribution in conceptualising communication is so important that it has helped in formulating a more acceptable explanation about the working of the communication process. Wilbur Schramm adapted Shannon and Weaver's model to human communication and introduced two concepts of encoder, decoder, redundancy, feedback and noise into his model to explain the communication process.

In this model, Schramm has stressed the importance of feedback and noise which are considered essential elements of communication process. The feedback refers to the response that a receiver makes to a source's communication. He has formulated the following model:

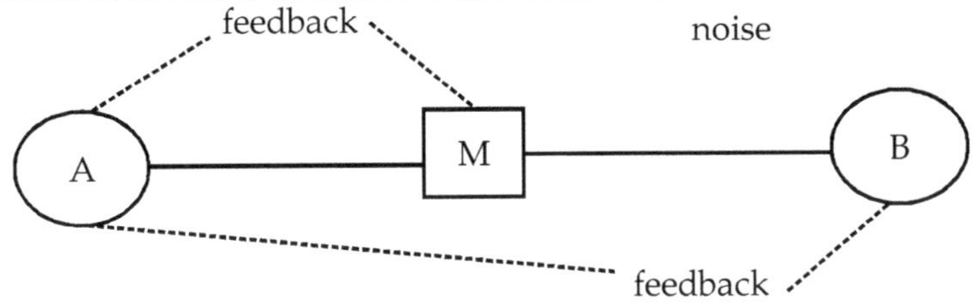

Fig. 1.8: Schramm's Model

The situation described in the above model is like a conversation between two people, where one is constantly communicating back to the other. The feedback obtained in such situation plays a very important role in the communication process because it tells the source how his messages are being received and interpreted. An experienced communicator is attentive to the feedback and may constantly modify his messages in the light of what he observes or hears from his audience. In face-to-face interpersonal communication feedback is instant.

The 'Noise' emphasised here may contaminate the message and make communication ineffective. The 'noise' concept is taken from electronics and adapted to cover a multitude of phenomena in human communication. Noise here is not anything that the sender has put intentionally into the communication channel but is actual physical noise which may come from the roadside or the passing of an airplane, or it may emerge from a faulty transmission, a blurred picture in the newspaper or a much used and faded film on screen. In many such instances a message is likely to suffer deterioration before it is decoded and interpreted by a receiver.

According to Wilbur Schramm, another form of feedback is getting response from our own messages i.e, we hear our own voices and correct our mispronunciations.

For example, we can see our own writing and can correct any misspelling or change the style. Similarly, we can edit our own audio/visual programme before presentation. Feedback of this kind is shown below:

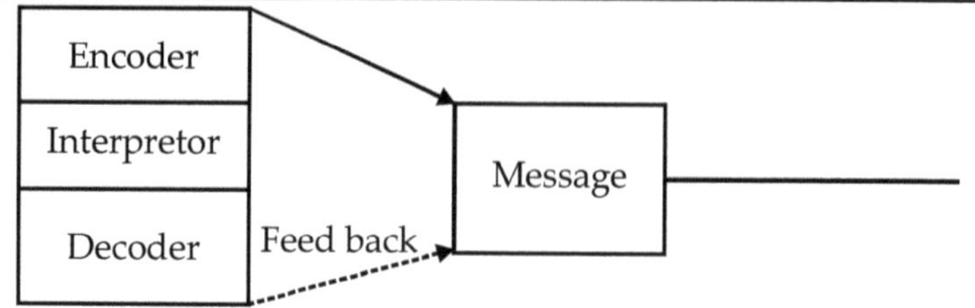

Fig. 1.9: Schramm's Model of Communication

Wibur Schramm further viewed the communication process as a complex one in the context of personal, social and cultural factors. He has visualised communication essentially as a process of sharing of experience, and how the shaping and reshaping of experience is. This is represented by him in a model as follows:

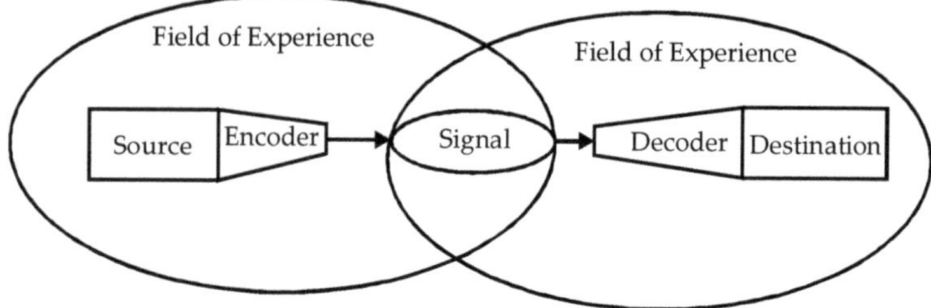

Fig. 1.10: Schramm's Model

The circles here indicate accumulated experience of the two individuals trying to communicate. The source can encode and the destination can decode only in terms of experience each has had. For example, if we have never learned French, we can neither encodenor decode in that language. If the circles have a large area in common, then communication is easy. If the circles do not meet, there has been no common experience, and then communication is impossible.

Schramm further elaborated this model by bringing into focus the frames of reference of the persons participating in the communication process. He also look into account the wider societal situation and relationship both of which influence the communication process. Diagrammatically, it can be shown like this:

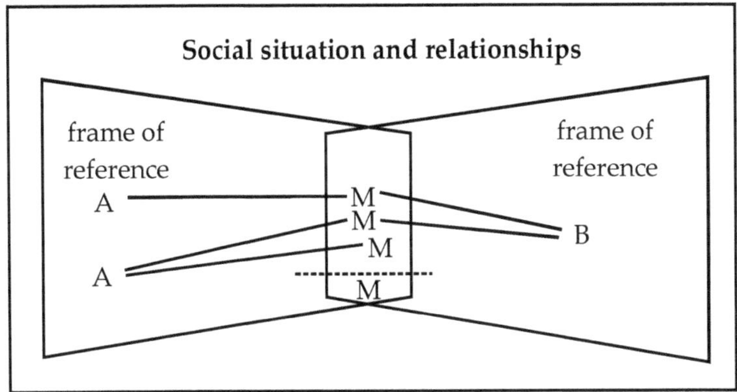

Fig. 1.11: Schramm's Model

A (source) and B (destination) have the same kind of situation, have the same social resources and face similar constraints.

Q12. Discuss George Gerbner's Model (1956).

Ans. Mr. George Gerbner is one of the pioneers in the field of communication research. His works are descriptive as well as very easy to understand any other before. He is working as a professor and head of the Annenberg School of Communications in the University of Pennsylvania. In 1956, Gerbner attempted the general purpose of communication models. He stressed the dynamic nature of communication in his work and also the factor which affecting the reliability of communication.

George Gerbner attempts to produce a general purpose model of communication in which the communication act is seen as a transmission of messages. The model assumes significance as it is seen as an advancement over earlier models in two ways. It relates the messages to 'reality' and thus enables us to approach the question of perception and meaning; further it sees the communication process as consisting of two alternative dimensions - the perceptual or receptive dimension and the communicating or means and control dimension. The complex model of Gerbner looks like this:

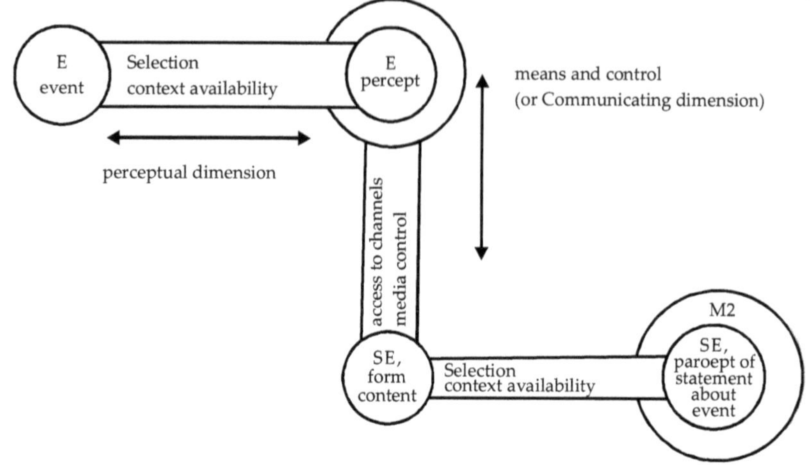

Fig. 1.12: Gerbner's Model (modified)

In this model, the communication process can be explained in three stages. The first step is referred to as the horizontal dimension. It starts with an event E (external reality) as perceived by M (Human being directly or through a machine such as a camera or a microphone). M selects E according to his perception of the event.

Since human perception is a complex phenomenon, the process involves interaction and negotiation. In this way, we try to match external stimuli with internal pattern of thought or concept and arrive at some perception of the event.

In the second stage, the vertical dimension, we give meaning to whatever we have perceived. It is then converted into a signal about SE. This is called message, that is, a singular statement about the event SE. Here, it is important to select the appropriate 'means' - the medium channel of communication. In this context, access to media assumes significance. So who makes the selection and whose picture of the world is transmitted as SE is obviously of prime importance. The media, especially television, often dubbed 'elitist', naturally would produce the elite biased version of an event.

The third stage of the process is again horizontal. M2 is not an event E, but a 'signal or statement about an event, or SE. The process here is something like we have explained in stage one, i.e. the meaning of the message is not 'contained' in the message itself, but is the result of an interaction or negotiation between the receiver and the message. M2 brings to SE a set of needs and concepts derived from his culture and sub-culture and if he can relate SE to them, we can say that he finds meaning in the message. And this can be realised only by interaction or negotiation between M2 and SF the resulting meaning is SE.

Q13. Discuss Theodore M. Newcomb's Model of communication.

Ans. The New Comb's model of communication was introduced by Theodore M Newcomb of the University of Michigan in 1953. He gives different approach to the communication process. The main purpose of this theory is to introduce the role of communication in a social relationship (society) and to maintain social equilibrium within the social system. He does not include the message as a separate entity in his diagram, implying it only by use of directional arrows. He concentrates on the social purpose of communication, showing all communication as a means of sustaining relationships between people. Sometimes it's called as an "ABX" model of communication.

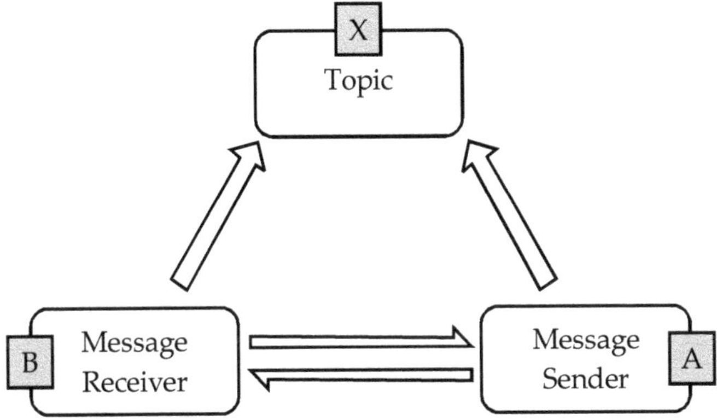

Fig. 1.13: The Newcomb's Model

Here A and B are communicator and receiver. They may be individuals, or management and union, or government and people. X is part of their social environment. ABX is a system, which means that its internal relations are interdependent: if A changes, B and X will change as well or if A changes his relationship to X; B will have to change either his relationship with X or with A.

The A-B-X system will be in equilibrium only if A and B have similar attitude to X. The more important a place X has in A's and B's social environment, the more urgent will be their drive to share an orientation towards it. Take the example of War time. During such a time, A, the government, and B, the public, need to communicate to establish their co-orientation to the War X because it concerns both A and B. Both A's and B's dependence on media is increased. This is because the War X is not only of crucial importance but also because the situation is constantly changing. So, government and people (A and B) need to be in constant communication via mass media.

Q14. Discuss Bruce H. Westley's and M.S. MacLean's Model (1957) of communication.

Ans. In 1957 Westley and MacLean's model of communication is proposed by Bruce Westley (1915-1990) and Malcolm S. MacLean Jr (1913-2001). Being one of the creators of journalism studies, Westley served as a teacher at the University of Wisconsin, Madison, between 1946 and 1968. Malcolm was director of University of Journalism School (1967-74) and co founder of the University College at University of Minnesota. The 'gatekeeper' concept is essentially sociological term applied to in mass media and is often associated with news. The model emphasises the role gatekeepers play within the media organisation. They decide on which messages are to be transmitted and how their content are to be modified. The model is explained as follows:

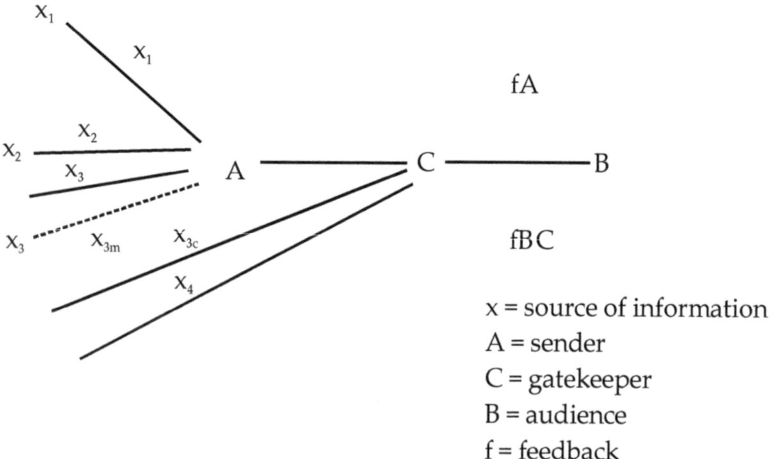

Fig. 1.14: The Westley and MacLean Model

A, here, is sender (e.g. reporter) who receives messages from many sources X1, X2, X3, X4 ...... X,C and according to his perception of event writes a report and sends it to gatekeeper C who performs the editorial-communicating function; that is the process of deciding what and how to communicate. C, therefore, keeping the specific audience in mind, may emphasise or deemphasise a certain point in the message to strike a balance and then sends it to the audience B. me audience, therefore, receives the reporter's and editor's versions of the day's events and not necessarily what may be the reality. In fact, interposed between the sender and the audience are the editors whether in print journalism, film, TV or radio who as gatekeepers, determine what the public reads, listens to or watches. Therefore, the audience's exposure to an event's reality is in the gatekeeper's hands.

The model designed by Bruce Westley and Malcolm MacLean is an extension of Newcomb's model and specifically adapted for the mass media. It is based on the assumption that messages in mass communication pass through different check points called 'gatekeeper' before they are actually received by audience. The 'gatekeeper' concept is essentially sociological term applied to in mass media and is often associated with news. The model emphasises the role gatekeepers play within the media organisation. They decide on which messages are to be transmitted and how their content are to be modified.

Q15. Explain the relationship between mass media and society. Also discuss its functions.

Ans. Mass communication influences both society and culture. Different societies have different media systems, and the way they are set up by law influences how the society works. Different forms of communication, including messages in the mass media, give shape and structure to society.

Some important theories of mass communication are discussed to understanding how mass communication operates in society. But later researches provide evidence against any direct cause and effect relationship between mass communication and society; rather they underline the importance of individual differences and personal influences on transmission, acceptance and retention of message. Socio logical theories portrayed mass media as an outcome of changes in society. There are other theories that express ideas on how the mass media ought to or can be expected to operate under prevailing political and economic circumstances. Some of the important theories discussed here will provide you insights into this role of mass communication in society and the way in which an audience utilises different mass media.

Mass media today are inextricable form of modern society. Without these media, society probably cannot conduct its affairs effectively. On their part, mass media, in a bid to serve the people, play a significant role in spreading new ideas, new forms of behaviour and information about a variety of products.

Society, whether simple or complex, needs some communication system so that its various organisations may perform their designated functions. Mass media do what is demanded of them and while doing that they draw strength and support from society for their survival.

Functions: Mass media perform many functions in society. The most important ones of these are information, education, motivation, persuasion, entertainment, cultural promotion and integration. Harold Lasswell defines these functions as 'surveillance of the, environment', 'correlation of the components of society in responding to the environment' and 'transmission of social heritage'. Wilbur Schramm has used simple terms of watcher, forum, and teacher. For instance, mass media not only inform the members of society about the threats and dangers, good omens and opportunities but also provide forums where. debates and discussions on relevant issues can give direction for change in society.

Another function of mass media in modern 'society is to provide entertainment. They are a source of personal and collective recreation and enjoyment. Newspapers, radio, television and other media help in promotion of cultural heritage and play an important role in integrating people, community and society for harmonious living.

Mass media use subtle means and persuasive techniques to mould opinion and induce changes. The question of media effect on society has been dealt with in several studies and' writings but not one of them provides a clear-cut view of media effects.

The information function of mass media has assumed a significant dimension at present. Society cannot survive today without being informed about international and local events, about political, economic, social and cultural affairs or even about weather conditions. People need varied information on practically all aspects of the lives in order to plan for the future.

Q16.Explain Interactive Perspective.

Ans. According to Denis McQuail's interactive perspective, that mass media are primarily moulders of society as well as reflectors of it. According to him, "society produces demands for information and entertainment to which media respond. It provides resources and time needed for the growth of media industries and freedom to operate. Mass communication in turn stimulates changed accelerates and demand for its own services, contributes to the climate of cultural and political freedom in which media can themselves better operate, diffuse new ideas and innovations. The two influences are so bound together that neither mass communication nor modern forms of society is conceivable without the other and each is a necessary but not a sufficient condition I for the other". In short, in his thinking, the mass media may equally be considered to mould, mirror and follow social change.

The portrayal of mass media as interactive with changes in society can be seen in the ways the two have evolved together. The origin, development, and ultimate use and influence of mass media have been in conformity with the changing conditions in society. As society has evolved towards industrialisation and modernisation and become complex, communication systems too have developed into highly intricate technical operations to cope with the ever increasing demand and for information and interpretation of events. The dynamic relationship between the two gets further strengthened if mass media functions are closely linked with people needs, interests, aspirations, etc. in a highly diversified society.' As long as mass' media give what people need or want, they remain a potent force, in society. But the moment they, with acquired power and control, give what they think people want, they become manipulative and may be working towards the taming of mind and indoctrination. Mass media are powerful instruments. In the recent past, quite a few leaders of the Third World countries have used these instruments to attain their own personal goals.

Mass media have to function with restraint and responsibility in accordance with the changing modes of society to become credible instruments of social change.

Q17. Write a note on hypodermic or bullet theory.

Ans. The "Magic Bullet" or "Hypodermic Needle Theory" of direct influence effects was based on early observations of the effect of mass media, as used by Nazi propaganda and the effects of Hollywood in the

1930s and 1940s. People were assumed to be "uniformly controlled by their biologically based 'instincts' and that they react more or less uniformly to whatever 'stimuli' came along". The "Magic Bullet" theory graphically assumes that the media's message is a bullet fired from the "media gun" into the viewer's "head". Similarly, the "Hypodermic Needle Model" uses the same idea of the "shooting" paradigm. It suggests that the media injects its messages straight into the passive audience. This passive audience is immediately affected by these messages. The public essentially cannot escape from the media's influence, and is therefore considered a "sitting duck". Both models suggest that the public is vulnerable to the messages shot at them because of the limited communication tools and the studies of the media's effects on the masses at the time. It means the media explores information in such a way that it injects in the mind of audiences as bullets.

If one believes in Bullet theory one has to maintain that the audience is made up of an enormous undifferentiated mass of humanity and that each member of the audience would react identically to the mass mediated messages. If that is so, thousands or millions of people who receive messages by watching horror movies or about dreadful events like war, drugs, AIDS, etc. would ultimately become potential victims of mass media. But researches and even our own experiences with mass media do not support this view of mass audience.

Q18.Briefly discuss Psychological or Individual Difference Theory.

Or

Write a short note on Individual difference theory.

[Dec-2019, Q.No.-10 (a)]

Ans. A theory of mass communication that proposes that individuals respond differently to the mass media according to their psychological needs, and that individuals consume the mass media to satisfy those needs. The need may be for information (e.g. providing statistics about players and teams), integrative (offering a sense of belonging to a group of similarly interested people), affective (e.g. by providing excitement), or escapist (helping to release pent-up emotions). Compare social categories theory. According to this theory, different personality variables result in different reactions to the same stimuli. In other words, an individual's psychological mechanism accounts for his reactions to media messages. In other words, the reaction to media content differs according to motivation of audience members, their predisposition to accept or reject a given message, their intelligence, beliefs, opinions, values, needs, moods, prejudices, perceptibility, etc.

From the voluminous psychological studies, two important concepts that have emerged - selective exposure and selective perception, need special consideration.

Selective exposure and selective perception act as barriers between message and effect, thereby limiting the scope of direct impact of mass communication on people.

Selective Exposure: Selective exposure occurs when people tend to expose themselves selectively only to communications which are in general accordance with their established convictions and avoid communications which seem to challenge their beliefs. For instance, Communists are far more likely than Congressmen to attend. Communist rallies, read Communist literature and discuss Communist policies. If, by chance, people are exposed to contrary opinions, they are able to perceive selectively in order to invest these hostile arguments with acceptable meanings, us narrowing the gap between what they believe already and what they are invited to believe.

Selective Perception: Once the individuals have selectively exposed themselves to the messages. In accordance with their preferences, they tend to "read into" the message whatever suits their needs. This process is called selective perception.

Selective perception also implies the tendencies of media audience members to misperceive and misinterpret persuasive messages in accordance with their own predispositions. The "Mr. Biggo experiments" are classic examples which show that prejudiced people twisted the meaning of anti-prejudice propaganda so it ended up reinforcing their existing biases.

Melvin L. De Fleur and Sandra Ball-Rokeach have concluded that "from the vast available content, individual members of the audience selectively attend to, interpret and retain messages, particularly if they are related to their interest, consistent with their attitude, congruent with their beliefs and supportive of their values" (1981).

Q19. Discuss different type of Personal Influence Theory.

Or

Mention the primary elements of the two-step flow of information theory.

Ans. The informal communications' network, in which audiences talked to one another and sought advice from opinion leaders, had led to two-step flow influence of mass communication.

Two Step Flow: The information received was mostly through other people, called "opinion leaders", who had first hand access to mass media information. It was explained like this: the information often flowed from mass media sources directly to opinion leaders, who passed it along to less active sections of the population. Thus, the majority got information this way. The study revealed that the information received by the audience this way was secondhand and could be different from the original because the opinion leaders might add their own interpretation to it before conveying it to others.

The opinion leaders, therefore, from valuable linkers in the two-step flow of information. This led to many studies on opinion leaders: who are those opinion leaders? What do they do to get information? How are they important to the opinion leaders, although not elected members in society, were more knowledgeable, Theory or educated, influential both socially and economically, and more modern in outlook than other fellow members in society. They were held in high esteem by people who relied on them greatly for ideas, information and guidance.

Like other theories, two-step flow has its shortcoming too: first, it diminishes the original, direct influence of mass media; secondly, its effects are evident only in political studies that were conducted decades ago when there was no television influence and, therefore, may not be as applicable to the contemporary political scene.

Multi- step Flow: Studies on opinion leaders led to the modification and reconceptualiation of the two-step flow concept into multi-step flow - because of the multi-directional influence of opinion leaders, not necessarily only downwards, when they interpreted the media messages for audiences. The influence was seen to be "upwards" or back towards the media sources, when they sought to tell gatekeepers (editors of newspapers, news editors of radio and TV news, producers, etc.) how to do their job. Also, the influence was "sideways" when they shared insights with other opinion leaders. Moreover, the multi-step flow concept was seen as having many relay points, i.e. information reaching a member of the audience directly or reaching him secondhand, third hand or fourth hand, and sometimes in a form considerably different from the original.

Q20.Discuss the various theories of mass communication.

Or

Among various Sociological theories of mass communication which one do you consider most relevant in the present Indian context and why? Substantiate your answer.

Or

Among the normative theories of mass media, which according to you is more relevant in the Indian context. Substantiate your answer.

[Dec-2019, Q.No.-2]

Ans. The sociological approach to communication theory is based on the assumption that there exists a definite relationship between mass communication and social change.

(1) Cultivation Theory: This theory, developed by George Gerbner (1967), is based on the assumption that mass media have subtle effects on audiences who, unknowingly, absorb the dominant symbols, images, and messages of media. He calls it " Cultivation of dominant image pattern". According to this theory, a long, persistent exposure to TV is capable of cultivating common beliefs about the world. Gerbner and his associates are of the view that the messages of television do not portray reality in society; repeated exposure to such distortions leads to development of particular beliefs about the world; and these beliefs get reinforced once they are developed.

For example, repeated viewing of glamorous locales, big houses, clothes, toys, chocolates, fast foods, electric and electronic gadgets may lead viewers to believe that they can expect such things in life but such message? are not beneficial for the poor and underprivileged majority. Gerbner also strongly suggests that the powerful effect of mass media act as moulders of society.

(2) Agenda-Setting Theory: The term was coined by Maxwell McCombs and Donald L. Shaw (1972) in the context of election campaign where politicians seek to convince the voters about the people's most imminent issue. Agenda-Setting Theory maintains that the media are more successful in telling people "what is to think about" than in telling them "what to think". This hypothesis is based on a whole series of studies showing a correspondence between the order of importance given in the media to 'issues' and the order of significance attached to the same issues by the public and the politicians. Over a period of time, according to this theory, the very priorities accorded by media to issues become the public priorities as well. But the critics argue that the evidence is insufficient to show a causal connection between the various issue 'agendas' of the media and the public.

They suggested the need for a study that combined analysis of party programmes, evidence of opinion change over time in a given section of the public: a content analysis showing media attention to different issues in the relevant period: and some indication of relevant media use by the public concerned. In the absence of such evidence, the hypothesis of agenda setting remains unproved.

(3) Uses and Gratification Theory: The Uses and Gratifications Theory arose out of the studies which shifted their focus from what the media do to the people to what people do with the media (Katz 1959). The "uses" approach assumes that audiences are active and willingly expose themselves to media; and that the most potent of mass media content cannot influence an individual who has "no use" for it in .the environment in which he lives. The uses of mass media are dependent on the perception, selectivity, and previously held beliefs, values, and interests of the people.

The term "gratification" refers to the rewards and satisfaction experienced by audiences after the use of media; it helps to explain motivations behind media use and habits of media use. Davison (1959) has shown that many research findings make more sense if communications are interpreted as a link between man and his environment. He suggests that communication effects can be explained in terms of the role they play in enabling people to bring about more satisfactory relations between themselves and the- world around them. Three distinct groups of uses and gratifications studies can be distinguished. The first of these groups conducts inquiries into the range of satisfaction derived from mass media material. The second group looks at the social and environmental circumstances that are responsible for people turning to the media in the first place. The third looks at the needs audience members are attempting to satisfy.

(4) Dependency Theory: Melvin De Fleur and Sandra Ball-Rokeach have proposed an integrated dependency theory of mass communication in which they recognise various psychological and social factors that prevent the media from exercising arbitrary control over their audiences. De Fleur and Ball-Rokeach describe it like this: "Mass media not only lack arbitrary influence powers, but their personal lack of freedom to engage in arbitrary communication behaviour. Both the media and their audiences are integral part of their society. The surrounding socio-cultural context provides controls and constraints not only on the nature of media messages but also on the nature of their effects on audiences". In fact, communication in all its forms has a very important role in holding society together. The need to belong to the society, to understand the society, and to keep up with society has increased our dependency on media and, in that sense, media enjoy certain powers.

Normative theories explain how the media 'ought to' or can be 'expected to' operate under the prevailing set of political-economic circumstances. Since each society controls its mass media in accordance with its policies and needs, it formulates its own separate press theory. Therefore, each theory is connected with the kind of political system in which the society has to conduct its socio-economic political affairs. Siebert et al., in 1956, mentioned four theories, based on classification of the world's national media systems into four categories. DenisMcQuail, in the 1980s, considered it appropriate to add two more theories to the original set of four. He concedes that these theories "may not correspond to complete media systems" but "they have now become part of the, discussion of press theory and provide some of the principles for current media policy and practice".

(5) Authoritarian Theory: The term used by Siebert refers to an arrangement in which the press is subordinated to state power and the interests of a ruling class. The theory holds that Press and other media should always be subordinate to established authority and should do nothing to undermine it. Media should avoid offence to the majority of dominant moral and political values. The Authoritarian Theory justifies advance censorship and punishment for deviation from externally set guidelines. Unacceptable attack on authority, deviation from official policy, or offences against moral codes should be criminal offences. The theory is easily identified in a dictatorial or repressive society. Under certain circumstances, media are subjected to authoritarian tendencies in democratic regimes as well, especially in times of war and during internal and external emergencies. For instance, in India, broadcasting is under direct control of government and works according to its guidelines. Other media like film, video, etc., are subjected to censorship. Even the press, which is free, lost its independence and freedom during the emergency (1975-77). The authorities can and do use the provisions of Officials Secrets Act to deny free access to information, thereby hampering the freedom of the press.

(6) Free Press Theory: This theory, also called "Libertarian Theory", (Siebert et al.) is based-on the fundamental right of an individual to freedom of expression, which is regarded as the main legitimating principle for print media in liberal democracies. In its simple form, it prescribes that an individual should be free to publish what he or she likes; it is thus extension of other rights to hold opinions freely, to express them, to assemble and organise with others. The free press theory needs no elaboration as is evident from the First Amendment to the American Constitution which states that "Congress shall make no law, abridging the freedom of speech or of the press. It is thus simply an absolute right of the citizen".

But the application of press freedom has hardly been straight forward. Milton, Stuart Mill and many others argued that if freedom is abused to the extent of threatening good morals and the authority of the state, it must be restrained. According to deSola Pool (1973), "No nation will indefinitely tolerate a freedom of the press that serves to divided the country and too pen the flood gates of criticism against the freely chosen government that leads it". Moreover, much difficulty has arisen because press freedom has become identified with property rights (private ownership) and freedom from interference in the market. The free press theory thus protects the owners of media but fails to give equal expression to the rights of editors and journalists or of the audiences.

(7) Social Responsibility Theory: The 'social responsibility' theory owes its origin to the Commission on Freedom of the Press (Hutchins 1947) that was appointed in the United States. The commission's main finding is that the free market has failed to fulfil certain obligations to society. According to it, the press has not met the informational, social, and moral needs of the society. In fact, it has increased the power of a single class.

The Social Responsibility theory is based on the assumption that media serve essential functions in society. Therefore, it should accept and fulfil certain obligations to the society. These obligations are to be met by setting up high professional standards in communication of information: truth, accuracy, objectivity and balance. In accepting and discharging these obligations, the media should be self-regulatory within the frame work of law and established institutions. In the public interest, the media should underplay that news which might lead to crime, violence, and social tension or cause offence to ethnic or religious minorities. The media should be pluralist, should reflect the diversity of their society and allow access to various points of view, including the right to reply.

This theory has lead to the establishment of self regulatory bodies like the Press Council which is responsible for drawing up of statutes to protect editorial and journalistic practice; framing of codes of ethics; ensuring implementation of anti-monopoly legislation; and regulation of advertising.

(8) Communist Media Theory: This is also known as the Soviet Media Theory. The Russian media were reorganised after the Revolution of 1917. This theory is derived mainly from the basic tenets of Marx and Engels. It envisages media to be under the control of the working class whose interest they are meant to serve. Private ownership of the pressor other media is ruled out. The media must serve positive functions in society relating to information, education, motivation, and mobilisation. The media must project society in accordance with the Marxist-Leninist principles. They must support progressive movements in the country and abroad.

The media, according to this theory, are subject to the ultimate control of the State and are integrated with other instruments of political life. Within these limits, the media are expected to be self-regulatory, They must:

(i) act with responsibility.

(ii) evolve and follow norms of professional conduct; and

(iii) respond 'to people's needs and aspirations.

The media, as per this theory, are not' subject to arbitrary interference as in the case of the authoritarian theory;

(9) Development Communication Theory: The limited application of the four established theories of the press to Third World countries, which are vastly different from each other and western countries, and with fast changing economic and political conditions, has led to the birth of a new

Theories of approach whereby communication is used to carry out development tasks in line Mass Communication with nationally established policy - hence the formulation of development communication theory. The best source for information on this issue is the report of the UNESCO sponsored International Commission for the Study of Communication Problems.

Some common conditions of developing countries that limit the potential benefits of other theories are-

(i) the absence of communication infrastructure;

(ii) a dependence on the developed world for hardware and software;

(iii) the commitment of these societies to economic, political and social development as a primary national task; and

(iv) the developing countries' awareness of their similar identity and interest in international politics.

Because of these differing conditions, the developing countries' overriding objectives would be to use mass media for nation-building. In the interest of this task of national development, the freedom of the media and of journalists needs to be curbed to an extent.

The major thrust of development communication theorists has been on the use of media as a support to national development programme - poverty alleviation, population control, literacy drive, employment generation schemes, etc. But the effectiveness of this 'theory depends on how governments exercise their right to restrict freedom or to intervene in media operations and how they use devices of censorship, subsidy, and direct control.

(10) Democratic-Participant Media Theory: This most recent addition to the list of normative theories, is relevant to the developed liberal societies but has some elements of the development media theory. McQuail notes that it is most difficult to formulate this theory "partly because it lacks full legitimisation and incorporation into media institutions and partly because some of its tenets are already to be found in some of the other theories". In his opinion, this theory represents a challenge to the reigning theories and merits separate identification.

The main feature of the democratic participant theory relates to the needs, interests, and aspirations of the active receiver in a political society. It is concerned with the right to information, the right to answer back, the right to use the means of communication for interaction in the small-scale settings of the community. The theory favours:

(i) multiplicity of media;

(ii) smallness of scale, of operation; and

(iii) a horizontality of communication at all levels. It opposes uniform, centralised, high cost, highly professionalised and state-controlled media.

Q21. Discuss some other theories of mass media

Ans. Some other theories are:

(1) Mass Society Theory: Mass Society Theory, according to Denis McQuail, emphasises the inter-dependence of institutions which exercise power in the society and mass media are deemed to be integrated into the sources of social power and authority. The media content loosely serve the interests of those who wield economic and political power. People are offered the means of relaxation and diversion. This theory gives a primacy to the media as cause and maintainer of mass society. The theory invokes the images of control and portrays the vertical direction of influence - from above downwards.

(2) Political Economic Media Theory: This theory's focus is on the economic structure of the media rather than the ideological content of the media. Here the ideology depends on the economic base and research attention is directed to analysis of ownership structure and operation of media market forces. Thus, the media institution must be considered a part of the economic system, though with close links to the political system. Economic interests of media owners, that is, the need for profit for media 'operations', are important. The consequences are-

(i) the reduced independences of media sources;

(ii) concentration on the largest markets; and,

(iii) neglect of small and poorer sections of the potential audience.

One weakness of this theory is that the working of public media cannot be analysed solely in terms- of the free market.

(3) Hegemony Theory: The "Hegemony" Theory, unlike the political economic, concentrates less on the economic system and more on the ideology itself. Here, a greater degree of independence of ideology from the economic base is emphasised. The relationships between the capitalist and working classes are legitimated by the media in terms of the voluntary consent of the working class itself.

(4) Culture and Semiotic Theory: This theory is derived from Saussure's and Peirce's studies of signs and meaning and their relation to culture, people, and objects. Saussure (1935), a linguist, stressed on texts and its meaning in the light of the "host" culture. It is thus concerned with explanation of cultural as well as linguistic meaning. Semiotics is the general science of signs, developed by philosopher and logician Peirce (1931-35), which deals 'with how signs signify.

Deriving largely from both Saussure and Peirce, Fiske (1982), describes semiotics a shaving three aspects; the signs and the way they relate to people who use them; the codes or system into which signs are organised to meet the needs of a society or culture; and the culture within which these codes and signs operate. It is only when meaning is conveyed from sender to receiver, that communication has taken place.

Semiotic theory, thus, is not concerned with transmission of message- is the case, in process approach, but with derivation or transfer of meaning in communication.

'The focus here is on the role of communication in establishing meaning and/maintaining values and on how these values enable communication to have meaning.

Q22. Discuss major areas of communications research.

Ans. Each medium has its distinctive characteristics facilitating or impeding communication effectiveness. And, therefore, the channel through which messages are transmitted is important in producing the effect.

The other dimension relates to the differences between written and spoken forms of communication, and their differential impact on attention, comprehension, and pressures to comply with the message. A tremendous amount of applied research has been carried out to test the effectiveness of mass media channels and interpersonal communication channels. The diffusion researchers are interested in the role of mass media and interpersonal communication channels at different stages of diffusion process. The greater availability of feedback in face-to-face communication situations is its obvious advantage. Comparison of various modalities - print, radio and audio-visual - has generated a lot of research. The importance of 'silent language' non-verbal or gestural communications also has received some attention. The role of folk communication, especially in the context of developing countries, has received a lot of attention from the communication scholars. Much research has been conducted in the Third World countries to study the role of folk communication in various development projects. Advertisers are much interested in this area of research as it offers suggestions on how to take a decision on selecting the right medium to reach their target audience.

- **Communication/Source Analysis:** The nature of the communicator and those characteristics which make him effective in his persuasive attempts, have traditionally attracted the attention of communication researchers. To begin with, one looks for the essential characteristics of a good reporter, editor or other media personnel. But, at the theoretical level, one explores how the source characteristics such as credibility, expertise, intent and attractiveness affect the acceptance of the message by the receivers. The classic example of this kind of research is found in the studies of the Yale Communication Research Group of the United States of America. Hovland and Weiss, for example, conducted an experiment in which they presented an identical communication to two groups of subjects. But the messages were attributed to high and low credibility sources. They found that when a communication was attributed to low credibility source, it was considered to be more biased and unfair in the presentation than when it was attributed to high credibility source. Further, the high credibility source had considerably greater immediate effect on the opinion of the audience than the low credibility source. There has been abundant research in this tradition, exploring the characteristics of the communicators and how these characteristics affect the receivers.
- **Message Analysis:** The quality and kinds of messages are often studied in terms of their comprehensibility, interest arousal, and attention value, and the final impact. Variations in style, length, readability, emotional appeal, rationality, and the content characteristics of message have been the focus of a number of research studies.

  Analysing the content of messages - a methodology which has become a favourite of communication researchers and relating it to other elements in the process, especially their impact on individual behaviours, attitudes and values, and the consequences in terms of social developments and cultural change, forms a major chunk of communications research.

- **Channel Analysis:** Each medium has its distinctive characteristics facilitating or impeding I communication effectiveness. And, therefore, the channel through which messages are transmitted is important in producing the effect. The well known communication theoretician, Marshall McLuhan, goes to the extent of advocating that the medium through which the message is communicated has more impact on the receiver than the message itself. One of his books is appropriately entitled "The Medium is the Message". He makes a distinction between 'hot" and 'cold' media, that is, whether the medium stimulates active participation or induces a passive and receptive state of mind in the audience.

  The other dimension relates to the differences between written and spoken forms of communication, and their differential impact on attention, comprehension, and pressures to comply with the message. A' tremendous amount of applied research has been carried out to test the effectiveness of mass media channels and interpersonal communication channels. The diffusion researchers are interested in the role of mass media and interpersonal communication channels at different stages of diffusion process. The greater availability of feedback in face-to-face communication situations is its obvious advantage. Comparison of various modalities - print, radio and audio-visual - has generated a lot of research. The importance of 'silent language' non-verbal or gestural communications also has received some attention. The role of folk communication, especially in the context of developing countries, has received a lot of attention from the communication scholars. Much research has been conducted in the Third World countries to study the role of folk communication in various development projects. Advertisers are much interested in this area of research as it offers suggestions on how to take a decision on selecting the right medium to reach their target audience.

- **Audience Analysis:** The ultimate aim of communication is to produce the intended effect on receivers. As such, the audience (a general term inclusive of the readers, listeners and viewers) characteristics - its size, composition, geographical distribution, interests, attitudes, opinions, and behaviours have been the main focus of a large number of communication studies. Media owners are particularly interested in knowing the nature of their audience in order to provide the content appropriate to their tastes and needs. Similarly, advertisers need to have the knowledge about the size and composition of audience of various media. This knowledge is necessary to reach the largest number and the right kind of people for their products and services.
- **Process and Effects Research**: Communication is a process involving several elements. The process is broken into elements in order to have a better understanding of it. However, the dynamic nature of the process is to be studied not by analysing the elements, but through a consideration of these elements interacting with one another to produce the final product, viz., the effect. The effect can be studied at several levels - exposure, comprehension, recall, acceptance, and action. Each level is a necessary pre-condition for the occurrence of the next level. Also, it is important to note there is a gap between acceptance (a cognitive chance) and action (an act of behaviour); acceptance of message need not necessarily result in behavioural changes. Further, mass media effect is not automation once it was assumed to be under the hypodermic needle model, or the magic bullet theory conception of massmedia effects. Mass media audiences are not just passive agents reacting to what they see and read. People's needs, biases, and interests affect the way they perceive, interpret and react to media communications.

Q23. Critically examine the different approaches of communications research.

Or

Write a short note on content analysis. [June-2019, Q.No.-10 (a)]

Ans. Each approach has its unique applications and its inherent strengths and limitations. No method is uniformly applicable to all kinds of communications research situations; each problem requires the application of a method or combination of methods suitable to its solutions. The different methods available to the communications researcher and their general procedures, merits and weaknesses are discussed here as:

(1) Historical Method: Although history was once considered the queen of the sciences, the method of history is essentially different from that of the sciences. The scientist makes direct observations, while the historian focuses on the past events. But history is not just a list of chronological events, it is rather an accurate interpretation of relationship between persons, places, times, and events. Historical research mainly depends on documents and records and less upon direct observation. The investigator analyses documents and records and draws inferences. The primary sources of data in historical method are the firsthand accounts reported by an actual observer or participant in the event. These may take several forms: official records, autobiographies, letters, diaries, newspapers, magazines, pictures, paintings, and soon. In the absence of primary sources, historical method often resorts to the use of secondary sources.

In the historical method, the most basic thing is the genuineness of the sources, and the admissibility of data as evidence. The researcher attempts to find out the meaning of the assertions contained in the sources, and the truthfulness of such assertions. Finally, he offers explanations for or tries to understand past events in the light of evidences available in his sources.

Since mass media materials - newspapers, magazines, programme transcripts, and soon - are in themselves primary sources of data, application of the historical method in communications research is popular and widespread.

(2) Experimental Method: Experimentation is the most favoured method of all sciences, and it is regarded as the method par excellence. The method, by its very operations, tends to be objective. It uses procedures of 'control' to rule out alternative explanations.

The starting point of any experimentation is formulations of a hypothesis. A hypothesis is a tentative proposition about the relationship between two or more observed phenomena. In research terminology, these phenomena are called variables.

For example, one may hypothesis a relation between age and movie attendance by posting that movie attendance is lower among older people. Age and movie attendance are the two variables, and the relation between the two forms a hypothesis.

An experiment is designed and conducted in order to test the hypothesis. The experimental procedure involves manipulating the variable to see the effect of this manipulation on some other variable of interest. The manipulated variable is called independent variable, and the other variable on which the effect of manipulated variable is observed is the dependent variable. The objective of the experiment is then to establish causal links between independent and dependent variables.

The experimental method, in its simplest form, proceeds by -

(i) administering the independent variable to one group of subjects, called the experimental group, and

(ii) withholding the application of independent variable to another group, the control group,

(iii) and observing the differences between the two groups on the dependent variable.

There may be more than one experimental group, if different levels of independent variables are applied to different groups to test the effects of different "dosages" of independent variable on the dependent variable. The experimenter keeps all other things constant or under control except the manipulated variable so as to ensure that the observed differences in dependent variable can be attributed to the manipulated variable. Thus, experimentation makes possible statements of cause of effect relationship between variables.

The method can best be illustrated through a couple of examples. The classic experiment by Hovland and Weiss was conducted to study the relationship between credibility of the sources and opinion change among the receivers. The experimenter selected certain issues which were current at that time and measured the opinions of 'their subjects on those issues. The subjects then read identical messages on a given issue, but the credibility of the sources of these messages was manipulated by attributing the authorship of these message to different sources. For example, on one issue, one group of subjects was told that the source was

Robert Oppenheimer, the Nobel Laureate, and the other group was told it was Pravda, the communist newspaper. Again, the opinion of the subjects was assessed after reading these messages. The changes in their opinion from 'before' to after was compared and it was found that those who read messages attributed to credible source changed their opinions more than those who read messages from a less credible source.

Another study by Freedman and Fraser was designed to investigate how to make, people comply with one's requests. They went by the logic that it was easier to induce people to accept larger requests, if one could make them accept smaller requests to start with. The investigators first went to housewives and said that they wished to enlist women's co-operation for a safe driving campaign to submit to the legislators (inducement to accept a small request). Several weeks later, the representatives of these investigators went to the same housewives, and also to another group of housewives who were not contacted earlier for the signature campaign, with a request to put up an ugly looking, unattractive signboard, "Drive carefully", in their front yards (asking for a bigger request). The investigators compared the number of compliances to the second request (i.e. the bigger request) by both the groups. They found that 55 per cent who had agreed to sign the petition (who had complied with the smaller request) also agreed to display the signboard (the large request), but only 17 per cent of those who were not contacted earlier with the small request agreed with the large request, viz., displaying the sign board. This led to the conclusion that inducing people to accept small requests facilitates in getting them to accept bigger requests. Here also, the investigators manipulated the independent variable (approaching with a small request or not doing so), and measured its impact on the dependent variable, this is, compliance with the larger request.

Although both the preceding experiments followed the same logic, there were vital differences in their procedures. In Hovland-Weiss experiment, the study was done within the four walls of the laboratory, whereas the Freedman - Fraser experiment was conducted in a real life situation. The former was a controlled laboratory experiment and the latter 'was a field experiment. Also, in Hovland-Weiss experiment the dependent variable (opinions of the subjects on issues) was measured twice: Once before the manipulation of the independent variable, and again after the manipulation. On the other hand, in the Freedman-Fraser experiment, the dependent variable was measured only once.

These two methods were called, "before-after" and "after-only" designs respectively.

There are inherent strengths and limitations in the laboratory and field experiments. It is possible to impose rigourous controls in the laboratory context, but generalisation from the laboratory to real life is rather limited. On the other hand, in a field experiment It is difficult to impose experimental controls, but the findings of a field experiment have greater scope for generalisation compared to those of contrived artificial laboratory studies.

(3) Survey Research: Survey research is one of the most familiar research method in social sciences. The methodology is quite common among communications researches also as they indulge in readership surveys, audience analysis, programme ratings, opinion polls, consumer and market research, and other kinds of investigations requiring survey research methodology.

The general objective of survey research is to obtain accurate information about people's attitudes, beliefs and behaviours by asking them appropriate questions. The data usually collected by administering questionnaires individually or in groups, through mailed questionnaires, or by telephone or personal interviews.

The success of the survey in terms of obtaining reliable and valid results depends on the right choice of people from the intended population (i.e. sampling), the quality and the relevance of questions, and proper interviewing procedures. Therefore, a brief consideration of each of these aspects of survey research is in order.

Sampling: In survey research, the investigator is interested in observing the distribution or occurrences of certain characteristics in a population of interest. For example, one may be interested in knowing how many and what kind of post-graduate students read newspaper editorials regularly, or how many and what type of housewives watch the TV serials regularly. In the foregoing examples, the post-graduate students of a university or a particular region and the housewives in a given city or a geographic area may constitute the population of interest to the respective investigators. Thus, a sample population is the aggregate of all the cases that conform to certain stipulated set of specifications.

School students in a given state, members of a political party, TV owners in a given city are all examples of a survey populations. There may be different subpopulations within a given population called the population strata. For example, the secondary school children in a given state may be stratified in terms of geographic location as urban and rural or in terms of sex as boys and girls, or combinations as urban boys, urban girls, rural boys and rural girls.

If we enumerate the entire population to study its characteristics, it becomes a census. However, to study the entire population is often laborious, time consuming, and expensive. The same outcome can be obtained by selecting a sample of the population, and inferring the characteristics of the total population from the sample findings. The correspondence between population findings (called population parameters) and its sample findings (called sample statistics) depends on how well on has selected the sample. There are a number of ways of selecting samples. Broadly, these are classified into two methods: probability sampling and non-probability sampling techniques. The essential feature of probability sampling is that each element in the population or every combination of elements has the same probability of being included in the selected sample. But in the non-probability sampling, there is no guarantee that every element has the same chance of being included in the sample. One must bear in mind that probability sampling is the only approach that makes possible representative sampling plans. The non-probability approaches are only procedures of convenience and much reliance cannot be placed on their findings.

The commonly used probability techniques are -

(i) simple random sample,

(ii) stratified random sample, and

(iii) cluster sample.

The non-probability techniques include-

(i) accidental sample,

(ii) quota sample, and

(iii) purposive sample.

Simple random sampling involves listing of all the elements in the population and taking a lottery to select the desired. number of elements from the totality. The same result can be obtained by selecting cases from the list using a table of Random Numbers. Before using the Table, all the elements in the population are to be listed; then, enter the Table at some random starting point, and move in any direction from that point; then select all those cases that come up until the desired number of cases are obtained.

Stratified random sampling is similar, excepting that following the procedures detailed above, the required number of cases are selected from each of the strata in the population, thereby ensuring adequate representation from each strata of the population.

Cluster sampling, also called multi-stage sampling, involves arriving at the ultimate set of elements to be included in the sample by first sampling in terms of larger groupings (the 'clusters'), again by following procedures of random sampling.

The non-probability procedures are not systematic and may lead to gross errors.

Accidental sampling, as the name suggests, picks up cases from the population that happen to be accidentally available to the investigator. Quota samples provider presentation to each strata, but within the strata the selection is again accidental. Purposive sampling involves picking up cases that are judged to be 'typical' of the population.

(4) Content Analysis: Content analysis is another commonly used research method in social science, and particularly in communication science. It involves analysis of documents and written records with the objective of describing and classifying. It is regarded as an objective, systematic, and quantitative technique. Although qualitative analysis is permitted at times, qualification of materials is often insisted upon. Essentially, the researcher constructs a set of mutually exclusive and exhaustive categories to analyse documents, and then records the frequency with which each of these categories appears in the documents under analysis.

The first step in content analysis is the selection of a sample of materials for analysis. This requires deciding what materials are relevant to the research topic, and then sampling the actual materials from the totality of the relevant materials following the procedures of sampling described earlier in this unit. The next step is to define the categories that are to be analysed. Examples:

(i) **Editorials, subject-wise**: Political. Economic and Financial, Law and Order, Social and Culture, Sports, etc.,

(ii) News: International, National, State, Local.

The unit of analysis must be selected; the unit may 'be each word, each sentence, each paragraph, each theme, each character or actor, or the entire item. The analysis can be made in terms of:

(i) presence or absence of a content category, the,

(ii) frequency with which each category appears (for example: the news items in which our Prime Minister figures),

(iii) the amount of space allotted to the category, or

(iv) the strength and intensity with which the category is represented.

Content analysis is done to study diverse kinds of problems relating to the:

(i) characteristics of communication sources,

(ii) messages,

(iii) causes and antecedents of these messages, and the

(iv) effects of such messages, Thus, the technique has wide applicability in communications research.

(5) Case Study and Anthropological Approaches: The case study approach; which is quite common in clinical settings, is used to make an in depth analysis of one subject-to examine several aspects or many characteristics of a single case. By comparison, in survey research, the investigator focuses on fewer characteristics of a large number of subjects. The case study is Communications Research undertaken to learn all about a particular case at a given point of time. Although the case studies may provide valuable insights about the subject matter, the findings cannot be generalised to other similar cases. However, the method provides a host of observations, ideas and insights; these can be followed with other types of investigations leading to generalisations.

Anthropological method, like the case studies, involves an in depth analysis of communication behaviours and their contexts. It looks at the situation in a unified way, conceiving it as a whole. The emphasis is on the totality, the underlying, assumption being that parts can never be properly understood apart from the whole.

Data Analysis: The data usually take the form of numbers through some measurement operation; this measurement may be of different kinds and at different levels. At the basic level, measurement involves classification or categorisation.

Classification of programme as 'good' or 'bad'; newspaper editors as 'liberal' or 'conservatives'; opinions on an issue as 'pro', 'con' or 'neutral' - these are all examples of classification. Classification only implies that one is not the same as the other, but it does not say that one is greater or better than the other. There is no implication of the magnitude of the characteristic under measurement. At the next level, ranking of objects in terms of magnitude of the characteristic they posses is involved. For example, boys spend more time with newspapers than girls; paper X has better circulation than paper Y. At the highest level, the measurement will be in terms of 'intervals' and ratios. Statements such as boys spend 30 minutes with newspapers and girls spend only 20 minutes; or the younger people attend twice as many movies as the older people, represent measurement at the interval and ratio levels.

Q24. Briefly discuss some common technique of data analysis.

Ans. Data analysis is defined as a process of cleaning, transforming, and modeling data to discover useful information for business decision-making. The purpose of Data Analysis is to extract useful information from data and taking the decision based upon the data analysis. These are some of the commonly used technique of data analysis.

(1) Frequencies and Percentages: To reduce the data to make some sense, one may begin with a frequency count. In other words; count the number of times each observation has occurred in the set of data. For instance, how many respondents have agreed with an opinion statement, how many housewives watch the TV serials regularly, how many times sex themes appear in commercial movies and so on. Consider this hypothetical example. An investigator has asked 300 post-graduate students on a university campus how many times they attended movie shows in a given year. The answers, range from zero to 50. The frequency analysis takes into account how many among these three hundred respondents, how many have not attended any movie shows at all, how many have attended just one, how many two and so on. One may even group these scores into what are called class intervals, and have categories like those visiting fall between the following ranges 0-4, 5-9, 10-14, and so on. Then count how many cases fall within each of these intervals. This scheme helps to summarise data from the 300 respondents to a manageable size, and provides information as to what number of cases attend how many movies.

The frequencies for each score or for a given class-interval can also be converted into percentages, multiplying the frequency by 100 and dividing the product by the total number of cases. Suppose there are 30 cases out of 300 attending between 10-14, movies in an year, then 10 per cent of the cases (30 x 100/300) attend between 10-14 movies.

Counting" frequencies and calculating percentages, although a simple affair, provide a good deal of information on the sets of data collected.

(2) Averages and Dispersion: The two aspects of any set of data that are basic and important are its central location and its spread or dispersion. Averages are measures of central location, and they typify the whole set of data. Any particular score in the set may be viewed as a certain distance above and below the average. Commonly used averages are: Arithmetic Mean, Median, and Mode.

An Arithmetic Mean is the sum of a set of measurements divided by the number of measurements in the set. In the hypothetical 300 postgraduate students have given actual or estimates of the number of movies they have to Communications visited during a year. Add up the numbers given by these 300, and divide it by 300, the resulting value is the Mean number of movies attended by the group. That gives a central reference value with which the scores of the respondents may be compared. Another commonly used measure of central location is the Median. It is the mid-point of a set of observations arranged in order of magnitude. In the set of data, half of the observation fall above and the half fall below' this mid-point.

Mode is another quick, but rarely used measure of central location. Mode is the 'most frequently occurring value in the set.

The other aspect of a set of data is how the measurements are distributed, i.e. the spread or dispersion of scores in the set. It is possible that there may be heavy concentration of 'scores or wide variations in a given set of measures. The common indices are the Range and the Standard Deviation. The Range is simply the difference between the highest and the lowest score in the set. The Standard Deviation, on the other hand, is the square root of the mean of the squared deviation scores about the mean of a distribution. This measure, often considered a cornerstone of modern statistics, gives us a basis for probability estimates.

(3) Correlation: Correlation is a measure of relationship between variables. Say we have two sets of measurements taken on the same sample. One measure is an assessments of school achievement and the other is time spent every day on studies. If one students has spent more time on studies, he is likely to have a better measure of school achievement. Similarly, a student spending less time-with his studies would be expected to have a low measure of school achievement. In this case, the two measure vary together - increment in one measure is associated with concomitant increment on the second measure - and we would say that the two variables have a positive correlation. Let us look at another two sets of measurement taken on the same sample. One measure is again an assessment of school achievement and the other is the number of movies the student attends every week. A student who attends a higher number of movies has a lower achievement score, while the one who watches a lesser number of movies has a higher achievement score. Here, the two measures vary inversely, that is, a high score on one is associated with a low score on the other, and vice versa. We would say that the two measures have a negative correlation. The correlation is thus an index of relationship, and the index is called correlation coefficient. Correlation coefficients indicate both the degree and direction of relationship. The degree of relationship can range from no relationship to perfect relationship between variables. The direction of relationship may be positive (if two variables vary together) or negative (if they vary inversely). Thus, the coefficients can take on the following possible range of values:

+ 1.0 (perfect positive correlation)

0.0 (no correlation)

- 1.0 (perfect negative correlation)

This would mean, that a correlation of + .25 is a slightly positive correlation and a - .80 is high negative correlation.

There are different techniques for working out correlation coefficients. The choice of technique depends on kinds of measurements we have. If the data are category/classification type, the investigator uses chi-square (x) or contingency coefficients. In the 'case of rank order type of data, rank order correlation is used. At the higher levels involving interval and ratio measures, product-moment correlation is appropriate.

(4) Statistical interference and Tests of Significance: An investigator rarely studies an entire population of his interest, rather he takes a sample of the population for his study. Say, for example, the investigator wants to know the time spent by the university students on TV viewing. He takes a sample of the university students and he ascertains from the sample how much time they devote to watching the TV everyday. The purpose of the study is to make an inference about the viewing time of the students at the university. He calculates the mean, and this sample value is called statistic. The values based on the entire population are called parameters. The statistic, which is characteristic of sample, provides the basis for estimating population parameters. The process of estimating parameters from statistics is referred to as statistical inference.

Q25.Discuss communications research applications in the Indian context.

Ans. The use of a scientific reason for the establishment of speech as a separate department had important implications for the growth of Communication Research. Speech scientists pursue the more recognised human sciences, such as Psychology and Sociology, which had follow such physical sciences as Biology and Physics. Speech scientists take up their research methodologies, as well as many interdisciplinary concepts and perspectives for studying communication phenomena, from the physical and other human sciences.

Research and evaluation in the field of communication in India, especially in, applied areas, such as rural communication and extension, family welfare and planning, industrial and organisational set-up, have been going on for the last three to four decades. The enormous research output eludes easy generalisations.

Nevertheless, some notable trends may be observed.

Most of the studies conducted so far in India are descriptive in nature. History of individual newspapers, biographies of known journalists, debates on issues of freedom of the press and autonomy of the media, problems of professionalism and such issues are the dominant themes of these descriptive studies. Sample surveys on the media audience, their media behaviours, and opinions on various issues form another dominant category of studies. Readership surveys, audience profile studies, opinion polls, media effect studies, (using sample survey techniques), are quite common. There is an abundance of content analysis studies of the media messages, often lacking in practical relevance: Experimental research to test theoretical propositions or hypotheses is sadly lacking.

Altogether, much research has gone into the role of communication in the national development process. Diffusion of agricultural innovations, problems of rural communication, extension education, family planning and welfare have been popular areas generating a vast amount of research and a fund of information. But these research facts have not been systematically collated and theoretically integrated, thus limiting the utility of these findings. A landmark in the Indian communications research is the Satellite Instructional Television Experiment (SITE) which was "one of the largest techno-social experiments ever conducted in human history". It assessed the use of technology for instructional purposes.

Analysing the trends in communications research in India, Yadav made a series of observations, and some of them are reproduced here:

- The studies on newspaper and press in general were more in number than the studies of the other media. But in recent years, the number of studies on the TV and the mass media for communication in general, have substantially increased.
- The sample survey was by far the most common research method followed.
- Traditions of empirical research have gained strength over the years.
- Such issues as rural communication, extension, and family welfare have received a fair amount of attention from communication researchers.
- Although there is now, comparatively, a lot more sophistication in research approach and methodological rigour in the way communication studies are conducted, yet there is a lot more to be desired in this regard.

Q26. Critically examine the impact of mass media.

Ans. The various functions of mass media, the four primary ones are (1) to inform (2) to entertain (3) to educate, and (4) to promote culture, goods and ideas. These functions overlap at times. Each medium tends to emphasise one of these more than the others. The print media tend to emphasise information.

Whereas the broadcast and film media stress entertainment. Advertising is the most blatant form of persuasion, but much of the persuasion in mass media is concealed, and some is passed off as news.

Finally, the media preserve the culture by furnishing a record of events and by noting changes in the social structure.

There searchers underlined individual differences and personal influences on the transmission, acceptance, and retention of mass media messages. Denis McQuail, as pointed out, proposed an interactive perspective. He held that mass media may equally mould, mirror, and follow social change.

Consequently, the origin, development and ultimate use and influence of mass media are in conformity with the changing complexion of society. Though the industrial and communication revolutions have changed the face of our country, it still remains largely an agriculture-based socio-economic entity. Thus, the impact of mass media in India has to be seen in the background of our tradition and value=bound social structure.

Nature of Mass Media Effects: While new media technology is sweeping across India, many questions about the precise impact of mass media remain unanswered. We 'know that the mass media have an impact, but the answers to questions such as what impact they have, why they have impact and how all that happens remain elusive scientists are examining the effects of mass media; we know that we can predict certain out comes in certain situations. But the variables are-numerous. Two social scientists,

Bernard Beralson and Morris Janowitz, once summarised knowledge about the effects of mass media thus in Readers in Public Opinion and Communication.

"The effects of communication are many and diverse. They may be short-range or long-run. They may be manifest or latent. They may be strong or weak. They may derive from any number of aspects of the communication content. They may be considered as psychological or political or economic 'or sociological. They may operate upon opinions, values, information levels, skills, taste, or over behaviour."

Questions on Media Effects: What are the effects of the mass media on our society? To what extent are we moulded and shaped by the media? Are we informed? Or are we manipulated? Are we in control? Or are we merely dancing at the end of strings pulled by mass communicators?

Then, there are allied questions. Should the mass media be as free as they are in our society? What rights should they have? And what limits should be placed on them? Should they be responsible to the government, the society, the audience or themselves?

Should there be any ethical guidelines or standards for mass media operations? Where do the mass media overstep the ethical boundaries? How can pressure be brought on the media to make them perform in accordance with norms acceptable to the society? For instance, what about crime and violence depicted in the mass media? Have we become a violent society because we read about crime in our newspapers and see violence on television? Do news stories about terrorism inspire terrorists? Do stories about airplane hijacking inspire hijackers? What about stories relating to dowry-deaths and suicides? Do they inspire women to take such extreme steps? Do the mass media create violence in our society by reporting it, or do they merely reflect the violence that is already there?

Are mass media in any way responsible for the increase in sexual promiscuity? What have the mass media done to us politically? Can one be elected to a political office without the endorsement of mass media? And are media giving us an accurate picture of our politics and politicians? When going to the polling booth, can we rely on the information we have received from mass media?

To what extent does our government control the mass media and vice versa? To what extent do the media control business and vice-versa? Do the mass media present a fair and accurate picture of women in our society? Are they adequately represented in the mass media? What are the results of the media's distortions of the image of women in society or its version of women's issues? And there are similar questions about other underprivileged and neglected segments of the society.

How have the mass media affected religion in our society? How have the mass media affected our culture as a whole? Are we becoming a classless or a class conscious society as a result of what is served out by the mass media?

And finally, the media themselves are changing because of the new technologies. What impact will this have on our culture and our society? What will satellite cable television, laser beams and computers do to us? And what can 'we do-about them, if anything?

Mass Media Effects and Society: There are no clear-cut and final answers to most of these questions. The growth of mass communication has made it possible for us to get far more information today than any time before. Information is indispensable in a complex, advanced society. We are an information-hungry society; we need an ever-increasing amount of facts in order to maintain and enhance our standard of living.

Information today is a commodity we are willing to pay for. The mass media today are not only entertaining the masses; they are selling information as well. We have often been told that information is power.

Q27. Outline the development of journalism in India from a mission to an industry and explain its present impact on people.

Ans. India, towards the end of the 20th century, still largely remains an oral society. We spend more time communicating interpersonally rather than through the channels of mass communication. The situation in the West is different. There, an average person daily spends at least six hours "consuming" mass media products, mainly TV, radio, film, and newspapers.

Impact of Journalism: In India, the Press has been closely associated with the freedom struggle. This association further intensified as the freedom struggle gathered momentum. In the nineteenth century, the press fought for the freedom of information and the right to criticise. But in the early twentieth century, the freedom struggle took a new turn.

It was no longer petition-making and asking for small mercies from the British Government. When the press projected these changing attitudes, censorship and other restrictions were imposed on it. The revolutionary movement by the active Bengal youth and, particularly, by the intellectuals, led to the suppression of national aspirations and the beginning of distrust by the British. The seeds of Hindu-Muslim disunity were sown, leading to the division of the Indian Press into two categories, i.e. nationalist press, supported by the nationalists and the Anglo-Indian press, supported by the Government.

The Jallianwala Bagh massacre, Gandhiji's Non Co-operation movement, and Civil Disobedience movement soon spread all over the country through the press. The Gandhi-Irwin pact and the Government of India Act, I935 made big headlines in the press. The national press also made people aware of the activities of these paratist Muslim League, started under the leadership of M. A. Jinnah, with the strong support of the British Government. During the Second World War, memorable and extraordinary events took place in India, starting with the Quit India Movement in 1942. The British Government tried to deal with the India problems by sending the Cripps Mission to India. The Mission was opposed by Lala Lajpat Rai and others. This incident convinced the British that it was no longer possible to keep India under subjugation, resulting in the historic announcement regarding the British withdrawal from India. An interim Government was formed which took over in 1946, and continued up to 15 August, 1947. In all these extraordinary events and developments, the press was a direct participant. The Nationalist press under went the same kind suffering as the freedom-fighters.

Changing Face of the Press: Newspapers in India have undergone revolutionary changes, both in form and content, since the eighties. Today, there are hundreds of dailies and magazines crying for attention. Splashes of colour and slick typography based on computer technology, are making them brighter and visually more appealing. To keep up with TV, contemporary journalism has increasingly become more pictorial. While still clinging to the traditional news coverage formula with its emphasis on politics, they have also started discussing social economic, and environmental issues. This has resulted in a drastic jump in circulations and revenues. In 1985, there were 3,000publications with a total circulation of over 26 million. In 1993, just six publications, namely, The Times of India, Indian Express, Malayala Manorama and Ananda Bazar Patrika (dailies) and Malayala Maaorruna Mamgalam and Kumudam (weeklies) have a combined circulation of five million, while 150 other publications have a total circulation of 25 million.

Today, as compared to 1950, the number of publications has increased seven times and the circulation by ten times. The press occupies a commanding position in India despite the low level of literacy, (52.11 per cent) and circulations remaining confined to metros, cities, major towns and district headquarters. There are over 30,000newspapers (daily newspapers and journals of periodicity of different kinds) with over 60 million circulation. The press remains the principal information medium, in the private sector.

Effects of the Press: Newspaper readers, though numerically small in India, largely constitute the intelligentsia. The influence of the press is decidedly far wider than reflected by mere circulation statistics. It has a "multiplier effect", its message spreads far and wide, even into the villages. The Bofors-Sofma field gun controversy snow-balled in such a manner that even Rajiv Gandhi later admitted in an interview that the press was an important factor in turning public opinion against him. The impact of the press can be judged only in the perspectives of current developments and pace of change in the country. Despite its predominantly urban and middle class moorings, the press has done a reasonably good job in highlighting the issues of poverty, corruption and unemployment, and has given the ruling class a sense of guilt. The power of the press is also seen to be mainly responsible for the major political developments in India during the nineties.

Devilal's weekly interview led to his eventual removal. So was an interview published in an obscure weekly which led to veteran C. Subramanian giving up his gubernatorial robes in Maharashtra, or the telephone tapping story which led to Ramakrishna Hegde's downfall. The Harshad Mehta and Gold star scandals are all the contributions of the 'press. The capacity of the Indian press to generate a healthy debate on public issues has been only partially realised. But with increasing literacy, it holds out infinite possibilities in the future.

Q28. Describe the reach of radio and its impact on the masses.

Ans. Radio encouraged the growth of national popular music stars and brought regional sounds to wider audiences. The effects of early radio programs can be felt both in modern popular music and in television programming. The Fairness Doctrine was created to ensure fair coverage of issues over the airwaves.

There are external services broadcasts in 17 foreign languages and 8 Indian languages for about 75 hours daily. The external service is designed to give India's viewpoint on important-issues to listeners abroad, and project the cultural heritage of the country, its art, literature, music and socio-economic developments.

Radio: Medium for the Masses: Radio can justifiably be called the medium for the masses. In India, the three major hurdles to meaningful communication are mass illiteracy, lack of efficient means to reach the remote places and poverty which prevents access to mass media. Radio has the inherent advantage to overcome these barriers. Radio, unlike the print media, can overcome the obstacle of illiteracy. It also does not recognise the barrier of rivers and mountains can reach people in the farthest corners of the country. Thanks to the transistor revolution, this is perhaps the only mass medium which an average Indian can afford.

Local Broadcasting: Local broadcasting is a new concept in participative communication and focuses on the local community. Here, the barefoot broadcasters and the community together initiate the quest for a better life. Several local stations have been 'set up in remote locations in different states in India and some of them have succeeded in striking an immediate understanding with the local people.

Q29. Explain the role of film as a mirror of social realities and its effects on the society.

Ans. Since its beginning with the film 'Raja Harish Chandra' (1913), the cinema has remained the most powerful media for mass communication in India. Cinema has the ability to combine entertainment with communication of ideas. It has the potential appeal for its audience. It certainly leaves other media far behind in making such an appeal. As in literature, cinema has produced much which touches the innermost layers of the man. It mirrors the episodes in such a manner that leaves an impact on the coming generations. Cinema presents an image of the society in which it is born and the hopes, aspirations, frustration and contradictions present in any given social order.

Films can carry not merely information; they can even create a yearning for change and modernisation. By dexterously employing the mechanical tricks of photography and camera angles, by exploiting the ingenious use of close-ups, by building up of suspense and illusion, and by weaving human elements and stay in appropriate sequences, films can create social awareness and even arouse strong emotions. Films can Inform inspire and express feelings and emotions most dramatically with lasting impact.

A film calls for creative collaboration between the film-maker and other performing and visual artists. Films fired the imaginations of people by the closing years of the nineteenth century. Fostered by Edison, Lumiere brothers and George Melies, the film grew rapidly in stature-with the work of Edwin S. Porter and Griffith. By the twenties, the film came to be recognised as an art form, a distinct mode of creative expression. It is also earned universal acclaim. It is a versatile means of communication. It can be produced on all subjects of human interest and includes, broadly speaking, feature films, documentaries and newsreels.

The Indian Cinema: The Indian film industry remains a paradox in many ways. India is going to enter the 21st century with the largest number of illiterates in the world. Therefore, there is an urgent need to have proper communication among these illiterate people. The films in many way meet this need. Because the only meaningful access to audio visual entertainment for the poor people is the film. Films are extremely popular among the masses. And the Indian film industry continues to be the world's largest producer of films, releasing on an average 750 films every year in 16 languages.

The Indian films followed the Hollywood model right from the start with heavy emphasis on entertainment. But individual film-makers, away from the main stream, have always made socially purposeful films, even in the thirties. The Indian cinema discovered its native genius with the advent of Satyajit Ray, RitwikGhatak and Mrinal Sen in the fifties who have earned international acclaim. But it was BhuvanShome, made in 1969 by Mirnal Sen, which ushered in a new consciousness for the whole country. It paved the way for a bunch of talented filmmakers to make their mark. There was meanwhile a southern wave, led by Gopala krishnan, Vasudevan Nair, Girish Karnad and G. Aravindan.

Q30. Describe the role of TV among the Indian elite and masses.

Ans. It's better to begin with this assertion – even if the advent of television in the Indian scenario is a recent phenomenon, it has already made steady advances and profound impacts in the Indian society. There was indeed a time when television in India was a wonder and people of the neighbourhood used to gather in the evening at the owner's house to take a view of the most popular shows of those days. It would be wrong to say that the situation is quite different these days. In reality, there has been a radical transformation by now and television has become part of the life of the Indian populace, especially the urban and semi urban ones.

Developmental Use of TV: An experimental television service was introduced in India with the inauguration of Delhi Kendra, with a UNESCO grant, on September 15, 1959. Entertainment and information programmes were introduced from August 1965. A number of other television centres (Bombay, Srinagar, Jalandhar, Calcutta, Madras and Lucknow) came into existence, from 1972 onwards in quick succession.

SITE: The most momentous development in Television in India was the one year Satellite Instructional Television Experiment (SITE) which was inaugurated on August 1, 1975. The SITE Programmes generated tremendous interest among the people of the six states in which it was launched.

Effects of TV: TV can transport the viewers to the actual scene of action to see things as they happen. But many have also come to hold TV responsible for inciting violence, corrupting the young and creating a make belief world of illusion to keep us away from the realities of life. But if TV can distract and distort, it can also instruct and inspire. The Joshi Committee (1982) expresses, the view that Doordarshan was a faceless medium. It promoted cheap entertainment and cultural rootlessness and sadly neglected the myriad diversities of the Indian cultural tradition. Doordarshan, therefore, has come to represent the unusual case of growth without improvement.

As an instant medium, TV is ideal for news presentation. TV news is unsurpassed in its ability to transport viewers to the scene of action, giving the audience a sense of excitement and involvement that cannot be matched by any other medium.

Q31. Describe the new technologies like Video, Cable, and Satellite, and identify their relevance to the Indian media scene.

Ans. During the mid-eighties video immediately caught the fancy of the affluent section of the Indian society. It holds out infinite promises of entertainment and information. Its potential to enrich the lives of the people, both culturally and economically, has been so far realised only to a very limited extent.

Though better known as an entertainment medium, video has immense possibilities as an educator and commercial persuader. Video on a wide range of subjects, and with interest and appeal to specialised audiences, is increasingly being shown to the professional people, students, technical workers and other group, It also promotes interaction-based programme production. Its safe and easy facility for stop, go, forward and reverse viewing is invaluable for teaching and learning. Naturally its use as a tool for teaching in the classroom is catching. With improved technologies and reduced cost, video is fast becoming one of the most pervasive forms of communication in education, entertainment, business and industry.

According to a survey, (by the end of 1972) there were an estimated 50 lakh videocassette recorders (VCRs) and video cassette players (VCP) in the country.

Secondly, (by the beginning of the nineties) India had an estimated 15,000 video parlours, 60,000 video libraries, 15,000 video buses and about 15,000 hotels showing videos. Video libraries circulate 4.8 crore cassettes every month through more than 30 lakh VCRs. Renting of VCR is as common in India as watching a video in a community function or restaurant. Viewing a film on video is a usual feature in the long-distance buses.

The new audio-visual space that the video has created for itself will be the most deeply explored avenue in the coming years, possibly obviating the need for the costly conventional technology of broadcast television. But more importantly, the technological criteria may no longer be the only determining factor in the transmission of a programme. With the relative simplification of video production and the overall easy access to video technology, it will finally be the content rather than the electronic quality that will dictate matters. The video will wield immense political power and is likely to be transformed into a political weapon like none other in history.

Video Magazines: By the end of eighties, video had discovered an extremely enterprising and innovative mode for dissemination of information through a new genre called the video news magazines. Just as the early eighties had seen a boom in print magazines, the nineties witnessed an explosion of video magazines. The video newsmagazines, a totally new concept in the field of mass communication, have flourished and met with amasing success. Obviously, the coverage of contemporary affairs has taken a new dimension with the advent of the video newsmagazines. The most important reasons for their resounding popularity are their credibility, spot, coverage, comprehensive reporting and their extended focus on matters of immense public concern.

Video and Political Campaigns: Electioneering in India took a new turn with the appearance of video. The potential of video for rousing the masses and for political campaigning was first demonstrated in India during the Andhra Pradesh Assembly elections in 1983. Video I was also used on a large scale (for political advertisement) in the eighth Lok Sabha elections in 1984. About 5,000 video prints of a 20-minute video film, entitled Ma, based on Indira Gandhi's life, were extensively shown in the villages.

It was believed to be one of the major factors behind the sweeping victory of Congress (I). But it was only during the ninth Lok Sabha elections in 1989 that the full impact of the video as a medium of mass communication was first realised by most of the leading national parties.

Cable Television: Cable TV has literally brought the world to our parlour and made a viewer truly an international citizen without my frontiers. Sitting in a remote comer of India, one was able to experience all the horrors of the Gulf War beamed by the Cable News Network (CNN), the 24-hour global television news and feature service. Besides, the viewers can also tune into World net, Arabsat, Intelsat, BBC Sports, Japans at and TV stations in China, the USSR, Saudi Arabia, Pakistan, Singapore and Hongkong, thanks to the dish antenna of the cable operators.

The growth of cable TV is directly related to the inadequacies of Doordarshan programmes - the same factor which is behind the mushrooming of video magazines. Doordarshan is no longer being accepted as the primary source of TV viewing and its role may be further marginalised unless it infuses a new air of vitality in all its programmes. Another reason for the growth of Cable TV is that the cost of having access to a dish antenna what has been steadily coming down.

Basically Cable television is a system of delivering television programming to consumers via radio frequency (RF) signals transmitted through coaxial cables, or in more recent systems, light pulses through fibre-optic cables. This contrasts with broadcast television (also known as terrestrial television), in which the television signal is transmitted over-the-air by radio waves and received by a television antenna attached to the television; or satellite television, in which the television signal is transmitted by a communications satellite orbiting the Earth and received by a satellite dish on the roof. FM radio programming, high-speed Internet, telephone services, and similar non-television services may also be provided through these cables. Analog television was standard in the 20th century, but since the 2000s, cable systems have been upgraded to digital cable operation.

Q32. 'The communication explosion has created areas of danger'. Comment.

Ans. The negative effects of mass media on society can lead people towards poverty, crime, nudity, violence, bad mental and physical health disorders and others as such severe outcomes. It is claimed that this proliferation of information and the swiftness of its distribution would certainly improve the human condition. However, along with the positive values it fosters, the communication explosion has created areas of danger that must be recognised and controlled.

Among them are these five major concerns -

- Perversion of the truth by electronic trickery
- Invasion of privacy
- Violation of security, both governmental and institutional
- Impact on the democratic process
- Isolation of people.

Manipulation: Clever users of electronic devices can alter the meaning of recorded visual and audio material, making it appear to be what it really isn't.

Privacy: There have been innumerable complaints about the invasion 'of privacy.

The whole question of co-relating the right to privacy with public interest has 'become a vexed problem for policy planners and social scientists alike.

Security: Protection of secret government information, private financial transactions, and institutional records In computer systems has become a matter of concern.

Democratic Process: It is democratic that democracy functions best when voters are widely informed on all problems and issues. Given power to select the information they desire with the aid of new technologies, will citizens be exposing them selves to a sufficiently broad range of knowledge? By choosing to see and hear only what interests them most - for example, sports, stock market quotations, and entertainment - will they be able to vote intelligently?

This power of selectivity might actually serve, under some circumstances, as a limiting factor (rather than as a broadening one) in the education of the citizenry.

Isolation: While the communication revolution has the power to draw the global community closer together, simultaneously, it also isolates individuals and small groups. Instead of mingling with crowds at movie theatres, couples and families stay home to watch television and video on their TV screens. Both adults and children sit for hours, aware only of what appears on the small screen. Often they seem visually damaged, almost bewitched. A owing number of workers do their jobs at home, linked to their offices by personal computer. This isolation from comarades, this loss of the group dynamics, has forced some intense media users to seek psychiatric help. The negative influence of such aloneness of a large number of people has not been felt yet in our country.

2 ELEMENTS IN MASS MEDIA

INTRODUCTION

This chapter describes the position of the press in India, especially taking note of post-Independence trends of commercialisation, the concentration of power in publishers hands, and the introduction of new printing technologies, after that the characteristics of radio, television and film. This chapter also discusses the study of the nature, origin, features and behaviour of the audience of mass media. And in the last, we are going to consider the characteristics of mass media messages. With a discussion on the media messages.

Q1. Describe the current status of the print media in India.

Ans. The Indian media consists of several different types of communications of mass media: television, radio, cinema, newspapers, magazines, and Internet-based websites/portals. Indian media was active since the late 18th century. The print media started in India as early as 1780. Radio broadcasting began in 1927. Indian media is among the oldest in the world. It dates back even before the reign of Ashoka. Many of the media are controlled by large, for-profit corporations, which reap revenue from advertising, subscriptions, and sale of copyrighted material. India also has a strong music and film industry.

As of 31 March 2018, there were over 100,000 publications registered with the Registrar of Newspapers for India. India has the second-largest newspaper market in the world, with daily newspapers reporting a combined circulation of over 240 million copies as of 2018.India has over 1,600 satellite channels (more than 400 are news channels and is the biggest newspaper market in the world—over 100 million copies sold each day.

The first Indian media were established in the late 18th century with the newspaper Hicky's Bengal Gazette, founded in 1780. Auguste and Louis Lumière moving pictures were screened in Bombay during July 1895; and radio broadcasting began in 1927. Indian media—private media in particular—have been "free and independent" throughout most of their history. The period of emergency (1975–1977), declared by Prime Minister Indira Gandhi, was the brief period when India's media were faced with potential government retribution.

In India, book printing/publishing has come a long way since 1556 when Portuguese Jesuits set up a printing press in Goa to print religious books for free distribution. Later, printing/publishing efforts were accelerated by the East India Company and the British government to print government texts, circulars and government notifications in the form of Gazette publications and booklets side-stitched or glued together.

The first newspaper printed in India was Hicky's Bengal Gazette, started in 1780 under the British Raj by James Augustus Hicky. Other newspapers such as The India Gazette, The Calcutta Gazette, The Madras Courier (1785), and The Bombay Herald (1789) soon followed. These newspapers carried news of the areas under the British rule. The Bombay Samachar, founded in 1822 and printed in Gujarati is the oldest newspaper in Asia still in print. On May 30, 1826 UdantMart and (The Rising Sun), the first Hindi-language newspaper published in India, started from Calcutta (now Kolkata), published every Tuesday by Pt. Jugal Kishore Shukla.

Even after independence from Britain in 1947, the English-language papers were prominent due to a number of reasons. The telegraphic circuits of news agencies used the Roman alphabet and the Morse code, giving the English press an advantage in speed. The speed of typesetting was also much slower in Indian languages because of the diacritics. Also, the press largely relied on advertisements of imported goods for revenue, and the foreign advertisers naturally preferred English-language media. The language of the administration had also remained English.

Currently India publishes about 1,000 Hindi dailies that have a total circulation of about 80 million copies. English, the second language in terms of number of daily newspapers, has about 250 dailies with a circulation of about 40 million copies. The prominent Hindi newspapers are Dainik Jagran, Dainik Bhaskar, Amar Ujala, Devbhumi Mirror, Navbharat Times, Hindustan Dainik, Prabhat Khabar, Rajasthan Patrika, and DainikAaj.

In terms of readership, Dainik Jagran is the most popular Hindi daily with a total readership (TR) of 70,377,000, according to IRS Q1 2019. Dainik Bhaskar is the second most popular with a total readership of 51,405,000. Amar Ujala with a TR of 47,645,000, Rajasthan Patrika with a TR of 18,036,000 and Prabhat habar with a TR of 14,102,000 are placed at the next three positions. The total readership of the top 10 Hindi dailies is estimated at 188.68 million, nearly five times that of the top 10 English dailies that have a 38.76 million total readership.

The prominent English newspapers are The Times of India, founded in 1838 as The Bombay Times and Journal of Commerce by Bennett, Coleman and Co. Ltd, a colonial enterprise now owned by an Indian conglomerate; The Times Group. The Hindustan Times was founded in 1924 during the Indian Independence Movement ('Hindustan' being the historical name of India), it is published by HT Media Ltd. The Hindu was founded in 1878 by a group known as the Triplicane Six consisting of four law students and two teachers in Madras (now Chennai), it is now owned by The Hindu Group.

In the 1950s, 214 daily newspapers were published in the country. Out of these, 44 were English language dailies while the rest were published in various regional and national languages. This number rose to 3,805 dailies in 1993 with the total number of newspapers published in the country having reached 35,595.

The main regional newspapers of India include the Marathi language Lokmat, the Gujarati Language Gujarat Samachar, the Malayalam language Malayala Manorama, the Tamil language Daily Thanthi, the Telugu language Eenadu, the Kannada language Vijaya Karnataka and the Bengali language AnandabazarPatrika.

Newspaper sales in the country increased by 11.22 per cent in 2007. By 2007, 62 of the world's best selling newspaper dailies were published in China, Japan, and India. India consumed 99 million newspaper copies as of 2007—making it the second largest market in the world for newspapers.

The whole world is trending towards a technology era with immersive experiences being more popular among users, but print will still have its own position in advertising. The reason for this is that print has personal impact that people can touch and feel. Fine art is created when paper and ink come together in a powerful way. This is why the Columbia Journalism Review refers to print ads as the "new media".

In 2006, newspaper circulation in India was about 39.1 million copies, yet until 2016, this number has grown to 62.8 million – a 60 per cent increase. Comparable data for the most recent year available, 2015, show that although circulation fell in almost every major media market (by 12 per cent in the UK, 7 per cent in the US and 3 per cent in Germany and France), the newspaper circulation grew by 12 per cent in India. Why print media show good performance in India? Probably because of the primacy of the written word and the home delivery of the newspaper. The bulk of paid circulation is dominated by dailies in English and other languages. These now account for nearly 56 million of the total circulation in the period under study. The highest circulation of 22 million copies a day comes with Hindi language dailies, followed by English at 8.55 million, Malayalam (4.55 million) and Marathi (4.33 million).

Q2. Identify the developments of commercialisation and new printing technologies after Independence.

Ans. In India, printing came first to Goa in 1556 and then moving along the coastal towns, it finally penetrated into Calcutta and inland provinces. The first English newspaper, James Angustus Hicky's *Bengal* Gazette was published in Calcutta in 1780. The first language book was the grammer of the Bengali language. Although the first Bengali language newspaper appeared in 1816 for a short while, the regular Indian owned language newspapers were started by Raja Ram Mohan Roy in 1822; he is rightly known as the father of Indian language journalism in India.

Since Independence, printing/publishing in India is pulsating with charged energies of professionalism and technology, which has resulted in well-designed and well-produced newspapers, magazines, books. This considerable change in printing/publishing was possible because of the availability of expertise provided by the professionals produced by Regional Schools of Printing Technology sponsored under the First Five Year Plan.

Over the years, more such institutions were opened, besides one IIT (Indian Institute of Technology, Bombay, which runs an advance course on design), two universities at Jadavpur and Chennai offering graduate and post-graduate courses of late Guru Jhambeshwar University in Hissar, Haryana, is offering graduate and post-graduate courses. Although the progress has been substantial, when we take the overall picture of the publishing industry into consideration, it has not been uniform all over the country; in fact rather uneven in certain states.

In the first three decades of 1900, when independence movement was gathering momentum and so was publishing and distribution system of the printed word in the form of books, journals and newspapers and the clandestinely printed newsletters, in came the influx of various publishing houses involved with printing and publishing of textbooks for schools and colleges, religious books, books on literature, both oriental texts and newly penned books in various regional languages infused with national feelings.

Publishers like Moti Lal Banarasi Das (MLBD) established in 1903; Anjuman Taraqqi Urdu (Hind) established in 1903; Nagari Pracharini Sabha established in 1910; Oxford University Press (Indian Branch) established in 1912; and Gita Press in Gorakhpur established in 1927; gave a great push to the Hindi publishing trade in the heartland covering Bihar, Uttar Pradesh, Madhya Pradesh, Punjab, parts of Andhra Pradesh and Bengal.

Deep in the south, several printing/publishing houses like Vidyarambham Press and Book Depot established in 1931 in Alleppey; KR Brothers established in 1925 in Calicut; Prasad Printing & Process established in 1935 in Madras; and Commercial Printing Co established in Madras in 1936 played a key role.

Sri Saraswaty Press in Calcutta, established in 1932, played a crucial role in the printing of underground publicity materials for the freedom movement. While the freedom struggle was on the printing/publishing trade in India was dragging its feet due to constant harassment by the British Raj and the lack of essential ingredients needed for the progress and survival of the trade – paucity of funds, as the government assistance was almost negligible and private investors had diverted funds to the cause of the freedom struggle on the sly. The printing/publishing industry did not keep pace with the technological developments in the west – so very few printers/publishers could match their products with the products printed/published in Europe and other western countries.

Q3. Underline the role of small newspapers in enlightening readers on how to exercise their right to emphasise the need for maintaining professional and ethical discipline in media operations and note the role of the Press Council of India in this connection and indicate the future prospects of the print media.

Ans. Although some of the newspapers have adopted desk top publishing technology, the overall cost is mounting. The cooperative type of management has not gained ground. The development council, as envisaged by the Second Press Commission, has not yet been constituted. As no significant measures have been taken to revitalise the sinews of the grassroot newspapers, the bottom line of the Indian newspaper industry remains weak. The government's existing concessions, in terms of supply of newsprint and advertisements, are not enough by themselves to sustain their professional health.

At the same time, it is well known that small newspapers are not all paradigons of virtue. Some of them have been censured by the Press Council for having succumbed to temptations of different kinds. This is a serious problem. It is necessary to take steps to ensure that the small and medium newspapers become financially viable and do not resort to malpractices of any kind. Only then the press would be in a position to discharge its obligations to people in rural India.

Professional discipline is necessary for all media. Realising the importance of this obligation, the Western press has evolved codes of ethics to ensure discipline. The first Press Commission had envisaged that the proposed Press Council of India would evolve such a code. We have a code only on the coverage of communal riots.

The Press Council, the press barons and the high browed journalists claim that matters of professional discipline should be left to the conscience of individual media institutions and practitioners. The Press Council, which can censure the erring newspapers, finds it difficult to enact an enforceable formal code. It has, however, of laid down certain guidelines in its decisions taken from time to time. The council considers this should be good enough. One of the council's decisions enjoins that it is the duty of the press "to serve the people with news, views, comments and information on matters of public interest in a fair, accurate, unbiased, sober and decent manner. Publication of inaccurate, baseless, graceless, misleading or distorted material should be avoided". The second important induction is that newspapers should not publish anything which is per se defamatory or libelous against any individual or organisation unless such a publication is in public interest.

Likewise, the Press Council has forbidden any intrusion or invasion of the privacy of individuals unless it is outweighed by genuine overriding public interest. Among other taboos prescribed are, not to jeopardise the present state, and society, and the rights of individuals, and not to resort to vulgarity and obscenity.

The Press Council believes that by obeying such rules a newspaper will not only command social respectability but will draw good business too.

When TV came on the scene, Marshal McLuhan Prophesied the doom of the print media. TV turned from black and white to colour and yet the print media survived.

Now the cable TV and satellite cable TV pose danger to routine TV. It is feared in our country that Doordarshan may be gobbled up by the satellite cable TV despite the remedial measures proposed by the government. Perhaps nothing of that sort may happen. Whatever may be the future possibility, at least no visual media can replace or uproot the print media. You know that the print media have built their niche in the society and their role or providing exhaustive and interpretative information cannot be completely taken away by other media. They have played their role well in the past. This they will continue to do irrespective of Speed and glamour of the new communication media.

Q4. Discuss the new trends in Print media with suitable examples.

[Dec-2019, Q.No.-3]

Or

Critically examine the characteristics of print media.

Or

"Print media serve the information needs of audience better than television.' Do you agree with the statement? Substantiate your answer.

[June-2019, Q.No.-3]

Ans. Trends in print media come and go. And while it might have seemed like the introduction of the digital age would have heralded the end of print marketing as we know it, modern printing trends highlight the best of what can happen when you combine digital innovations with traditional print techniques.

Print is always going to have benefits for brands, in particular when it comes to building trust and nurturing relationships with potential and existing customers. And today, the most effective trends in the printing industry are the ones that bring together the best of both the print and online worlds.

The print media have an added advantage; ease and convenience in using them.

People can read newspapers and magazines wherever and whenever it is convenient to them- at home, in transit, in office or back at home in the evening. That is not possible in case of the electronic media, for they are time scheduled. If one fails to see a programme on TV at a given time, one misses it forever unless the programme is recorded. The old issues of printed media can be easily preserved in the libraries.

Current issues of prominent or well produced magazine are displayed even in the drawing rooms of the urban elites. The actual number of readers of the magazines and periodicals is more for they change hands at the magazine parlours as also among the subscribers. In our country, interestingly, even the old issues of newspapers and magazines are saleable at a discounted price.

New-Trends in Print Media: After Independence, certain innovations in the printing technology and other socioeconomic developments have had a significant effect on the role and functions of the print media. The two notable developments are shift towards commercialisation and introduction of new printing technologies.

Commercialisation: The national newspapers, during the British period, functioned primarily with a missionary zeal and acted as the voice of the freedom fighters and stimulated the movement through advocacy journalism. They underwent a significant change after Independence. Having successfully helped the nation to win freedom, the missionary zeal of the newspapers evaporated. Journalism in India, like elsewhere, had already become a publishing industry. The cost of production and distribution was increasing fast in India; so were wages of journalists and others engaged in newspaper production. The competition too was growing. Although the two Press Commissions stressed "public utility service" as the main attribute of a good press, they did not completely sidetrack the financial aspect because without financial viability the freedom is not possible. The theory of delinking of the press from business houses engaged in other industries was not accepted by the newspaper magnates.

New Printing Technologies: The induction of modern printing technologies has brought about a new climate of working in the print media organisations. It of course varies from unit to unit, depending upon the nature of technology employed. In big organisations, reporters now type their copy straight on the computer linked with video terminals (that is, the electronic type-setting machines) and not on the mechanical typewriters. Copy, after corrections, is stored in a small computer where it can be retrieved by the desk for final selection and electronic editing. The next stage is to prepare the layout, page by page, again by the video process. The final copies of pages are sent to the bigger computer which transmits them to the specially sensitive plates for printing. The desk is no more clustered with edited copies or proof read material. There is no noise of whirling machines or that of the deafening rotaries. No storage of galleys or stereo plates used in the former rotary printing. No spoiling of hands by the lead. The front portion of a newspaper or a printing press resembles the office of a bank or any other corporate office.

The copies of newspapers, you read at home, are now elegantly printed, bearing creative typrographical and layout designs. In fact printing today has became a graphic art. Whether you are browsing through **The Times of India, Saptahik Hindustan, India Today, Swagat, Nai Duniya, Aaj or Tribune,** it **is** a pleasing exercise in eye scanning.

The newspapers at the stalls today are nearly as tantalising as the glittering magazines. There are elegantly produced morning papers accompanied by colourful supplements on fixed days, especially on Saturdays and Sundays. The seductive tabloids called the 'eveningers', both in English and Indian languages, have flooded the metropolitan towns. Their consumers are largely the train and road commuters who are anxious to know about the latest news. The lure of their catchy titles and big size pictures, along with the ever-present sparkling magazines, has so far enabled the print media to hold well in competition with the electronic media.

Need for Content Evolution: However, merely good looks cannot be a substitute for professionalism and high quality, reader-oriented journalism. The content analysis of newspaper and magazines has revealed a lack of uniform professional excellence in the press. Most of the newspapers concentrate on political issues and negative news (like disasters).

High class specialised or feature journalism, investigative and research-based depth or development reporting, and incisive analysis of current national and international news are lacking. The same few high profile commentators dominate in all the newspapers and magazines. To win over a large section of people, the printing revolution must be accompanied by a content revolution so that the newspapers play a more robust role in the coming days of intra-media competition. Regular readership surveys will be of great in achieving this goal.

Profession Suffocation: The trend towards commercialisation became even more pronounced as the newer, printing technologies were increasingly adopted by big and medium sized newspapers, both English and Indian languages, as also by magazines and journals.

These technologies were capital intensive and pushed the press further in the grip of commercialism. The computer controlled photo composition, multi-coloured offset, facsimile, desk top publishing and laser printing added colour, gloss and a variety of typographical designs and made old drab newspapers look attractive. This bestowed power on the investor and his managerial staff. As a result, contract journalism is gaining ground and the instances of deviant editors being fired are becoming more common. This trend of the editors being "cut to size" and diminishing value being attached to objective and truthful reporting because of political and commercial pressures has been considered a retrogressive development by leading media observers. The changing relationship at the top managerial and editorial levels has adversely affected the morale of the journalists at the lower levels within the media organisations. Many have complained at media seminars of professional suffocation.

Role of the Press: The press is widely acknowledged ka watch-dog in a democratic country. The diversification and segmentation of reading material, together with the emergence of .new styles of reporting, writing, and editing have help the print media to flourish.

Today the press is not merely informing, illuminating, investigating, and exposing but even warning and biting. Particularly when acting in the public's or reader's interest, all these roles are justifiable and perhaps axiomatic. According to Dinning and Backer, all media in the emerging society act as:

- purveyors of information,
- provides of pleasure and enjoyment,
- furnishers of channels of expression and interaction,
- economic activists and changers of perception, influences of behaviours,
- builders of institutions, and
- shapers of the future.

Some researchers may not agree with these big claims, but all the print media meant for mass communication have subtle potentialities in this respect; they must of course be used professionally and according to well planned strategies.

Q5. Write a short note on:

(a) Small newspapers

Ans. A small newspaper is a newspaper with a circulation less than 2500. The newspaper organisation also needs to deal with import duties, credit restrictions and importing licence. Many newspapers never have enough revenue to run the paper efficiently, as they sell copies at low rates. The development council, as envisaged by the Second Press Commission, has not yet been constituted. As no significant measures have been taken to revitalise the sinews of the grassroot newspapers, the bottom line of the Indian newspaper industry remains weak. The government's existing concessions, in terms of supply of newsprint and advertisements, are not enough by themselves to sustain their professional health. At the same time, it is well known that small newspapers are not all paradigons of virtue. Some of them have been censured by the Press Council for having succumbed to temptations of different kinds. This is a serious problem. It is necessary to take steps to ensure that the small and medium newspapers become financially viable and do not resort to malpractices of any kind. Only then the press would be in a position to discharge its obligations to people in rural India.

(b) Professional Discipline

Ans. Professional discipline is necessary for all media. Realising the importance of this obligation, the Western press has evolved codes of ethics to ensure discipline. The first Press Commission had envisaged that the proposed Press Council of India would evolve such a code. We have a code only on the coverage of communal riots The Press Council, the press barons and the high browed journalists claim that matters of professional discipline should be left to the conscience of individual media institutions and practitioners. The Press Council, which can censure the erring newspapers, finds it difficult to enact an enforceable formal code. It has, however, laid down certain guidelines in its decisions taken from time to time. The council considers this should be good enough. One of the council's decisions enjoins that it is the duty of the press "to serve the people with news, views, comments and information on matters of public interest in a fair, accurate, unbiased, sober and decent manner. Publication of inaccurate, baseless, graceless, misleading or distorted material should be avoided". The second important induction is that newspapers should not publish anything which is per se defamatory or libellous against any individual or organisation unless such a publication is in public interest. Likewise, the Press Council has forbidden any intrusion or invasion of the privacy of individuals unless it is outweighed by genuine overriding public interest. Among other taboos prescribed are, not to jeopardise the present state, and society, and the rights of individuals, and not to resort to vulgarity and obscenity.

Q6. Write a note on the beginnings of radio, television and films.

Ans. The first degree programme in broadcasting began in 1939. In 1965 the School of Journalism, the Department of Speech, and a newly formed Department of Radio-Television-Film became the three departments officially organised as the School of Communication.

In 1896 came the film, in which the performance was caught by the camera and preserved on the celluloid. It could be shown again and again, without any variation(which is not possible in stage medium), to different audiences. So, the film could reach vast masses. Till 1927, it was the era of the silent film. In 1927, sound was added to the film and we got talking films or talkies. In India, the first talkie was released in 1931.

The 1920s witnessed the coming of radio broadcasting in many countries, including India. The silent film had no ears. Now, the new medium, radio had no eyes. And, yet, both media excited the people. Lack of ears was a limitation and a challenge for the silent film. Lack of eyes was a limitation and a challenge for the radio. But both film and radio converted the challenge into an opportunity. That was accomplished through creative imagination of talented men.

In the 1930s, the television made its bow in the West. Its true development took place after the Second World War. In India, the new glamour medium came in 1959.

Today, TV pervades the life of people-in most nations. It has become a very powerful medium of information, education and entertainment. Like the film and the radio, TV has its unique process of communication and psychology of reception. All the three media (like the stage medium) have their relevance and utility.

Radio and TV are called the electronic media because they are electronically operated. Today, they are the supreme media of mass communication, leaving the other media far behind.

Q7. Discuss the characteristics of Radio.

Ans. Radio is a linear medium. The selection process takes place in the studio and the listener is presented with a single thread of material. Radio has boundation of time and lack of space. It can allow less space to advertisement and personal announcements than paper.

- **A Medium of the Sound:** It is an exclusive medium of the sound. It is an aural or auditory medium, a medium of the ear. There are three elements of a radio broadcast. They are the spoken work, music and sound effects. They are all sounds carried on the air waves to the listener. To be acceptable, all these sounds must be pleasant and expressive for the ears of the listener. They must be artistically integrated or mixed to provoke the imagination of the listener. Otherwise, the intention of the broadcast would be defeated.
- **A Medium of the Voice:** Radio is a medium of the voice. The performer can use only his voice in a broadcast. The producer mixes his voice with music and sound effects. But it does not mean that a broadcaster, say, an actor, has only to learn a few tricks of the voice. An actor, using only vocal tricks, would soon start sounding fake or untruthful to the listener. A radio listener has a highly developed ear or sound sense. It has been correctly said that an actor or any other performer must broadcast with his mind. An actor, for example, must express all the emotions through his voice alone - the torture of the soul, the pleasure, the laughter and so on. He is not wearing any costume or make-up; there is no scenery or properties. Neither he nor his co-actors are seen by the listener. So he must imaginatively give cues or intimations only through his expressive voice. This he will be able to do only if he mentally gets under the skin of his character and dialogues or speeches.

  Vocal tricks will fail a broadcaster because voice does not exist autonomously or independently. It is a part of the total person of the performer. A truthful vocal expression will come only if the whole person's mind, soul, psyche and imagination and his body are all in tune with one another. That explains the difference between a good and a bad radio broadcaster.
- **Microphone:** The Link between Speaker and Listeners 'Microphone is the only instrument through which a radio broadcaster speaks to his listeners. And, microphone is a devilish precision instrument (G.B. Shaw, 1925). It is a hi-fi (high fidelity or faithfulness) instrument that patches the softest sigh, the minutest shade of the voice, the tiniest rustle of the

paper. It exposes all vocal lies or untruthful expressions. It amplifies even the feeblest hiss or a sob. Microphone will tell all, the truth from a lie. So, only truthful vocal expressions can go well with the ear of the listeners. Because of the microphone, the broadcaster must speak into the mike as if the listeners are sitting by his side. He must not speak like the stage performer. The stage performer has to reach out to the last man in the last row. The stage performer has to project himself outwards because the auditorium diminishes him, his voice and body. But the radio performer must project himself inwards because the microphone amplifies or magnifies him, his voice.

- **An Intimate Medium:** Radio is an intimate medium. The broadcaster must imagine as if the listeners are sitting by his side, shoulder to shoulder. To the listeners, it sounds as if the broadcaster is speaking from within the sound box, the radio set or the transistor. It is as if the broadcaster and the listeners are made for each other as if the broadcaster is broadcasting for each listener individually.

  Because the radio is an intimate medium, the best subjects for radio broadcasts are those which intimately concern the listener like the personal, the private and the family problems, the family relations, the working of the soul, the innermost feelings.

  Intimate subjects are especially relevant to good radio drama. And intimate style of acting is especially relevant to the radio. Words, which are supreme or sovereign on the radio, too, must evoke intimate images on the stage of the imagination of the listener. (Silence or absence of words on the radio is fatal. It is like an empty stage). Like the words, the manner of expressing or articulating the words must also be intimate. The words and the manner of their expression or articulation must be intimate also because the condition in which broadcasts are received are very informal. May be one or two or three listeners are sitting by the fireside or in bed or moving about the house, doing all sorts of things. Sitting in the informal conditions of the home, they are casually dressed. The communication must be informal and intimate.

The broadcaster must build an instant equation or rapport with the listener. The listener, sitting in informal conditions, is casually dressed and has not spent any money for the radio show, a talk show, a quiz show or a drama show. If he does not find the show or the broadcast interesting enough for the first two or three minutes, he will switch off the broadcast. It does not cost him anything to dial out the performer who is not interesting enough.

A radio listener is not sitting in an auditorium along with so many others. In an auditorium, he may not get up to get out for fear of disturbing his neighbours even if the stage performer is not interesting enough. But in radio's reception conditions, he will not disturb anybody if he switches off the uninteresting performer. So, the rule of the oil industry applies here:if you cannot drill in the first two minutes, stop boring.

So, the text of the broadcast, a talk, a discussion, a documentary, a feature, a docu-feature, a docu-drama, etc. must get into the subject informally, intimately and interestingly right at the start.

- **A Mass Medium:** Radio is a medium of mass communication. Its broadcasts reach hundreds of thousands in one go. On the one hand, as we said above, it is as if the performer is communicating with a vast mass of people collectively. His task is to find out the lowest common denominator to communicate well with the largest number of listeners. Because hundreds of thousands of listeners, listening to the same broadcast simultaneously, belong to different classes and groups of society, they have different educational, social, economic and cultural background. It is a much cheaper medium of mass communication. Hence, it is very relevant to developing countries like India. A radio set or a transistor is far cheaper than a TV set. It costs much less to set up a radio station as compared to a TV station. Not only the capital cost, but recurring expenses to run a radio service are less. A large number of people can afford a radio set but not a TV set.
- **Simple Language:** A very large number of people are illiterate or semi-literate in India and other developing countries. So, the

language of radio broadcasts must be simple, must contain the idiom of the common masses. It must be closer to the spoken language that the common people use than to the literary language. The literary and the technical words must be avoided because the common people, specially the illiterate or semi-literate segments, do not understand them. The broadcast language must be simple, lucid and direct which can be commonly understood.

This medium of mass communication has the potential of becoming an important medium for informal information and education and for dissemination of ideas. It has the potential of transforming a traditional society into a modem society.

- **A Mobile Medium:** Radio is a mobile medium. You can have it at home, take it to the picnic resort, listen to it while driving, have it on land or under the sea, in public or in private. So, it is a most convenient medium for anybody. It can accompany you and entertain you anywhere. It can be, and is, a never-failing companion. It does not respect unities of time, place and action as prescribed by Aristotle, more than two thousand years ago, for dramatic communication. Stage drama may, even now, respect these unities because of the obvious limitations of the stage medium. But radio drama, which is drama of the mind, may hop from any period or place to any other period or place. Because the radio player performs on the canvas of the listener's mind, so to say. And the mind, truthfully sparked off by the player, can construct any period, any place.
- **A Cheap and Quick Medium:** Radio is a medium of immediacy. It can report the events almost instantly, as they are happening. So, it is a medium of the "here and now". Even for TV, it is more difficult to take the camera immediately to events as they are happening. It is the radio which can be the first to report the happenings.

  Radio is a much cheaper and quicker medium than television for production of programmes. For example, it requires a performer and a producer who may also be a recordist and an effects man. As against this, a TV production (tele-production) would require a costumes man, a make-up man, two or three cameras and cameramen, a dolley man who assists the cameraman, in moving the cameras, a scene designer, a carpenter, several lights and light men, several monitoring sets, engineers, a producer, performer, etc.

Since the cost and time required to produce a programme are much less, radio can produce a wide variety of programmes. It can also afford to experiment with new and innovative programmes.

- **No Shared Experience:** Radio listeners have no shared experience, like the stage medium's spectators have in an auditorium (the auditorium could be a closed one or an open-air auditorium). Radio listeners are sitting all alone or with one or two members of the family. In the stage medium, spectators are sitting a crowd, a sort of social gathering in an auditorium. The psychology of reception for a radio broadcast is much more informal than the psychology of reception for a stage performance or a show. The spectators for a stage show are governed by a crowd psychology. They are specially, formally dressed up for the show. They may have also spent some money for the ticket for entry. They come for witnessing the stage show in a social gathering Psychologically, they are in a mood to accept the make-believe on the stage. As the poet-critic Coleridge said, they "suspend disbelief' and are forgiving. They are prepared to believe the illusion or magic of the stage performance. They are ready to suspend their critical faculties to enjoy or experience the performance.

Q8. State and elaborate the characteristics of Television.

Or

Critically analyse the potential of television as a medium of education in the present media scenario, with suitable examples.

Ans. Television is a system for transmitting visual images and sound that are reproduced on screens, chiefly used to broadcast programs for entertainment, information, and education. The television set has become a commonplace in many households, businesses, and institutions. It is a major vehicle for advertising.

(1) An Audio-Visual Medium: TV is audio-visual but predominantly visual, proportionately much more visual than audio. A TV broadcast is conceived and produced and received in audio-visual terms.

A radio broadcast is conceived, produced and received entirely in terms of sound, for 'the ear only.

A TV broadcast directly affects two senses simultaneously, those of hearing and seeing. It is more effective than the radio broadcast. Radio is a unisense medium, affecting only one sense, hearing. TV broadcasts can have greater effect or influence on the receiver of the broadcast, called the viewer.

The potential of TV to have greater effect or Impact is because, according to psychologists, the eye absorbs much more than the ear in the same time. The eyes also retain the seen image much longer than the ears can.

(2) Features of Other Media: TV has borrowed certain features from the earlier media of communication like the stage, the film and the radio. But it has so mixed up these borrowed features as to make something uniquely different, uniquely its very own. For example, from the stage it has borrowed movement, from the film the camera, from the radio the microphone. But TV has integrated all these into a whole that makes TV a uniquely new medium, different from all other media, thoroughly telegenic. In nature, in idiom of expression, in conditions of reception, in its arithmetic of communication, it is different from the other three media.

(3) Wide Reach and High Credibility: The TV camera, today, goes to the planets, it goes under the earth and into the sea and throws light on the dark areas of knowledge about our world, the universe, and the total environment. It has brought about an information revolution and has turned our society into an information society.

Because of its reach. TV has widened the mental horizons of man. It has become the supreme educator of man. It has the potential of humanising knowledge. The man can be educated to feel as a citizen of the world. He can be educated by TV to look at the entire environment sympathetically and to think of himself as a part of it. TV has a great potential for imparting fruitful lessons on One World education to mankind.

TV is a credible, a believable medium. Seeing is believing. Things that few people might believe otherwise become believable when shown on the TV screen. Stories of man's poverty and richness, of the beautiful and the ugly, of m6anness and nobility, of despair and exultation, when seen with naked, open eyes, become absolutely true. They become effectively truer than those that one reads in the print medium or listens to on the radio or learns through hearsay or word of mouth. Just recall the tele-pictures of the upheaval in Russia after the collapse of Communism. Or, the visuals of uprising at the Tienanman Square in China or those of the Iraq war. Or, of the havoc done by earthquake in Maharashtra.

Because of its reach and believability, it becomes a powerful medium for projecting the world, of politics, sports and art, personalities, events and ideas. You have surely watched international sports meets and sportsmen becoming super-super stars overnight. It is sometimes said that to a large extent, Presidential elections in the United States of America are won or lost on the TV. Politicians in power cleverly use the TV medium to promote their party and their own political career.

(4) A Glamour Medium: TV Is a glamour medium. You watch on TV glittering personalities and events, international conferences, sports meets and festivals, fashion shows and banquets, travel shows and interviews with world leaders, bold and beautiful personalities as well as rich and famous people. The great convenience of, watching all this, sitting back at home, adds to its glamour. The facility of watching almost round the clock enhances the glamour appeal still more.

Because of its glamour, TV has also been called the magic box. All sorts of people at all sorts of times, almost magically, seem to be appearing on the screen from within the box. It has also been called a toy, a toy with which adults get fascinated, like the child's toy which fascinates the child. Incidentally, some critics have also called it an idiot box. Perhaps, TV "idiotically" churns out at all sets of times all sorts of programmes, good, bad and indifferent, watchable and unwatchable. Also, perhaps, because It shows only those things which the programmers, and men behind the camera, in their wisdom think should be shown.

Very few can resist the glamour and magic of TV. It has a habit of attracting people to the point of addiction. Tele-addiction, in fact, has become the greatest addiction of our times, of most people including the children, the young, the adults and the old; sitting by the TV set has become a second nature with them. The programme, its nature or content does not matter with them. They seem to be happy with some pictures, any pictures appearing on the small screen.

(5) A Medium, of the Close-up: TV is the medium of the close-up. Its stage is its screen which is small. Because of the small screen, it is not an ideal medium for spectacles or huge pageants. It is ideal for close-up of human faces, for long shots of scenery.

It is an ideal medium for expressing reaction and interaction between people in a tele-drama, for presenting an interview and a discussion, etc. That is why you would find the camera catching the reaction or expression of the man who is talking at a particular moment. If something has happened or somebody has said something, the camera would show the reaction of several people, one by one, in close-up. According to artistic necessity, the camera would take full close-up or half or quarter close-up of a character or a man.

(6) A Living Room Medium: TV is a medium of and for the family. It is a medium of entertainment and information at home. The whole family or some members. of it sit by the screen to watch TV shows.

TV watching brings together the family increasingly. There is likelihood of increasing interaction between members of the family, especially in developing countries like India where people cannot afford a TV set In every room.

TV brings theatre and cinema auditorium to the living room: Stage drama has become drawing room theatre. Film drama too has become drawing room cinema auditorium. Fewer people now go to witness stage performances. Also, fewer people go to the cinema theatre for a movie.

Earlier, people used to get specially dressed up to witness a stage drama or a film. It is the reverse process now. The film or the theatre comes to you in your drawing room under home conditions. Just think of street theatre in the context of stage drama. Instead of the people going to the theatre, the street drama takes the theatre to the people.

Since TV is watched by the young and the old members of the family sitting together, the tele-subjects have to be in tune with the culture of the particular society. In our country, the subjects must be treated with restraint. They must respect our cultural heritage. They should not be very explosive or provocative. Since young girls and boys are sharing the viewing with their elders, parents, grand-parents and parents-in-law, the consideration of good task, of our cultural taste cannot be overlooked.

Also, the subjects should not spread communal hatred, conflict, enmity between countries. The government in which certain subjects are prohibited.

Since it is an intimate medium for the family and the home: some of the ideal subjects are those that handle intimate human relationships, relationships between the members of the family, between neighbours, friends and the over-all pattern of relationships in the society.

(7) A Democratising Medium: It is a democratising medium. It is available to all people. Since it is a medium of mass communication, it has to deal with the problems of all sections of the society. It democratises information and informal education, reaching out to one and all. It also tends to democrate literature by discussing it in broadcasts or by telecasting it in a dramatic version. Even those who have not read literature or are illiterate or semi-literate come to know of it.

Since TV, a mass medium, has to cater to all sections of the society, it is not generally and uniformly very artistic, Highly artistic things might go over the heads of the common viewer. As against TV, the stage can afford to be highly artistic because its audience is selective. Only those people go to the theatre who are ready to pay for the show. Theatres like off-Broadway and Off-Off-Broadway have select audiences who are ready to pay for artistic productions as against commercial productions.TV cannot choose its viewers. And TV does not charge ticket money for entry into its shows. So, most TV programmes are for the common people. Exceptions are there, as they have to be.

TV productions, at least a majority of them, cannot be of high artistic value because TV is a medium in a hurry. It has to fill almost 24 hours, at least a large pan of the waking time every day. It has to meet schedules. Day after day a producer has to produce all sorts of programmes, news, views, documentaries, features, quiz shows, dramas, serials, soap operas, etc. In mass production, the quality cannot be uniformly high.

On the other hand, the above situation gives the producer scope for experimentation and to touch excellence in some productions. Since he makes so many programmes, he can afford experiments, even failures.

As against this, a stage theatre producer, just cannot afford failures. He produces one, two or three shows in a year for the professional stage.

(8) A Medium of Immediacy: TV is a medium of immediacy. It captures the events even as they are happening, much before the newspaper comes out with information on events next morning. Yesterday's news is no news on TV. It will make TV look outdated. TV is a supreme reporter. In audio-visual terms, it reports the events "here and now". Remember how the CNN or BBC reports minute-by-minute Presidential election results or Olympics or Gulf war.

TV operates in fixed time units. Every programme slot has a time chunk. The time unit must be respected. Otherwise, all time schedules for all programmes would be disturbed.

Because of fixed time units for slots, the performers and the writers of the scripts have to be disciplined. So also must be the producer. For example, a tele-play is usually scheduled for 29-1/2 minutes or 59-1/2 minutes (at least half a minute is kept for the announcer). The writer, the performers and the producer must say what they have to do in the allotted time.

(9) Advertisers' Influence: TV is the great salesman of modern times. The businessman sells his products and service through TV. This medium is much more effective for him to reach out to a vast number of potential and actual customers than the newspapers, hoardings, etc. TV advertisements or programmes sponsored by businessmen can reach tens of millions of people. No newspaper can ever dream of reaching out to such large numbers. The implication is that he who pays the piper will call the tune. The tune may be bad, socially and culturally. It may be without taste, artistically. The advertiser, the sponsor, is interested in only selling his goods and services. He may be irresponsible in his advertisements, in their content and presentation. But to make the content and presentation of advertisements tasteful and that do not offend the culture and morals of viewers, Sponsors and advertisers should prescribe a code.

Q9. Discuss the characteristics of Film.

Ans. Film, also called motion picture or movie, series of still photographs on film, projected in rapid succession onto a screen by means of light. Because of the optical phenomenon known as persistence of vision, this gives the illusion of actual, smooth, and continuous movement.

Film is a remarkably effective medium in conveying drama and especially in the evocation of emotion. The art of motion pictures is exceedingly complex, requiring contributions from nearly all the other arts as well as countless technical skills (for example, in sound recording, photography, and optics). Emerging at the end of the 19th century, this new art form became one of the most popular and influential media of the 20th century and beyond.

As a commercial venture, offering fictional narratives to large audiences in theatres, film was quickly recognised as perhaps the first truly mass form of entertainment. Without losing its broad appeal, the medium also developed as a means of artistic expression in such areas as acting, directing, screenwriting, cinematography, costume and set design, and music.

Film is a continuous strip of exposed celluloid. Celluloid is composed of several reels. Reels have several shots. Shots have several frames. Frames have only images which are static and do not move. So, film is only a sequence of static images, recorded by the camera. These images move and come to life through projectors, running one after the other at the end of each reel.

Actually there is no real movement of images when the projectors project them on the cinema screen. It is only an illusion of movement of images. This illusion of movement is made possible by the property of quality of the viewer's eye. We humans have in our eyes the faculty which is called persistence of vision. Persistence of vision in the ability of the retina of our eye to retain the image due to the stimulus of light.

So, film strips contain on!: static, frozen movement and action. Fast projection of images on the screen gives an illusion of movement and action to the eye which has persistence of vision.

A motion picture is not shot as continuous whole. It is photographed in bits and pieces. Final scenes may be shot first and the opening scenes later. Intervening or middle scenes may be recorded in a jumbled sequence. This shooting process is understood completely by the director alone. Later, he may create any effect by joining scenes in a certain sequence, through what is called the editing or "cutting" process.

An actor is also a creature of the machine in cinema. The success of effectiveness of his performance mainly depends on the director and how he gets the film edited, how he gives meaning and depth to various shots and sequences, how he mixes music and sound effects with the spoken words. The actor may know the script of the film drama as a whole but may not know the position or purpose of individual scenes. So, he is completely dependent on the film director. He must, almost blindly, follow the directions and suggestions of the dictator of the cinema, the director.

Although the film actor and the stage actor are both artists of acting, the stage actor is much less dependent on the machine like lighting and sound effects. He has more freedom. No doubt, like the film actor, the stage actor too is dependent on the director but only during rehearsals. Once the curtain goes and the show starts, he is absolutely free. In fact his performance keeps on varying from one show to another. This is because of several factors, like the type of theatre space, the type of audience, his own mood, mental state, the feedback he gets from the live audience, etc. That is why it is said that a stage actor keeps on making "statues of snow". It means his performance dies the very movement he performs just as statues of snow melt the moment they are made. In the next performance, his statues of a snow are also different. The film actor's performance is captured and recorded on the film. He cannot vary his performance. He makes statues of marble, so to say.

(1) A Mass Medium: Film is a medium of mass communication. Millions of cine-goers watch the movie in a country. The same movie may be seen by a very large number of people in several countries (like Richard Attenborough's "Gandhi"). Although in a cinema hall only a few hundred or, at the most a few thousand people, can watch a-film at one time, it can be shown in many cities, towns and villages at the same time. Any number of copies can be made of the film for screening. Today, a film can also be transferred from the celluloid to the video cassette. The cassette can be played at home through the VCR (Video Cassette Recorder). The cable operators can transmit the film on to the TV sets of a large number of their customers at the same time. So, a film can reach out to a very large number of people.

(2) Mechanically Reproducible: Film is a mechanically reproducible medium. So it can be preserved. It can be seen again and again. It can be useful for research on a relevant subject. It is very useful as a mirror of society at the time when the film was made. It describes the political, social, economic and cultural scene of a country. It describes the customs, fashions and attitudes of people at a particular time. It also throws light on the style of acting, music, dance, direction, etc. of the times.

Films can be watched and understood even by illiterate people. They may not have the fortune to go to the books for information and to enrich their personalities. But they can understand and entertain themselves with the films.

(3) A Collaborative Medium: Film is a collaborative medium. So many people collaborate to make the film and to reach out the film to people. Producer, director, writer, actor, art director, music director, dance director, fight director, lights man, costume man, make-up man, scene designer, sound man, cameraman, clapper boy, etc. work together to make a film.

After a film has been made, the financier, the distributor, the exhibitors, etc. work together to make it available to the common people. No other medium depends so much on so many people.

It is the director's medium. Although a team of so many artists and technical people have to work in a true team spirit, the director is the boss in film-making. It is his word, his conception which must prevail. It is he alone who conceives and visualises the film in its totality. So, everybody must obey him. Everybody must carry out his directions. He is the dictator in cinema.

The director, with his artistic and technical skill, can make a good film out of a bad script. (A bad director, similarly, can kill a good script). He can, by using several devices like different camera angles, editing, re-recording, re-processing in the laboratory, can make an average performance look great on the screen. In the cinema, camera is very important, next only to the director. But it is the director ultimately who gives orders to the camera too.

The director orders several "takes" of a scene or a sequence. He finally selects the most effective take. He sits along with the editor on the cutting table and arranges the shots, joins the sequences, mixes them with music and sound effects, dubs the scenes and manipulates the shots in so many ways. He does all this with the help of so many machines and technical devices. All this is done to give meaning, logic, rhythm and depth to the story and the performance. Some of the great names who have used the technical devices to great advantage are Griffith, Eisenstein, Steinbeck, Pudovkin, Cecil D'Melle, Hitchcock, Godard, Melies. Some great directors in India have been Satyajit Ray, RitwickGhatak; Mrinal Sen, Shantaram,

Raj Kapoor, Hrishikesh Mukherjee, Bimal Roy, Kedar Sharma, Mehboob, Basu Chatterjee and 'shyamBenegal.

(4) An Art Medium: Film, today, has become an art medium. It is in the last decade or two that cinema has come to be considered an art form. In the beginning it was considered a medium only of cheap entertainment, even of escaping from harsh realities of life into the world of fantasy and dream for two to three hours. In our times, intellectuals and serious thinkers have associated themselves with cinema. In fact, today, cinema is considered the seventh art like the earlier arts of painting, sculpture, architecture, drama, poetry, and music.

Pudovkin, the great Russian theorist of cinema, had pleaded in 1933 that cinema is a synthesis of the oral, the visual and the philosophical elements. He called for making the greatly effective cinema as an art form which will leave behind all the older arts. He called it a supreme medium to express yesterday, today, and tomorrow with its own unique language.

Satyajit Ray made a passionate plea to introduce cinema as an art discipline at the universities. It should be studied by serious scholars and developed further. It should not be treated as a sub-culture and only as an entertainment medium. That is how it was treated in the earlier years in India and elsewhere. Devices like montage, double exposure have made it very artistic.

(5) Government's Role: Our government must remove high taxes on cinema. It must relax the licensing rules for cinema theatres. Harsh rules and high taxes give an impression that cinema is treated as an activity which is undesirable. However, it must be said to the credit of our government that it has set up some organisations to promote cinema as a worthy and artistic activity. Important organisations in this respect are the Film and Television Institute of India at Pune, the National Film Archive, the National Film Development Corporation, the Directorate of Film Festivals, the National Film Awards and the Children's Film Society. It has also indirectly supported the Film Society Movement.

The Working Group on Cinema, set up by the government, has recommended the establishment of a Chalanchitra Academy, a Film Educational Advisory Service, a Film Information and Documentation Centre, a National Film Museum, and Children's Film Centre.

(6) A Medium for Development: Film is an effective medium for development. Development, in the broad sense, means the growth of the individual and the growth of the society in all aspects. These include political, economic, social and cultural aspects. Film can contribute to modernising the traditional society by helping to change the attitudes of people. For example, a change in attitudes relating to work, sex, religion, customs, communities, beliefs, etc. can be brought about films.

Films can promote national and emotional integration. They can bring about a creative understanding between different regions and their people. They can be a medium for educating the people against superstitions and for promoting scientific, modern ideas.

Film is a very effective medium of communication. We have already noted that film can be a medium of education and development. It is particularly true because its impact on people, good as well as bad, is substantial. We are talking about the ability or potential, of the medium. What the impact will be depends finally on how the medium has been used.

The capacity of the film to do good or ill for the society is generally well recognised.

You must have surely heard parents complaining that their children pick up ideas from films about clothes, about hair style, about manner of greeting or about their general behaviour towards others, including teachers, parents, etc. It means that they tend to initiate what is portrayed or depicted in films. Obviously, films should set good standards for imitation.

(7) A Medium that Demands People's Concentration: The conditions under which a film is screened and is received by the cine-goers in a cinema house demand concentration of different sections of society, sitting together in the same hall and constituting the audience. All these people tend to be unified, so to say. Everybody's motive is the same, to watch the film drama. The lights are put out. Suddenly there is total silence. A sort of magic atmosphere. There is expectation and anticipation on the part of everybody. Concentration is centred on the screen and the audience almost appears as a unified mass.

The images, the words, the music, the sound effects are skillfully integrated. For the audience, the integrated whole or the film becomes a total experience. This demands great concentration from the audience. Sitting in the dark silence of the hall, audience is mysteriously affected by how the story and scenes are presented. In a very indirect way, the director communicates his or camera's point of view. He has various means to communicate his viewpoint.

(8) A Realistic but Expensive Medium: The film can be effective in hitting the consciousness, sometimes conscience of the audience with the camera. The camera is mobile, is moved from, one angle to another. At one time, it is placed at the objective angle- at a distance from the object, say, a palace. At another time, the subjective angle is emphasised- that is the camera acts as the eyes of the audience. And, then, the camera is placed to give the actor's point of view. Generally, it is the director's point of view. He hides himself behind the actor hut speaks and sees through him. By clever change of camera angles, the audience is made to believe in the illusion that the film is speaking out their thoughts,-their very own. Film viewing becomes, thus, very convincing and effective. The large cinema screen helps to emphasise the effect, especially in close-up that fills the large canvas. In fact, the effect becomes so great that the viewer starts identifying himself with the hero or some other character. That is why the memory of certain scenes lingers on in the people's memory for long.

Film is a realistic medium. Camera and microphone can never be kind to any exaggeration. The body movements, postures, gestures and expressions, like the voice, must be life-like. They must be perfectly truthful. Any loudness of body or voice will appear fake, false. The camera and the mike will amplify and highlight any unreality in performance.

It is an expensive medium. Tens, sometimes hundreds of lacs of rupees are spent on a film. The actors and actresses, especially if they are stars, are very expensive. So are the raw film and all the processes of film-making. In spite of the fact that film-making is very expensive, it is a cheap medium of entertainment. Particularly in poor countries like India, it remains a popular medium for the vast masses.

In India, there is a dominating commercial cinema, art or parallel or "other" or off-beat cinema and middle cinema. Middle cinema takes care of the artistic as well as the commercial aspects. Therefore, cheap commercial cinema is not accepted in India.

Q10. What do you understand by the term Mass?

Ans. The term mass have different meanings. If we look at physics, the word mass refers to the quality of matter or material contained in an object. It may also mean a quantity of matter of indefinite shape and size-a lump.

Sometimes the word mass is used to refer to common people, especially the lower classes. Mass also has both negative and positive meanings. In the negative sense, it refers to the ignorant and unruly mass. Mass implies a lack of culture, intelligence and even of rationality. In socialist tradition, mass has a positive meaning. It connotes the strength and solidarity of ordinary working people when organised together for political ends.

In general usage, the word mass refers to people in a large number. If we say masses are ignorant, we mean that a very large proportion of the population is ignorant.

Similarly, when we say mass destruction, it means destruction on a very large scale.

Mass awareness programme refers to a programme that aims to create awareness amongst a very large number of people.

In fact, the most important feature of mass is its very large size in terms of the number of individuals. It will be appropriate if we say this mass refers to an infinite number of individuals. The size of mass is very large and unknown.

Secondly, masses are geographically distributed. Very large number of people may be attending a public meeting. They are physically present at one place and they are called a public. The individuals of mass may be present anywhere and everywhere.

When we say masses in developing countries are poor we refer to the people living in Africa, Asia, Latin America and perhaps some other pans of the world as well.

Since the masses are very large in size and in physical terms the people are distributed all over, they are anonymous to each other. The individuals in a mass society are not known to each other. They are not even conscious of the presence of one another. There may be a vague feeling of others like us but it is not well defined.

Since the people are anonymous to one another, the masses are unorganised. Unlike the people in a public meeting, the masses do not have any common goal to achieve. There is no organisation and therefore no leadership or hierarchy in mass. Further, the masses are not capable of behaving as one unit.

Scholars like Roymard Williams have summarised that masses actually do not exist, it is only a way of conceiving large groups of people as masses. As a conclusion, mass refers to an infinitely large number of people who are physically located at different places and are not organised at all as a group.

Q11. Critically examine the emergence of the theory of mass society.

Or

Write as short note on mass society. [June-2019, Q.No.-10 (b)]

Ans. The idea of mass society originated in the conservative reaction to the French Revolution (1787–99). For critics such as Hippolyte Taine, the real significance of the Revolution lay not in the constitutional changes it brought about but in the deep social upheaval it caused.

The concept of mass society is not to be equated with that of massive society. It is more than the massive society. There are many traditional societies that are very large in numbers but are not necessarily mass societies. The individuals in a traditional society behave more as members of the group rather than individuals.

Brown and Selznick have explained the concept of mass society as follows:

"Modem society is made up of masses in the sense that there has emerged a vast mass of segregated, isolated individuals interdependent in all sorts of specialised ways, yet lacking in any central unifying value or purpose. The weakening of traditional bonds, the growth of rationality and the division of labour, have created societies made up of individuals who are only loosely bound together. In this sense, the mass society is something closer to an aggregate than to a tightly knit group."

In fact, as stated earlier, mass society has no continuous existence, except in the minds of those who want to reach as many people as possible. It will be useful to further understand the concept of mass society using a set of contrasts with other kinds of units in social life, like group, crowd and public.

In a small group all members know each other. They are aware of their common membership, share the same values, have a certain structure of relationships which are relatively stable. The members of a group interact with each other for a purpose.

The crowd is a spontaneous collection of individuals. It is temporary and never reappears with the same composition. Members of a crowd may strongly identify with each other. More important, they share the same mood. But there exists no order or structure in the crowd. In many cases the actions of the crowd are emotional, sometimes irrational also. Crowd is physically present within observable boundaries, that is at a particular place.

Unlike crowd, public is widely dispersed. Its size may be small or large. Generally, public is identified with some cause, purpose or activity. Public may be quite heterogeneous and members may not be aware of each other. usually public is identified by the people who want to perceive a large number of people as targets.

Q12. Explain the concept of audience.

Ans. An Audience is the person for whom a writer writes, or composer composes. A writer uses a particular style of language, tone, and content according to what he knows about his audience. In simple words, audience refers to the spectators, listeners, and intended readers of a writing, performance, or speech.

There are four different ways of looking at media audiences. These are media reach, media access, media exposure and media effects. We shall discuss these approaches one by one:

- **Media Reach:** The owners and producers of the mass media conceive the total population whom their communications can reach. The signals of All India Radio are available to about 95 per cent of the population living in about 85 per cent of the country's area. So the total population of India may be treated as audience for All India Radio. Similarly, Doordarshan can claim more than 80 per cent of the population as its audience because its signals can reach that many people. For a newspaper, audience would be defined in terms of all individuals who are within the distribution range of the papers. For a cable TV system the audience reach will include all residents within the wired area.
- **Media Access:** Mass media may be available but the capacity or willingness to me the media may not be there. A large section of the population does not have the radio receivers or television sets. Thus, only those who own the radio sets may be treated as audiences of All India Radio. But access may not overlap ownership. In fact, there are many people who watch television

programmes at the houses of neighbours or friends or in community centres. Groups watching a popular television programme at a television shop is a common sight.

Many families do not buy newspapers but their members may read newspapers at various places like teashop, barbershop, library or even at neighbours' or friends' houses. This, those who have direct access by virtue of ownership along with those who are non-owners but get exposed in other ways constitute the accessible audience.

- **Media Exposure:** Everyone who has access to radio or television does not necessarily use them. In a family that subscribes to a newspaper, everyone does not read it. So only these individuals who actually expose themselves to the media are the media audiences. Again, no one is exposed to the total content of any medium. No one listens' to the programmes broadcast by All India Radio. Similarly, it is impossible to watch all the programmes of Doordarshan. Many people do not even glance at the commerce page of the newspaper. There are many young people, specially students, who read only the sports page. So audiences can also be seen as programme specific or content specific, that is, populations actually exposed to specific media content.

  Another important aspect of media behaviour is that all users of media content are not uniformly exposed. There are people who listen to news ever day without fail. Others may listen to news, say on an average of five days a week. Still others may be listening to news only once a week or even less often. And, of course, there are people whose exposure to news on radio is nil.

- **Media Effects:** Another way to think about audiences is in terms of individuals who have been exposed to mass communication products and have undergone a change in their knowledge, opinions, attitude or behaviour. A person may not recall anything of the information received after listening or watching a news programme. The same person, after watching an advertisement, may immediately rush to buy the advertised product. Voters generally do not change their voting preference after listening to election broadcasts by the representatives of political parties.

Q13. Critically Examine the duality of Audience.

Or

"The commercialisation of media has led to a situation where audiences are treated as markets. Do you agree with the statement? Give reasons for your answer with examples. [Dec-2019, Q.No.-4]

Ans. The history of mass media indicates that audiences can originate both in society and in media and their contents. People stimulate an appropriate supply, or the media attract people to what they choose to offer. If we take the first view, we can consider media as responding to the general needs of a national society, local community, or preexisting social group. They also respond to the specific preferences actively expressed by particular sets of individuals—for instance, the politically active, or business people, or youth, or followers of sport, and so on. Alternatively, if we consider audiences as primarily created by the media, we can see that they are often brought into being by some new technology.

(1) Rise of Audiences: The original audiences were the sets of spectators for games, stage plays or dispension of justice by the kings. Such pre-media audiences existed in all cultures in one form or another. Audience for religious discourses have played a very significant role in the spread of social and political ethos.

Invention of printing revolutionised the whole character of audience. This was the beginning of mass audience. The most important change that took place was that the audience participation as a private act became possible. People could now take the printed materials to secluded places and undergo a totally private experience. This led to another important change. The audiences become delocalised. It was no more necessary for all members of the audience to be present at one place. A book had readers spread all over the world.

The advent of newspapers created mass audiences in the real sense. Newspapers also converted mass audiences into potential receivers of commercial messages or advertising. The advent of electronic media further delocalised the audiences. The information carried by electro-magnetic waves could cross the national boundaries.

The audiences were now spread over the whole world. The members were separated from each other and their distance, physical and social, from the communicators also increased.

The audiences now not only took the form and character of masses but they also acquired the features of a mass society. The satellite communication, coupled with cable network on the ground, has brought a situation where the whole world population can be treated as one audience.

(2) Audience Types: The types of audiences can be distinguished based on their demographic characteristic and mental make-up.

(i) **Elite Audience**: Elite audiences are composed of the people who are decision-makers and trend-setters in the society. They are economically well to do and are highly educated. They have high status in the society. Their number is very small but their influence is very strong. They may also be the owners or controllers of the mass media institutions. The members of the elite audiences are the early adopters of communication technologies. Their actual media consumption is generally low.

(ii) **General audiences**: They are very large and highly diverse groups that represent the broad cross-section of the society. Majority of the people belong to this category. The media content is generally targeted at them. Their participation determines the success or failure of a content or medium.

(iii) **Specialised Audiences:** These audiences are composed of individuals who possess similar characteristics. They are relatively small in number. Mass media generate special contents for these audience groups. Programmes for tribals, for housewives, for college students, etc. are examples of programmes for specialised audiences. Similarly, journals like Mainstream, Femina and Economic and Political Weekly have limited but known readership.

(3) Audience as Markets: Rise of consumerism has led to a situation where audiences are treated as markets. The media product is a commodity or since offered for sale to a given body of potential consumers, in competition with other media products. Their potential or actual consumers can be referred to as markets.

With the commercialisation of broadcasting and telecasting in our country, the audiences are being treated more as markets. There is competition between Doordarshan, STAR TV, ZEE TV, MTV to capture as big an audience as possible.

Drastic changes in the programme content of Doordarshan main and Metro channels is an indication of the fact that even the state controlled medium is forced to view audiences as markets. Audience, according to the market concept, can be defined as an aggregate of potential consumers with a known socio-economic profile at which medium or message is directed.

Audience has a dual significance for the media. Firstly, as set of potential or actual consumers of media content and secondly, as the audience for advertising messages.

Thus a market for media content is simultaneously a market for other products; media serve as advertising vehicles for delivering messages to the potential customers of other products. Advertising is the largest source of revenue for all media.

In fact, no medium can survive if not supported by advertising or some other sources. Till the time AIR and Doordarshan were not commercial, the government used to subsidise their services. The most popular programmes of radio and television attract the maximum advertising. Not only that, advertising rates are the highest for prime time programmes.

The treatment of audiences as markets has social and moral implications as well:

(i) When the relationship between the media and audience is that of producer and consumer, the character of relationship becomes manipulative. The elements of accountability or even morality are reduced considerably. The aim is to sell as much as possible.

(ii) She members of the audiences are markets and are treated as passive receivers. The audiences are lured by cleverly designed messages.

(iii) Thirdly, the success of the media is measured not in terms of needs fulfilled but in terms of sales of the products.

(iv) The market view is that of the media owners and media producers. Audiences never see themselves as markets.

Q14. Briefly Discuss the nature of audience experience.

Ans. As the public grows less passive, the nature of communication and presentation must change to better accommodate the new audience demands that are placed upon experience providers. A revolution is taking place out there in the dark, and like all revolutions that matter, its effects are being felt one person at a time.

The development of the relationship between the mass media and the audience can be seen in two contrasting ways. We may consider the availability of a large number of media units as media explosion. In this conception, the media occupy the central position and information from the various media is seen as acting upon the audience.

But if we observe the media audience relationship carefully, we find that the audiences actually exercise their choice as to which medium is to be used and also which content they would like to be exposed to. Marshall McLuhan saw the audiences at the centre of the numerous attacks by different media. He referred to this as media implosion as against the media explosion. Rewards may be immediate or delayed but the focus is basically on the satisfaction of the audience needs. Individuals attend to a particular mass communication because it satisfies some needs.

The effort required for attending to mass communication may be considered in terms of the availability of the media and the ease with which we may use the media.

Expense involved and the time required are also important factors in "the effort required". Watching a film on television is less expensive, less time consuming and little effort is required for it as compared to watching a film in a cinema hall.

The uses and gratification theory of the media effects proposes that basic human needs motivate individuals to attend to particular forms of mass media and to select and use messages in ways they find personally gratifying. A conscious and motivated selection amongst the various mass media and also amongst the various item of content has been made by the audience.

Q15. Explain different type of audience feedback.

Ans. Listening to your target population means making sure there are open lines of communication between your audience and your organisation. Show the public you're interested in what they have to say, and then give them an outlet to voice concerns or get more information.

(1) Market-Based Feedback: Mass Communicators receive the following information through the market-based feedback system:

(i) audience access to the media

(ii) audience exposure to the media

The above mentioned information is received by the mass communicators by three methods:

(i) Audience Decision-making: Audiences decision to subscribe to newspapers or magazines is a direct feedback about the popularity of the publication. Rise and fall of circulation is a very important feedback that the market provides. More and more houses paying for cable TV connections indicates the increased popularity of the satellite channels. At the same time, it may also indicate that the audiences are not very happy with the Doordarshan programmes. Increased circulation of a newspaper implies endorsement of the style and editorial policies of the newspaper. Sales at box-office is a good feedback about the popularity of a film.

Sometimes, audience reactions to mass communication are very actively solicited. Coupons, rebate offers, bring-this-ad-and-get-a-discount and similar practices are used to measure the impact of particular promotional efforts.

For books, magazines, newspapers, video and audio cassettes, film and cable TV connections, the audience behaviour has a direct bearing. More consumers mean more revenue. In case of radio and television and even for newspapers and magazines, the largest share of revenue comes from advertising. But again the advertising rates are determined by audience sizes, and thereby audiences exert their influence, though indirectly.

(ii) Direct Feedback: Mechanisms of direct feedback are provided in each media system. Newspapers and magazines have columns reserved for letters to the editor sent by the readers. Similarly, radio and television networks have programmes reserved for comments, reactions suggestions from the audiences. Unsolicited letters and telephones also provide important feedback. In some cases, casual conversation between employees of mass media and members of audience may provide important feedback.

A careful observation of the mass media in our country over the last two decades would reveal that the felt needs for direct feedback from the audiences is increasing.

Space devoted to the letters to the editor column in newspapers and magazines has increased. Similarly, more and more air time is being given on radio and television for programmes where representatives of the audience are allowed to give their reaction and suggestions.

(iii) Media Reviews: Media give the greatest importance to the feedback received through the reviews. Every newspaper and magazine has a media review column written by a media critic. In these columns, the media critics examine the mass communication of radio and television. Similarly, there are regular reviews of films, audio and video cassettes published in newspapers and magazines.

The role of these media reviews is two-fold. One, the owners, controllers and specially the producers of radio and television programmes take the comments very seriously. Secondly, these reviews provide information to the audiences. They, in fact, provide expert opinion and influence audience to notice and use particular mass media content. A radio or television programmes or a film or book or a song sequence commented favourably becomes acceptable to the audiences. Many people buy or read a book after reading its review.

In our country, there were no reviews of the print media except in academic journals till recently. Now, some newspapers have introduced these. For example, The Pioneer has a weekly column Blue Pencil by G.S. Bhargava. It appears on every Sunday and critically comments on the coverage in different newspapers.

Firstly, the critic acts as a link between the producers and the audience. At this point, critic performs the role of calling attention to the availability of information and recommending responses. Secondly, the critic may provide his expert comments to the producers. At this point, the act is an interpretation of how and why the audiences reacted positively or negatively to the content. Various functions performed by the reviewers can be listed as follows:

(a) Informing audiences what is new and interesting.

(b) Raising the cultural level of the community.

(c) Advising the audiences on how to use their time and money.

(d) Helping artists and performers to understand how their efforts are being received by the audiences.

(e) Recording the history of mass communication.

(f) Entertaining audiences with their articles and reports.

(2) Research-Based Feedback: The market-based feedback and the reviews are more or less passive systems. Feedback information gets generated without the producers making effort for it. They leave many questions unanswered. A newspaper will get information that its circulation is decreasing but it is not known as to who are the people who have stopped subscribing and why have they done so. Similarly, media critics may hot comments at all on a programme or their comments may be considered subjective.

Research based feedback systems are created to provide systematic information about audience responses to a particular mass communication products of services. Many media organisations have their own audience research systems.

For example, there are Audience Research Units in All India Radio and Doordarshan. These units keep on collecting audiences responses to various programmes. Based on the research findings, the producers may improve their programme; some programmes may be discontinued or their timings may be changed.

Reliable and systematic information collected about the listenership or viewership leads to ratings of different programmes.

The use of the media by advertisers and media planners is based on such information. With this information, messages can be made to reach the desired audiences in a more cost effective manner.

Q16. What impact does the advent of television have had on the media habits of the audience of radio and films.

Or

Describe the audiences of various medias.

Ans. Audience is the important part of communication process. By media audience we mean the recipients of Mass Media messages. There is the audience of newspaper, television, radio, theatre, film and non-broadcast media. Audience of the above media re heterogeneously scattered. They are a mixture of age, sex, profession, education and social class etc and are strangers to one another. Audience is the ultimate source of Mass Media revenue. If there is no audience to purchase movie tickets and recording, subscribe to newspapers and magazines and attend to radio and TV programmes, no mass medium could stay in business. The messages of TV newspapers and film etc,. are determined according to the nature and behaviour of the target audience.

(1) Multiple Media Usage: Different media may attract different audiences but there is a considerable overlap between the audiences of one medium with those of the-other. Researchers have shown that persons who are above average in exposure to one medium are above average in exposure to other media as well. A person who reads a newspaper is likely also to read magazines, listen to radio and watch television. Lazarsfeld and Merton called this phenomenon as all-or-none principle. A person interested in escapist entertainment will find it in boob, magazines, films and televisions. Another person interested in public affairs will probably get exposed td newspapers, news programmes of radio and television. Anyone who has little opportunity to use one medium because of poverty, illiteracy, ignorance or lack of time or interest-will probably have little opportunity to use any medium.

(2) Newspaper and Magazine Readership: Newspapers attract very heterogeneous audiences. Children and young people generally do not read newspapers. Most of the readers read only the headlines or at the most read the introductory paragraphs. The finance page has a special readership composed of businessmen and those involved in economic and commercial activities. Sports page has an audience of predominantly young people. Editorials and edit page contents have a very small readership.

Magazines are generally read by people with more education and those belonging to higher economic strata, in general, young people are likely to use newspapers and magazines for entertainment, older people for information and views on matters of public life. Adults do more news reading than young people; the latter pay more attention to photographs and visuals like cartoons and comic strips.

More males read newspapers and also at greater length than females. Higher economic status is generally accompanied by increase in the reading of public news, sports news and society news. People belonging to low and very low socio-economic strata generally read local newspapers or they pay more attention to local news in regional or national newspapers. Middle-class readers tend to read national newspapers. Highly educated and rich people tend to read international newspapers arid magazines or the newspapers and publications of other countries.

(3) Radio Listeners: Before the advent of television, radio was the medium for all classes. However, many people neither owned radio sets nor did they have access to radio in any other way.

Transistor revolution spread the ownership of radio receiving sets very widely. But in our country at no time more than 60 per cent of the families owned radio sets.

Not-so-poor people and belonging to lower middle classes generally owned single hand or two band radio sets. As a consequence, their exposure was mostly confined to local radio station or medium wave stations. People with efficient receiving systems listened not only to AIR but also to foreign systems like BBC, Voice of America, Radio Moscow.

After the advent of television, radio listening in television owning households has fallen drastically. Many television owning households do not use the radio sets at all.

The predominant use of radio today is for music in the background while people are engaged in other work.

Many people use radio as an announcer of time. Unlike in US and other western countries, radio is not much used in motor vehicles in our country. Audio-tape players have become more popular in cars, buses and trucks.

Young persons use radio to listen to film and non-film music. Adults also listen to music but they tend to use radio as a source of news and information. Housewives may use radio as a companion during the day when they are alone. Young men and women appearing in competitive tests use radio as an important source of information, specially news and current affairs programme. Spotlight and Samayaki are very popular among those sitting in civil services examinations.

(4) Television Viewers: The tremendous popularity of television is at the expense of radio. With the advent of television, total time devoted to the media has increased. All sections of the population wish to watch television, Many have their own sets. Others watch television at neighbours or friends houses or at community centres.

News and current affairs programmes of Doordarshan are seen by more educated sections of the society. Common people tend to watch entertaining serials. Ramayana on Doordarshan had the largest ever audience. DD Metro is more popular than the main channel of Doordarshan.

Generally, people now subscribe to cable network systems. ZEE TV has a wide audience in Hindi-speaking middle and lower classes. The audience of Star TV is restricted to middle and upper middle classes. MTV has an audience of young and rich who are relatively more exposed to western culture and values. Research has shown that programmes like Krishi Darshan have very small audiences even among the farmers.

It is important to note that the viewers of television also become the audience of the films. A number of films are shown on various channels of television. Besides there are many programmes that are based on films. The television and film industries have become closely related and there are films now produced only for television. The premier of Mahesh Bhatt's film Phir Teri Kahani YaadAaiwas held on Zee TV. Even in radio, film music finds a wide outlet and thus audiences of radio and film music overlap.

(5) Film Audiences: Till television spread its network, films were the most widely used mass media. All sections of the population, very poor to very rich, went to cinema theatres to watch films.

With the advent of television, VCR, VCP, satellite transmission and cable networks, the film watching in cinema halls has decreased considerably. But the total exposure to films has perhaps increased.

Different types of films have different audiences. Common people generally like to watch masala-films that have an adequate mixture of emotions, comedy, violence, dance, music, sex, etc. The new-wave films, the art films and low cost films have an audience that is composed of more educated, socially conscious and intellectual sections. Religious films and films based on epics have an audience composed mainly of rural people, women, illiterate poor, etc. similarly, informative films or films with social messages have different audiences.

(6) Book Readers: Book-readers have a high exposure to other media. Books attract people who are above average in education and also in their use of the serious contents of other media. Books are more likely to attract young adults than older ones, people living in urban areas rather than in rural areas, people or high income rather than low income.

Books in Hindi and other Indian languages are read mostly by the people belonging to these language groups. Highly educated, well off people prefer reading English books.

Q17. Discuss the characteristics and elements of an effective media message with suitable examples.

Ans. Effective messages include a clear purpose to inform, persuade or collaborate with the intended audience. The message should be designed according to the audience's level of understanding, potential reaction and relationship with the composer. symbols or even through silence. But if it is not understood properly by the audience concerned, it is an exercise in futility. The difficulty in understanding the message properly can arise for a variety of reasons. May be the language is difficult. Or possibly the concepts are so complicated that the recipient cannot grasp them. The problem can also arise if the speaker doesn't draw clear conclusion. In that case, the listeners may draw different conclusions, depending on their background and their understanding of the issue.

There is an interesting story which explains this point. Once a biology professor was performing an experiment. He dropped a worm into a beaker of water and the worm continued to wriggle in it. The professor then dropped the same worm into a beaker of alcohol where it immediately died. The professor asked the class as to what conclusion they would like to draw from this experiment. 'One student in the last raw of the class room replied: "If you don't want worm, drink alcohol."

The message to be effective must have certain attributes:

(1) Clarity, Coherence and Consciousness: The message which is clear, lucid and concise is generally understandable. On the other hand, any message which is heavily loaded or is loose, jerky, overlapping, flabby or wooly becomes confused. Coherence is another attribute of a good message. The message should flow logically from point to point with proper links and examples. It should be a narration of story.

(2) Simple Language: The communicators should approach the concept of style warily and avoid the temptation to embellish the language with purple phrases. The path to good effective communication is plainness, simplicity, orderliness and sincerity. Messages with these attributes get understood and that is what the aim of an effective communication. There is a need for the communicators to take all precautions to ensure that messages are not misunderstood. Here lies the importance of pretesting and other forms of feedback. Pretesting minimises communication failures. This method can also help to pretest the following characteristics of a message: (i) effectiveness of appeal; (ii) readability; (iii) clarity; (iv) effectiveness of presentation; (v) acceptability (vi) appropriateness of length and layout of the message.

(3) Credibility of the Source: 'Who' in the communication process is another important factor in communication. If a famous historian tells how in the times of Jahangir the pulling of the silver chain in his palace would provide instant justice to any grieved person, people will consider that information to be correct, coming as it does from a historian of eminence. But if he recommends that the mechanism of distant communication adopted by Akbar to convey the tidings of the birth of Jahangir through physical chain transmission from Agra to Delhi is an ideal form of transmission and should be practised even today in our villages, the suggestion will fall flat on the students of modem telecommunications. That explains the importance of credibility of a speaker in respect of a particular topic. You will agree that the students of telecommunications will prefer to hear from an expert on telecommunications how a modem two-way telecommunication network could be installed in distant regions of our country.

(4) Persuasion: The message, to be effective, must be persuasive. This means that the contents and appeals should have the power to influence the receivers' attitudes. Communicators today are acquainted with the package of techniques which can endow that thrust to the message. But before we mention them, let us note the techniques which we should not employ.

(5) Rhetorics: At one time rhetorics (the art of oratory) was considered to be the source of persuasibility. The episode of Anthony diffusing the impact of Brutus through oratory in Shakespeare's drama entitled Julius Caeseris a good example of such a feat. In closed societies, propaganda is resorted to for that purpose. It implies drawing an iron curtain (not permitting people to get information or know about a situation from other independent sources). Then the communicators hide the other side of the picture, make repeated statements so that the news which they are disseminating is fully accepted and the cause which they are promoting gets an overwhelming support. They also use the techniques of associating the person, producer or organisation with favourable abstractions such as advocacy of freedom, justice, equality, etc. On the other hand, they would associate opponents with the terms charge with negative meanings such as fellow traveller, pervert, reactionary, war monger, etc.

(6) Modern Batteries of Persuasion: The batteries of persuasion used today are equally effective. They are even better techniques which work in the open and seek changes by consent. One of the techniques is that before starting actual communication, the source must resort to audience analysis. Audience analysis is knowing the attitudes of the recipients of the message on the issue, their socio-economic status, their exposure to media, etc. This audience analysis enables messages to be tailored more appropriately to the felt needs or problems of the audience. This orientation makes messages appealable to the psyche or economic and social requirements of the members of the audience. A good image of the source and his expertise in drafting the message skillfully help a great deal in the acceptability of the message by the audience.

(7) Audience Participation: The research bears out that the objective of communication- whether a change in the attitude or reinforcement of the existing belief- is well accomplished through audience participation. There are many findings which prove that if the management involves the workers in problem solving and makes the workers come out with a solution themselves, they will practise it willingly. This goal may not be attained by merely asking the workers to ensure quality production.

Q18. Explain how the impact of messages can be enhanced.

Ans. A human interest touch, dramatic and emotional appeal can make a normal message very interesting. They can become very convincing and credible if presented graphically and supported by statistics.

Pathetic Stories: One can narrate a pathetic story to evoke an effective human response. For instance, depicting the miserable life of a particular refugee family in famine ridden Ethiopia could touch the human chord of sympathy more intensely than making a flat appeal to donate and save four million people starving in that country. Individuals can be related to a family but not to four million people. Human misery can be vividly illustrated by a small documentary showing a few shots of some poor children picking up remnants of food from a dust bin near a rich man's house and contrasting it by depicting food being with on the dinner table of the rich family. The first part *of* the documentary could cause anguish and, the other part could evoke the concept of disparity and poverty-divide in the country. A photograph of a thin sick woman holding a child with a distended belly would prove the adage that a single picture is more eloquent than a thousand words.

Statistics in Support of Correctness: The use of statistics in an economic survey of a country can lend support to the correctness of conclusions drawn from the survey. The use of percentages and the details can show more convincingly the extent of rise and fall in the production of a commodity. Similarly, quoting feedback evidences or media testimonials in support of a cause can earn significant public backing.

Emotional Appeals: Emotional appeals, if properly used at an appropriate time, can stir imagination. The phrase 'Quit India' joined by Gandhi ji and addressed to the Britishers and 'AaramHaraam Hai', Pandit Jawaharlal Nehru's slogan to activise the nation are still in the minds of Indians. Prime Minister Lal Bahadur Shastri's slogan, Jai Jawan, Jai Kisan, electrified the Indian people during India's war with Pakistan. Churchill (UK Premier) and Roosevelt (USA President) could galvanise their countrymen by issuing well-chiselled appeals during world war II. Appeals, to the self esteem or social status have made people buy costly goods which normally they wouldn't.

Perception Filter: Any message is called a stimulus and a strong and emotion-laden message is termed as a strong stimulus. However, before any stimulus or message can transfer knowledge, create an image or change an attitude, or precipitate a behaviour, it must enter the mind of the receiver. Perception is the process whereby an individual receives stimulus through the various senses and interprets them. The factors which condition the perception of audiences are the information needs, attitudes, values, interests, learning process, social contexts, etc. The ability of the source to codify messages with the knowledge of the perception filter of the audience is, therefore, an important condition for a successful communication process.

Q19. Describe the importance of making messages relevant to the attributes of a particular medium, and to the socio-economic status, attitudes, and media habits of the target audience.

Ans. Mass media perform a vital and a crucial role in society. They are called the Fourth Estate, as they are one of the pillars of democracy along with the executive, legislature, and the other socioeconomic forces that bind a society together. In this context, it is important to note that they are both the watchdogs of public behaviour of elected officials and custodians of popular goodwill as they seek to report on the goings-on in society.

Hence, mass media are especially relevant to society because without the media, we would never know what is happening in the world around us and be without the moral compass and ethical conscience needed to hold society together. The point here is that like all opinion makers, the mass media has both a duty and a responsibility towards society and this is the reason it is considered a vital part of modern democracies.

Electronic Media Messages: The messages of the electronic media and the newer visual media like satellite TV, cable TV, video magazines, include the spoken word, sound inputs, and the action oriented visuals. The radio copy is to be read aloud. Its writing must follow the common speech pattern. It needs to be written in the conversational style because the ear is most uses to conversation. The conversational language is simple and informal. The simple sentence is the most effective tool for the writer of radio copy.

Likewise, simple and commonly understood words are to be used. Besides, an easy flow of the language has to be ensured. Informal words like house in place of residence and actor in place of thespian are preferred. In a broadcasting text, you are telling a story. We, therefore, use words and phrases that can be spoken naturally and relay the story in the form we are used to relating a story. If the language does not sound natural, if the meaning of words is not instantly clear to the listeners, it is not good radio style. One of the other important characteristics of the broadcast message is that spoken words must match with other audio elements.

Tongue-twisting alliterations or combinations of words which are jarring on ears are best avoided in radio copy. They create difficulties for news readers, announcers, and artists at the transmitting end and for listeners at the receiving end. Radio being an aural medium, fine statistics should be avoided in news or other informational programmes. There is no use, for instance, writing that according to the Department of Fisheries, 30,11,782 fish died in the tanks of (any city or state), during the year 1993. "That exact figure is not likely to register with the listener's ears. And that precise figure has no special significance. It is good enough to say that "more than 30 lakh fish ...." Giving of the exact figure is of course essential in announcing the result of a closely contested election. For example, X of the Congress Party defeated Y of CPI (M) by a slender margin of 55 votes. Likewise, in sports stories, the precise figures are necessary. For example: X remained unbeaten with 187 runs. Y took 4 wickets for 37 runs.

TV writing is picturised presentation of a story. Visual pictures replace verbal ones. Programmes are shown, not told. The TV copy is a split copy describing both the video and audio components. Words lose two-thirds of their value on the TV and the eye holds up the picture. What is being seen on the TV screen need not be described through words. TV has its own techniques of visual narration. No wonder that the viewers cling to the TV, absorbed in what is put out on the small screen.

In video magazines, interviews and articulate shots produce poignant or striking news stories. In films, the still pictures captured by the camera at a speed of 24 shots per second and projected at the same speed by the projector in the hall create an illusion of motion pictures on the wide screen, depicting a vivid human story, punctuated by dance and song sequences and scenes of touching and dramatic actions.

Q20. Identify the elements that go into the building up of creative advertisements for different media.

Or

Write a short note on creative ad message. [Dec-2019, Q.No.-10 (c)]

Ans. The production technologies and the availability of media forms constrains the copy writers of ad to create. Nonetheless, it is a creative exercise. A print copy is described as "salesmanship in print". Creativity in the ad format is required towards this end. The entire copy is to be structured along the AIDA line, that is for attracting attention, stimulating interest, creating desire and invoking action. According to Advertising

Manager's handbook, a good copy must do seven things in order to produce results. These are (1) create interest (2) inform the readers to the maximum about the product in an interesting way or in a display form, (3) highlight the solution which the advertised product or service offers, (4) help the readers to solve his or her problem, (5) convince the reader that the advertisement is truthful, (6) persuade the reader to buy the product, (7) to create such awareness of a product in the readers that the next time when they have a problem, they will remember the advertised product as the solution to the problem. In general, a creative copy style is one in which every word counts and communicates. It must speak the language of the market. The message must be concise, precise and eye-catching.

Radio Ad Copy: Radio copies, messages, slogans, jingles and musical commercials are very vigourous although they are oriented only to the ears of the listeners. Combining voices, spoken words, music and sound effects, the copies evoke various mental pictures. As radio gives the copy writer complete freedom of time, and better scope is available for ingenuity and creativity. Radio copywriting or message or slogan formulation, therefore, is an imaginative and professional job. As someone said, the acid test of a good radio copy is "put the copy on the tape and play it back". If it is not found effective, re-do the process until a radio commercial becomes a good package of sound, creativity and mental pictures and above all an order spinner.

TV Commercial: As TV is a combination of all the virtues, strengths and beauty that audio-visual technology can impart, the medium alone draws more ads than any other individual medium does. However, writing a TV script for a commercial is a complicated and highly professional task, since the medium involves moving pictures. Whatever be the type of TV commercial that is to be produced, the script writer has to include all the basic selling steps to cover attention, interest, desire, conviction and action. In fact, the script has to use the strongest attention-getting, attention-keeping and persuasive elements, including personalities and drama. The difference between the TV commercial and the print medium ad is that TV commercial must ensure that viewers grasp the entire story the first time they watch it. In case of the print media, the reader has a chance to look at it again and read it repeatedly. Recent research studies in India and abroad have clearly proved that even TV spots of short duration possess a formidable selling pull. There lies the strength and promotional potency of TV commercials, whether for selling products and services or for promoting non-profit social ideas or public utility causes.

Visuals with New Angles: Pictures and other visuals used in various media are not merely playing the role of supplementary for reinforcing a story but are giving new turns to stories. At times, they contain even independent or deeper versions. Whether it is the cropping, bleeding or placing of figures, they all add different moods to the pictures. Cartoons and other graphics speak their own language of satire or humour. The video and TV camera, through close ups or long shots, aerial or side views, add a new angle to a story. Illustrative or visual journalism is, therefore, becoming a powerful art. The video magazines, computer graphics and mixers add new dimensions to news coverage.

3 ORIGIN AND DEVELOPMENT OF MASS MEDIA IN INDIA

INTRODUCTION

In this chapter, the concern will be with the origin and development of the various mass media. Relating the story of the origin and development of radio, TV and film in India. These three media of mass communication were not born at the same time and have not developed at the same speed. Dwelling on the traditional folk media, which are deep-rooted in our culture and have been with us naturally for ages. This chapter will explain the nature of these folk media, enumerate the different types and suggest methods for increasing their efficiency. And also, the basic features concerning some of these technologies.

Q1. Describe how and when the press originated in India, and identify various stages of its development.

Ans. History of Indian Press accounts for the prestigious growth of Indian newspapers and its significance in Indian history as well. James Augustus Hickey is considered as the "father of Indian press" as he started the first Indian newspaper from Calcutta, the `Bengal Gazette` or the `Calcutta General Advertise` in January 1780. In 1789, the first newspaper from Bombay, the `Bombay Herald` appeared, followed by the `Bombay Courier` next year. This newspaper was later amalgamated with the `Times of India' in 1861. The first newspaper in an Indian language was in Bengali, named as the `Samachar Darpan`.

The first issue of this daily was published from the Serampore Mission Press on May 23, 1818. In the very same year, Ganga Kishore Bhattacharya started publishing another newspaper in Bengali, the Bengal Gazetti. On July 1, 1822 the first Gujarati newspaper was published from Bombay, called the Bombay Samachar, which is still extant. The first Hindi newspaper, the Samachar Sudha Varshan began in 1854. Since then, the prominent Indian languages in which newspapers have grown over the years are Hindi, Malayalam, Marathi, Tamil, Urdu, Telugu, and Bengali.

The status of Indian language papers have taken over the English press according to the latest NRS survey of newspapers. The main reasons include the marketing strategy followed by the regional papers, beginning with Eenadu, a Telugu daily started by Ramoji Rao. The second reason has been the growing literacy rate. Increase in the literacy rate had a direct positive effect on the rise of circulation of the regional papers. The introduction of mother tongue in the primary education stage brought about a great change.

The people who learned their mother tongue at the least could read the regional newspapers fluently and thus became aware of the national and regional scenario. During this developmental period, sale of the regional paper in the respective state rose to a great limit. Indian regional newspapers have several editions for a particular state for complete localisation of news for the reader to connect with the paper. Malayala Manorama has about 10 editions in Kerala itself and six others outside Kerala. Thus regional papers aim at providing localised news for their readers.

These newspapers carried news of the areas under the British rule. The first newspaper published in an Indian language was the Samachar Darpan in Bengali. The first issue of this daily was published from the Serampore Mission Press on May 23, 1818. Samachar Darpan, the first vernacular paper was started during the period of Lord Hastings. In the same year, Ganga Kishore Bhattacharya started publishing another newspaper in Bengali, the `Bengal Gazetti`. On July 1, 1822 the first Gujarati newspaper, the Bombay Samachar, was published from Bombay, which is still in existence.

As of 31 March 2018, there were over 100,000 publications registered with the Registrar of Newspapers for India. India has the second-largest newspaper market in the world, with daily newspapers reporting a combined circulation of over 240 million copies as of 2018.India has over 1,600 satellite channels (more than 400 are news channels) and is the biggest newspaper market in the world—over 100 million copies sold each day.

In terms of readership, Dainik Jagran is the most popular Hindi daily with a total readership (TR) of 70,377,000, according to IRS Q1 2019. Dainik Bhaskar is the second most popular with a total readership of 51,405,000. Amar Ujala with a TR of 47,645,000, Rajasthan Patrika with a TR of 18,036,000 and Prabhat Khabar with a TR of 14,102,000 are placed at the next three positions. The total readership of the top 10 Hindi dailies is estimated at 188.68 million, nearly five times that of the top 10 English dailies that have a 38.76 million total readership.

The prominent English newspapers are The Times of India, founded in 1838 as The Bombay Times and Journal of Commerce by Bennett, Coleman and Co. Ltd, a colonial enterprise now owned by an Indian conglomerate; The Times Group. The Hindustan Times was founded in 1924 during the Indian Independence Movement ('Hindustan' being the historical name of India), it is published by HT Media Ltd. The Hindu was founded in 1878 by a group known as the Triplicane Six consisting of four law students and two teachers in Madras (now Chennai), it is now owned by The Hindu Group.

In the 1950s, 214 daily newspapers were published in the country. Out of these, 44 were English language dailies while the rest were published in various regional and national languages. This number rose to 3,805 dailies in 1993 with the total number of newspapers published in the country having reached 35,595.

The main regional newspapers of India include the Marathi language Lokmat, the Gujarati Language Gujarat Samachar, the Malayalam language Malayala Manorama, the Tamil language Daily Thanthi, the Telugu language Eenadu, the Kannada language Vijaya Karnataka and the Bengali language Ananda bazar Patrika.

Newspaper sales in the country increased by 11.22 per cent in 2007. By 2007, 62 of the world's best selling newspaper dailies were published in China, Japan, and India. India consumed 99 million newspaper copies as of 2007—making it the second largest market in the world for newspapers.

Q2. Write a short note on the following:

(a) Censorship and Regulations

Ans. At that time, The East India Company had started taking a serious view of the contents of newspapers and imposed ruthless restrictions on the printing presses and editors. Censorship was introduced in Madras in 1795 when a newspaper entitled The Madras Gazette was required to submit for scrutiny all the material meant for publication. Similarly, in Bengal, several papers such as the Bengal Journal, Indian World and Bengal Harkaruhad incurred the displeasure of the East Indian Company's authorities in one form or the other. A number of legal restrictions were imposed on the press soon after.

As J. Natrajan says, "the first two decades of the 19th century saw the imposition of a rigid control of the press by Lords Wellesley and Warren Hastings. The May, 1799 regulations required the newspapers to carry the names of the printer, editor, and proprietor in every issue and to submit for scrutiny all material meant for publication. The censorship rules, however, were not strictly followed and also not so severely enforced. A lot of important developments took place between 1813 and 1818, and consequently, among others, a number of missionaries started publishing weekly and monthly newspapers in Bengal such as Dig Darshan, Samachar Darpan, and the Friend of India, the precursor of The Statesman of today.

A number of regulations known as the Adams regulations of 1818 were issued.

These gave enough freedom to the editors but a strict watch was kept on the contents of their papers. Around this time, Raja Ram Mohan Roy and James Silk Buckingham raised a voice for freedom of the press. Though pre-censorship was withdrawn, a number of rules continued to be in force to strictly deal with the press. Ram Mohan Roy's weeklies, Sambad Kaumdiin Bengali and Mirat-ul-Akhbarin Persian, and Bombay's noted paper, Mumbai Samachar, (which exists even today) started publication.

At this point of time, the press came out with some criticism of the administration. Therefore, the first press ordinance was issued in 1823. It laid down stringent regulations for the editors and heavy penalties and fines were prescribed for infringement. The East India Company staff was prohibited from having any relations with the newspapers. While political writings were forbidden, social and religious news, particularly those by missionaries, was encouraged. However, things changed when William Bentick became the Governor-General of India. He and Raja Ram Mohan Roy were instrumental in improving the social climate in the country and a somewhat liberal attitude was meted out to the press by the authorities. The press was allowed a measure of freedom. In 1835 when Charles Met cafe became the Governor-General, he relaxed several restrictions previously imposed on the press.

(b) The War of Independence

Ans. There was a setback for press at the time of war of Independence in 1857. The press freedom, consequently, was curtailed drastically. After the failure of the war of independence, the governance of India changed hands from the East Indian Company to the crown in England. In 1859, when Lord Canning became the Viceroy of India, the India Penal Code IPC) was adopted in 1860. A number of newspapers from Bengal, such as Nil Darpan, The Hindu, Patriot, Shome Prakash, Indian Mirror, Bengalee and several others influenced the Indian public opinion a great deal. With the appearance of the Amrita Bazar Patrika, first in Bengali and then dramatically changing over to the English language, the complexion of journalism in India transformed suddenly and radically.

It needs to be recorded here that around this time a number of noted English language newspapers were established. The Times of India came into being with the amalgamation of four papers - The Bombay Times, The Courier, The Standard and The Telegraph. Besides, the three other noted English newspapers - The Pioneer, Civil and Military Gazette and The Statesman - were born. In Madras, The Mail (an eveninger) and The Hindu, the largest circulated paper at present, also came into existence soon after.

This period witnessed a boom in the Indian language press in the country. Several newspapers in almost all major Indian languages appeared on the horizon. The Bengali language press was of course on the forefront followed by the press in Hindi, Marathi, Urdu, Tamil, Gujarati, Malayalam, Kamada, Punjabi, and other languages.

(c) Famous Leaders, Journalists and Newspapers

Ans. Several famous newspapers such as Bande Matram(Hindi), Kesari and Maratha (Marathi), Swadesamitran (Tamil), Amrita Bazar Patrika, National Herald, The civil and Military Gazette, Free Press Journal, Bombay Chronicle, The Leader, The Tribune, Madras Standard, The Hitavada, and a large number of other papers in English came to be set up. There were a lot of problems that these newspapers had to confront. Kaleidoscopic restrictions on news-gathering, printing and display were imposed. Vernacular Press Act, Official Secrets Act, Newspaper (Incitement to Offences) Act, the newly introduced sections of the Indian Penal Code such 124-4 153-A and 505, Defence of Indian Rules, Post Office Act, Press and Registration of Books Act, the Sea Customs Act and a large number of ordinances throttled the growth and development of the press in India in all respects from the very beginning.

Q3. Explain the concept of Nationalism in context of Indian Press.

Ans. Indian nationalism developed as a concept during the Indian independence movement which campaigned for independence from British rule. Indian nationalism is an instance of territorial nationalism, which is inclusive of all of the people of India, despite their diverse ethnic, linguistic and religious backgrounds. It continues to strongly influence the politics of India and reflects an opposition to the sectarian strands of Hindu nationalism and Muslim nationalism.

The rules and regulations promulgated during 1857, when the first of war of independence was waged against the British regime in India, were aimed at curbing the press. One of these laws was later known as the "Ganging Act" No. XV of 1857. This act revived numerous merciless measures against the press in the country.

Vernacular Press Act: When Queen Victoria assumed the title of "Empress of India" in 1857, nationalist leaders demanded a greater role in the conduct of government affairs in India. The newspapers and journals devoted liberal space to news and comments on such events. Lord Lytton, worried over the increasing impact of the writings in the press, particularly in the language press, and enforced the Vernacular Press Act on March 1, 1878, for stringently controlling the newspapers. The law came down heavily on the press. Under these regulations, any district magistrate or a police commissioner was empowered to force the printer and publisher of a newspaper to agree not to publish certain kinds of material, to demand security, and to confiscate any printed matter it deemed to be objectionable.

According to N. Krishna Murthy, the Vernacular Press Act of 1878 was the greatest blow to the freedom of the Press in India, and the Indian languages newspapers suffered most heavily because of this law. Again, according to him, "in order to keep the press fully posted with accurate and current information, Lytton instituted the post of "Press Commissioner for India". His main job was to liaise between the press and the government.

Some Great Newspapers: When the Indian National Congress was established in 1885, a number of newspapers in several languages had large readerships. The Tribune, Kesari, Spectator, Indu-Prakash, Maratha, Amrita Bazar Patrika, The Pioneer, The Bengalee, The Englishman, The Hindu and others in all prts of India enjoyed *B* high reputation and large circulations. Meanwhile, -the periodical journalism also surfaced at this point of time. The Illustrated Weekly was brought out in Bombay and the Capital was founded in Calcutta. Besides The Hindustan Review, and Indian Review also came into being as monthly journals.

In 1889, when Lord Curzon took over as the Governor-General of India, a number of new measures such as the partition of Bengal and enactment of the India Official Secrets Act, 1889, further estranged the people from the British government in India. The press opposed these steps tooth and nail. By that time, r number of draconian laws such as the Press and Registration of Books Act, and Sections 124-A and 505 of the IPC had created tremendous difficulties for the press. Numerous nationalist leaders such as Lala Lajpat Rai, Aurobindo Ghose, B.C. Pal,

Lokmanya Tilak, and several others had been arrested for their contributions in the press in diverse ways.

Q4. Describe the state of the press at the time of World Wars I & II.

Ans. At the time of World War I and world war II, the press was inclined to go along with the nationalists in their struggle for freedom.

World War I: When the First World War broke out in 1914, the British government released nationalist leaders from jail, with a view to soliciting their support in the conduct of war. But several newspapers such as The Madras Standard, New India, Bombay Chronicle, and Maratha took divergent stands. As *a* result, some 180 newspapers were asked to play security deposits and assure support to the Government in' 1914-1915. Meanwhile, the press also softened its stand vis-a-vis the British government in India. In 1918, the number of newspapers required to deposit security with government came down to only 30 from 180 in 1914.

However, after the conclusion of the war and during the 1920s the British government took a rather stiff stand on the question of granting freedom to Indian and several noted political leaders who had started the non-cooperation programme.

The press lent active support to the nationalists agenda. Mahatma Gandhi wrote in his Young India Ion July 2, 1925: "I have taken up journalism not for its sake, but merely as an aid to what I have conceived to be my mission in life." Again, in 1942, Gandhi Ji said::"It is better not to issue newspapers than to issue them under a feeling of suppression."

As the Indian press was passing through a most difficult period, a number of newspapers were set up by freedom fighters who functioned as proprietor-editors. Apart from Gandhiji's Young India, Motilal Ghosh was the owner-editor of Arnrita Bazar Pntrika, Surendranath Banejee of the Bengalee, Kasturi Ranga Iyengar of The Hindu. There were examples galore of such papers.

World War II: For about two decades during 1925-1946, Gandhi ji and his ideology of journalism dominated the Indian press in the development of opinion journalism with editorials overshadowing the news. The two decades also saw proliferation of newspapers in almost all Indian languages, particularly in Hindi and English. During the World - War II (1939-45), the press initially supported the stand of the British government in India. However, a conflict soon arose on reporting the war news in the newspapers. Gandhiji resorted to the civil disobedience movement and several newspapers supported him to the hilt. The government later came up with a notification "prohibiting the printing and publishing of any matter calculated directly or indirectly to foment opposition to the prosecu5tion of war " It was around this time that the All India Newspapers' Editors Conference (AINEC) came into being.

The main objective of the AINEC at the time was "to preserve high traditions and standards of journalism; to safeguard the freedom of publication of news and comment; to represent the press in India in its relations with the public and the government."

Meanwhile, the Second World War coming to an end and the rays of freedom's dawn started creeping slowly on Indian horizons. When Mountbatten came to India, he revealed the plan to partition Indian into two independent nations. The newspapers, according to Krishna Murthy, demonstrated "a general tone of acquisence with a satisfaction that after all freedom of the country was ultimately becoming a reality".

Q5. Describe how the Indian press has changed after Independence.

Ans. A new era arrived in India in which the role of the press changed slowly with the arrival of independence in August, 1947. It had to shoulder new responsibilities now. After assiduously contributing to the attainment of freedom, the press by and by assumed the role of an adversary.

The contribution of Jawahar Lal Nehru, Press Commissions and the Present Status of the Press India is as follows:

Nehru's Contribution: With the approval of Independence Act in August 1947 the role of Press changed. It had to shoulder the new responsibilities of national reconstruction. India's first Prime Minister, Jawaharlal Nehru was the champion of the liberty of press. About the contribution of Nehru in strengthening the Indian Press Chalapathi Rau says: In the period after independence, Nehru played a large part in shaping all thinking about the Press, as Gandhi ji had done before independence. He was opposed by powerful sections of the Press, but he could carry on easily because he was a product of adult suffrage, had mass appeal and vast majorities, while newspapers still represented a small segment of opinion. But he stood for tolerance and accepted that a vigourous critical Press was a vital part of democracy. He was a passionate defender of press freedom as of all other freedoms. The traditions which grew in his time are becoming deep-rooted.

He did not like press barons or barons of any kind, and he wanted editors to have the freedom necessary to function freely, to develop character, and impress their character on the newspapers they edited. The greater the freedom the greater the responsibility. He was looking forward to mass circulations, though he would not allow any pandering to the mass mind...He, of course, deplored misuse of freedom, but if it came to a question of action, he preferred self-regulation. He was a passionate defender of press freedom as of all other freedoms. The traditions which grew in his time are becoming deep-rooted."

The Press Commission: A Press Commission of 11 members was appointed under the chairmanship of Justice G.S. Rajadhyaksha on 23rd September 1952. It recommended for the establilshment of an All India Press Council of 25 members. The Press council was to safefuard and maintain the freedom of the press. The Press Commission wanted to make newspapers and journals a central subject. It suggested that the advertisements should not cover more than 40 per cent of the total space.

The Commission, however, pointed out that the well-established newspapers had, on the whole. Maintained a high standard of journalism. They had avoided "cheap sensationalism and unwarranted intrusion into private lives".

The Second Press Commission, in its report of 1982, strongly recommended the delinking of the press from its connections with other industries. It also called for greater diffusion of ideas in the society. The Commission clarified that it viewed journalism not merely as an industry but as a public service and profession.

One of the major recommendations of the Commission was for the setting up of a National Development Commission (NDC) to promote the growth of the entire Indian press. NDC was to set up advisory assistance specially to small and medium newspapers for the development of printing and other technologies suitable for them.

Thus, the Press in India had come to play an important role in the lives of the people of India. After Independence it is regulated well so as to serve the masses as well as their Government by their representatives. The press can look forward to a bright future in the 21st Century.

The Present Status: The newspaper in India in almost all languages are fully modernised in every area of their operation... news reporting, editing, design–layout, production, distribution, advertising, sales management and editorial contents. The standard match the best in the world.

Saturday/Sunday magazines and daily supplements in some newspaper such as. The Hindu and the Eenadu (Telugu daily) offer an enormous variety of feature ranging from facial make–up to quality management from religion to science.

Today, there are over 35,000 newspaper, journals and magazines in India Published in 92 languages and dialects. While most dailies and several periodicals in all Indian languages use the most modern computer and facsimile technologies, there are still newspaper which are written in hand, typed with manual typewriters, cyclostyled and photocopied; there are other which depend on hand composition or monotype or linotype composition and employ letterpress process of printing and use traditional outdated rotaries.

The industry employs the latest techniques in all area of management. With an increase in literacy rates, rise in income, greater thirst for news, newspaper in all languages can look forward to a bright future. Multiplying circulations and swelling advertising revenues now beckon the newspaper proprietors. During the last two decades, dailies in all languages have set up editions in such remote places where people could not even dream of seeing copies of newspapers earlier. For example the India Express group, besides its English daily published from to centres in the country, owns, a paper each in Tamil, Gujarati, Hindi, Telugu, Kannada, and Marathi. It also owns a financial daily, a weekly (in three languages) and a television monthly. Similarly, the Ananda Bazar Patrika group has a paper each in Bengali and English, a financial daily, a fortnightly each on cinema, sports, economics and commerce.

Hindi newspapers Aaj, Jagran, Bhaskar, Nav Bharat and many others come out from more than half dozen towns. One Can safely predict a bright future for the India press in the 21st Century; it is bound to attain new and great heights in all aspects of newspaper production.

The newspapers in India in almost all languages are fully modernised in every area of their operation... news reporting, editing, design-layout, production, distribution, advertising, sales management and editorial contents. The standards match the best in the world. Saturday/Sunday magazines daily supplements in some newspapers such as The Hindu and the Eenadu (Telugu daily) offer an enormous variety of features ranging from facial make-up to quality management from religion to science.

Today, there are over 35,000 newspapers, journals and magazines in India published in 92 languages and dialects. While most dailies and several periodicals in all Indian languages use the most modern computer and facsimile technologies, there are still newspapers which are written in hand, typed with manual typewriters, cyclostyled and photocopied; there are others which depend on hand composition or monotype or linotype composition and employ letterpress process of printing and use traditional outdated rotaries.

The press industry employs the latest techniques in all area of management. With an increase in literacy rates, rise in incomes, greater thirst for news, newspapers in all languages can look forward to a bright future. Multiplying circulations and swelling advertising revenues now beckon the newspaper proprietors. During the last two decades, dailies in all languages have set up editions in such remote places where people could not even dream of seeing copies of newspapers earlier.

Q6. Write a detailed note on origin and the development of radio in India. [Dec-2019, Q.No.-5(a)]

Ans. Radio broadcasting began in India on 1922.The Government owned radio station All India Radio dominated broadcasting since 1936 but through privatisation and deregulation has allowed commercial privately owned talk and music stations to reach large audiences. Radio Broadcasting began in June 1923 during the British Raj with programs by the Bombay Presidency Radio Club and other radio clubs. According to an agreement on 23 July 1927, the private Indian Broadcasting Company Ltd (IBC) was authorised to operate two radio stations: the Bombay station which began on 23 July 1927, and the Calcutta station which followed on 26 August 1927. The company went into liquidation on 1 March 1930. The government took over the broadcasting facilities and began the Indian State Broadcasting Service (ISBS) on 1 April 1930 on an experimental basis for two years, and permanently in May 1932 it then went on to become All India Radio on 8 June 1936. When India attained independence, there were six radio stations within Indian territory, at Delhi, Bombay, Calcutta, Madras, Tiruchirapalli and Lucknow.FM broadcasting began on 23 July 1977 in Chennai, then Madras.

The Indian Broadcasting Company: Organised broadcasting in India was started by the Indian Broadcasting Company (IBC) in 1927. Bombay and Calcutta stations were inaugurated in July and August, 1927. The first radio programme journal India Radio Times was started on July 15, 1927. Its name was later changed to The India Listener and again to Akashvani, IBC was a financial failure in spite of a loan from the government. It went into liquidation and was closed down in March, 1930. Under pressure from the radio-set dealers, programmers and the general public, the government took over the Bombay and Calcutta stations in April, 1930. The Indian Broadcasting Service was formed. Those were the days of world wide depression. The government too faced financial difficulties. Even otherwise, it was not very enthusiastic about broadcasting. So, it ordered the closure of the Indian Broadcasting Service on October 10, 1931. Representations and agitations compelled the government to reverse the orders on. November 23, 1931. The Government doubled the duty on radio sets. In. 1932, the British Broadcasting Corporation (BBC) started an Empire Service. The number of receiving sets, which were all imported, doubled in less than two years. This resulted in an increase in the government's income from licence fees. The increase in import duty on radio sets and components of the radio sets also enhanced the government's revenue. Broadcasting now became financially viable. It was decided to start a radio station in Delhi. It actually went on the air on January 1, 1936.

All India Radio: The BBC loaned the services of Lionel Fielden who became the Controller of Broadcasting. (Today the radio chief is called Director General). He persuaded the government to realise the potential of broadcasting and allot more money to the service. In his autobiography, The Natural Bent, he writes about financial problems and red-tapism. He also gives an interesting account of how he could persuade the then Viceroy to adopt the name All India Radio for the broadcasting service. The name was adopted from June 8, 1936.

Fielden got together a group of devoted young people. With the help of these and of Goyder, his Chief Engineer, he started short-wave service in 1938, to cover the entire country. Lucknow station went on air on April 2, 1938, and Madras on June 16; 1938. In 1939, the Tiruchi station came into being. The same year the External Service Division at Delhi was started. A.S. Bokhari, another dynamic administrator, took over from Fielden to become the first Indian Director General. He was the chief during all the war years and thereafter till the partition. A new Broadcasting House was built on Parliament Street, New Delhi. On June 3, 1947, Lord Mountbatten (the Viceroy), Jawaharlal Nehru and Mohd. Ali Jinah made historic broadcasts on the partition of India. In the midnight on August 14-15, 1947, Nehru broadcast his famous speech "Tryst with Destiny". It is preserved in the AIR archives.

First Three Plans: Following the country's partition; six radio stations came to the share of India (Bombay, Calcutta, Delhi, Tiruchi, Lucknow and Madras). When the princely states became a part of India, five more stations (Hyderabad, Aurangabad, Baroda, Mysore and Trivandrum) were taken over by AIR.

- **First Five Year Plan:** During the First Five Year Plan (1951-56) much development of broadcasting took place. In 1952, the first National Orchestra was set up with Pandit Ravi Shankar as its conductor. Regional news bulletins in Hindi and Marathi were started in 1953 from Lucknow and Nagpur respectively. The first National programme of Talks too went on the air in 1953. In 1955 the first Radio Sangeet Sammelan was broadcast. The same year the Sardar Pate1 Memorial Lectures and Radio Newsreel were started. In 1956, the first National Symposium of Poets war broadcast and also the National Programme of Plays, Operas and Features. By the end of the first plan, the number of radio stations had increased to 26. 3 Dr. B.V. Keskar, the Minister for Information and Broadcasting (1953-61), did a lot for Indian classical music. He &so brought eminent writers, poets, musicians and playwrights on contract as Producers.
- **Second Five Year Plan:** Finances for broadcasting for the Second Plan (1956-61) were' increased four times as against finances in the First Plan. In 1957, Vividh Bharati, an All India Radio Variety Programme Service, was started at Bombay. It provided light entertainment with a generous dose of film music. Over the years. it has become a very popular service. The service was started to counteract the increasing popularity of Radio Ceylon's commercial service. It has succeeded very well in its aim. 1957 also saw the start of an Inter-station Programme change unit at Delhi. An annual folk music festival, "Songs of Nation Builders", was started in 1958 but it was short-

lived. The scheme of Radio Rural forums was implemented in 1959, for two-way communication with rural listeners. In 1960, Jawaharlal Nehru's speech at the UN was directly relayed from New York. By 1961, radio covered 55 per cent of the population and 37 per cent of the area.

- **Third Five Year Plan:** The Third Five Year Plan (1961-66) saw much expansion of medium-wave broadcasting. As many as 26 transmitters were added to AIR stations for broadcasting Vividh Bharati Programmes. In addition, two independent transmitters were installed at Chandigarh and Kanpur. By 1966, 54 stations covered 70 per cent of the population and 52 per cent area.

Chanda Committee: A committee on Broadcasting and Information Media was set up in 1964 under the Chairmanship of A.K. Chanda. It gave its report in 1966. It recommended separation of radio and television with two independent corporations. It was not accepted by the government then. The separation ultimately came about in 1976 and the TV setup was called Doordarshan. Another recommendation was for the starting of a commercial service. Commercial service was started from Vividh Bharati in 1967.

Code for Broadcasters: A 9-point code for broadcasters, introduced in 1969, prohibits the following:

- Criticism of friendly countries
- on religion or communities
- Anything obscene or defamatory
- Incitement to violence or anything against maintenance of law and order
- Aspersions against the integrity of the President, Governors and Judiciary
- Attack on a political party by name
- Anything amounting to contempt of court
- Hostile criticism of any state or the Centre
- Anything showing disrespect to the constitution or advocating change in the constitution by violent means, but advocating changes in a constitutional way should not be debarred.

In 1969, a new channel "Yuva Vani" was started at Delhi. The sponsored programmes on the commercial service were introduced in 1970 and the Sanskrit news bulletins were introduced in 1974. Earlier, in 1971, the highest AIR station was set up at Leh. In the same' year, the first satellite link was established.

Verghese Committee: In 1977, the Janata government appointed a Working Group headed by B.G. Verghese, to suggest an autonomous set-up for AIR and Doordarshan. The Group recommended in 1978 the creation of a National Broadcast Trust or Akash Bharati to look after both radio and TV. A bill to create the recommended Trust, was introduced in 1979. The recommendations of the Working Group, however, were much diluted in the Bill. Eventually the bill lapsed when the Janata government went out of power. The Janata government also introduced party election broadcasts for the first time in 1977, on the eve of assembly elections in several states.

The Present State: By 1980, radio covered about 90 per cent of the population and over 78 per cent of the area in the country.

Expenditure on radio broadcasting in the first plan (1951-56) was just over 2 crores. By the 7th Plan (1985-90) it increased to 700 crores. In 1991, we had 102 full-fledged radio stations which were production centres. The number of broadcasting centres, which included relay centres, was 205. The population covered was 97.5 per cent. Area covered was 91 per cent. The number of transmitters was over 300. This number included short wave, medium wave and VHF (very high frequency) or FM (frequency modulation) transmitters. National AIR channel via satellite was started in May, 1988.

- **Vividh Bharati:** Vividh Bharati programmes are broadcast from 32 centres including two short-wave transmitters at Bombay and Madras. They are relay centre with low-power transmitters. They broadcast taped programmes. The tapes are sent to the various centres much in advances.
- **External Services:** The External Services Division broadcasts programmes in 24 languages (17 foreign and 7 Indian) for a total of 75 hours daily. A special weekly programme is prepared and is broadcast through foreign radio stations in UK, USA and Canada. These programmes are meant for a large number of Indians living in these countries.

- **Educational Services:** Several stations broadcast educational programmes for schools (school broadcasts), twice or thrice a week. The duration generally is 30 minutes. Unfortunately only about 20 thousand schools out of 7 lac schools have their own radio sets. Only about 40 per cent schools actually listen to school broadcasts. They too do not have the listening period in their regular time-table. Some stations help the Directorates of Correspondence Courses with University broadcasts. "Yuv Vani" provides the youth (15-30 years) with a channel to express themselves and for their talents to blossom.

Audience Research: Communication process is a two-way process. Unless there is feedback, the quality or effectiveness of broadcasts cannot be known. For this purpose AIR started an Audience Research Wing in 1946. But in 1952, just after six years, the Wing was closed. Some critics say that it was closed because the findings of the Research Wing were not very pleasant for the bosses.

Q7. Explain the origin and development of TV in India.

Or

Write a short note on Joshi Committee. [June-2019, Q.No.-10 (c)]

Ans. In January 1950, The Indian Express reported that a television was put up for demonstration at an exhibition in the Teynampet locality of Madras (now Chennai) by B. Sivakumaran, a student of electrical engineering. A letter was scanned and its image displayed on a cathode ray tube screen. The report said that "t may be this is not the whole of television but it is certain of the most significant link in the system" and added that the demonstration of the sort could be the "first in India".

In Calcutta (now Kolkata), television was first used in the house of the Neogi family. Which was a huge milestone for industrialisation In India. Terrestrial television in India started with the experimental telecast starting in Delhi on 15 September 1959 with a small transmitter and a makeshift studio. Daily transmission began in 1965 as a part of All India Radio (AIR). Television service was later extended to Bombay and Amritsar in 1972. Up until 1975, only seven Indian cities had television services. Satellite Instructional Television Experiment (SITE) was an important step taken by India to use television for development. The programmes were mainly produced by Doordarshan (DD) which was then a part of the AIR. The telecast happened twice a day, in the mornings and evenings. Other than information related to agriculture, health and family planning were the other important topics dealt with in these programmes. Entertainment was also included in the form of dance, music, drama, folk and rural art forms. Television services were separated from radio in 1976. National telecast was introduced in 1982. In the same year, colour television was introduced in the Indian market.

TV Comes to India: Television came to India rather late, on September 15, 1959. For years the debate went on whether a poor country like India could afford TV. It was also feared that TV might alienate us from our cultural roots, that it might spread a consumerist culture. Consumerism would increase the hunger for comforts and luxuries. It might increase frustration and lead to social conflict between the rich and the poor. But manufactures, businessmen, educational institutions continued to make strong demands for TV in India. UNESCO offered a grant of twenty thousand dollars to buy community sets. The USA also offered some equipment. Philip India offered a transmitter at a low price. Ultimately, the Government yielded. It set up a TV hid in station at Delhi on an experimental basis. The declared aim was to discover what TV could achieve in community development and formal education. The transmission could cover an area of 40 k.m. in and around Delhi. Programmes were beamed twice a week. Each programme was of 20 minutes duration. The viewers were members of 180 tele-clubs. These clubs were provided free TV sets for community view by UNESCO. Programmes were beamed from an improvised studio at Delhi. UNESCO conducted a survey in 1961 and its conclusion was that TV did make "some impact".

School Television (STV) was launched in 1961. It was meant to train science teachers of Delhi schools. Many schools which did not have laboratories, benefitted from the new transmission. On pressure from public ad TY set manufacturers, entertainment programmes were started on August 15. 1965. They were broadcast daily for one hour. The first Hindi news bulletin was also introduced on that very date. The Federal Republic of Germany helped in setting up a studio for production of programme.

The first rural programme "Krishi Darshan" was started from Delhi on the Republic Day, January 26, 1967. This programme was received by farmer-members of 180 village tele-clubs in Delhi, U.P. and Haryana.

Daily TV transmission was increased from one to one and half hours and to two hours on Sundays on August 15, 1968. On 3rd December 1971, the first English news bulletin was introduced. In 1972 (October) the inauguration of the Bombay TV centre came about. In 1973, Srinagar and Amritsar Kendras started producing tele programmes. Pune too started relaying programmes from Bombay that 'year. Calcutta, Madras and Lucknow TV centres were set up in 1975. So, we can see that the real expansion of TV in India came about in the seventies. For example, the number of TV sets, all of which were imported, was 22,000 in 1970. In 1975, the number shot to over one lakh. What is even more important is that now the Indian sets are available in the market.

SITE: In 1975, the Satellite Instructional Television Experiment (SITE) was conducted. It made a deep impact on the country and the world. The one-year SITE exercise proved to India itself that it was ready for the satellite television. In 1967, a UNESCO study was conducted in India on satellite TV's use in the country. The study concluded that India can and should use satellite for national development. Accordingly, our Department of Atomic energy entered into an agreement with the National Aeronautic and Space Administration (NASA) of USA for the loan of a satellite for one year. The satellite called ATS 6 was provided free of cost from August 1, 1975, to July 31, 1976, for SITE. Educational programmes were broadcast direct from a satellite to the TV sets for the first time. Direct satellite transmission means that it does not pass through the relay stations. The SITE programmes were received by 2400 villages in six states - Andhra Pradesh, Bihar, Karnataka, Madhya Pradesh, Orissa and Rajasthan. An additional 2500 villages and towns in these states received these programmes through earth transmitters.

The daily 4 hour programmes were on education, agriculture, health and family planning. The satellite provided for one video channel and two audio channels, so the various programmes could be telecast only in two languages at one time. According to surveys conducted by the Indian Space Research Organisation (ISRO) and others, the experiment had a fair, though not complete success.

National Broadcast Trust: On April 6, Doordarshan was separated from All India Radio or Akashvani. Now Doordarshan, like AIR, got a directorate of its own, with its own Director General as the chief. But, both AIR and Doordarshan continued to be under the Ministry of

Information and Broadcasting. There had been great demand from the opposition parties to be given time on the electronic media. They strongly criticised the ruling party for using these powerful media of mass communication for their own political ends. It was for the first time in 1977 that the opposition shared time with the ruling party for election campaign. It was a step forward for the growth of a healthy democracy. The Janata Party was the first non-congress party to come into power at the centre in 1970. It appointed a Working Group to find out how best Doordarshan and AIR could be freed from the government control and made autonomous. Opposition parties had always been against the government control of the electronic media. So, now that they were in power, they wanted to show their commitment to this conviction. They did so by appointing the Working Group. The Group is popularly called the Verghese since the Chairman of the 12-member group was B.G. Verghese. The Group submitted its report in March 1978. It recommended a single. autonomous National Broadcast Trust (NBT). It suggested that such an independent, impartial and autonomous Trust could be made by an Act of Parliament. National Broadcast Trust or Akash Bharati would look after the working of the both AIR and Doordarshan. It did not recommend two separate corporations for radio and TV. Because of their different nature, they would be two units no doubt, but at the apex level these two units would be integrated under the care of a single Trust. There would be Licensing Board to issue licences to franchise stations for institutions like the universities. These franchise stations could have their own transmitters for specific purposes. No commercial advertising would be allowed on the educational channel. Their licence would be renewable every three years. The Group also recommended the setting up of a Complaints Board, selected by the Chief Justice of India. This Board would deal with the complaints of unfair treatment of persons, subjects, events, etc. by AIR or Doordarshan. The Trust would be responsible to the Parliament through its budget, annual reports, auditor's report, reports of the complaints Board and the Licensing Board. The Controller General of Broadcasting (CGB), the chief of radio and TV broadcasting, would provide a link between the trustees and the entire broadcasting organisation.

Development in the Eighties: The year 1980 saw the start of the National Programmes of Music and Dance. The basic aims of radio and TV are to provide information, education and entertainment. It is also their responsibility to preserve and promote our culture and heritage. It is to fulfil this aim that Doordarshan started these National Programmes. The idea of National Programines was already existing at AIR. The National Programme for the whole of India began on TV on August 15, 1982.

- **Asiad and NAM:** In 1982, Doordarshan took to colour transmission on August 15. Then occurred two significant events in the development of Indian TV. In November 1982, the Asian Games were efficiently covered through colour transmission. The way the TV personnel handled this huge task was appreciated widely in India and abroad. In March 1983, Doordamban covered the Non-aligned Meet (NAM) held in Delhi. This was another feather in the cap of Doordarshan.
- **INSAT Launched:** The first domestic satellite was launched in 1982. This satellite, INSAT 1-A, was placed in geostationary orbit but it could not become operational. India's second I satellite, INSAT 1-B, was launched in August 1983. This made TV programmes available to a much larger segment of our population. It also improved the quality of reception of broadcasts.
- **Soap Operas:** The year 1984 was very important for our TV. The first sponsored serial, Hum log, went on the air in July. Higher Education TV (HETV). produced by the University Grants Commission, was started. Doordarshan celebrated its silver jubilee and Delhi Kendra's second channel started. Before our own Hum log, we imported serials, sitcoms (situation comedies). soap operas and similar other programmes. The name soap opera is given to sentimental, sob-and-sigh dramatic serials. Such serials first appeared on the radio in 1920s in America. They were sponsored by soap sellers and their sentimental stuff was mainly meant for women. Broadcasts like 'The Fox'. 'Sorry', 'I Love Lucy', and 'Star Trek' were all imported. The imports came mainly from the USA and Germany.
- **Education Television:** Educational TV(ETV) was started in 1961 from Delhi. The broadcasts, to start with, were meant for science teachers and students of Delhi Schools. Later, they

covered larger areas and more subjects. ETV was then extended to other kendras like Bombay, Calcutta, Madras and Srinagar. The service was also made available to higher secondary schools. We have already, noted that the Verghese Group recommended franchise stations for the Universities to prepare and broadcast their own programmes. Such programmes for higher education were started by the University Grants Commission (UGC) in 1984. UGC set up an ISAT Cell at Jamia Millia Islamia, New Delhi, to co-ordinate programmes prepared at different universities. The UGC transmission for higher education was called Countrywide Classroom. Several Audio-Visual Research Centres (AVRCs) and Educational Media Research Centres (EMRCs) were set up in different parts of India to produce programmes. The programmes are meant to supplement the old and formal process of education. They also try to promote the interest of students in seeking knowledge outside the syllabi.

- **Morning and Afternoon Transmission:** The Morning Transmission was introduced in 1987. Tk late night feature film project was also introduced that year. Besides, a weekly news bulletin for the deaf and dumb was launched. In 1988, Calcutta and Madras got a second channel. INSAT-1C was also launched. \ In 1989 came the Afternoon transmission. In 1990, INSAT-ID was launched. In 1993, Doordarshan started five Metro channels, including music, sport. entertainment channels. They were started under pressure from the foreign channels like the Hong-Kong based Star TV and the US based CNN.

Joshi Committee: First the Joshi Report on TV. The second was the video boom and the third was the appearance of Cable TV. The Joshi Committee on Software for TV, set up under the Chairmanship of P.C. Joshi, gave its report in 1985. The report is called "An Indian Personality for Television". The report criticised Doordarshan for concentrating mostly on the North for its programme content. It also criticised TV's attitude to make broadcasts predominantly in Hindi. The Committee said that Doordarshan has not been able to achieve-its aim of becoming a medium of public service and social education. The reason was that it did not have functional freedom. The Joshi Committee recommended the setting up of a National Doordarshan Council. Its aim would be (1) review and guide Doordarshan's performances, (2) to act as a guardian of functional and professional autonomy, (3) to act like Press Council to examine complaints of unfairness against the medium. The Committee also recommended decentralisation of Doordarshan. Local stations at district level should be set up to involve the local communities in the process of programme production. Every village must have at least one community viewing set, and the Audience Research Unit should be strengthened. Viewers should be encouraged to give views freely so that the organisation becomes democratic in its programming. The Committee did not ask for an autonomous corporation for Doordarshan. But it asked the organisation to find its roots in the rich Indian heritage and develop a strong Indian personality. Only then shall we be able to fight the foreign invasion of the Indian Skies.

Video Boom: When one go around any city or town, you find that many individuals possess video cassette recorders (VCR) or video cassette players (VCP). It appears like a situation of a video boom. Why only in cities and towns, even comparatively well-off villages in many states like Punjab, Karnataka, Kerala, Maharashtra seem to have a situation of that kind. Even the north-eastern states have not been left behind. The video seems to be even more active when you come across video parlours, video clubs, video restaurants and video buses. Video has become a profitable business proposition. It is shown to a fair number of people, who are charged tickets. And this activity of video playing and watching activity continue till late in the night. Video boom in India came in the early eighties, especially after the Asiad in 1982. No confirmed figures ere available for the number of video players in India. Similarly, correct figures are not available for the number of people who watch video daily.

Figures for players vary from the to four million and for watchers from one to two million daily. Estimates and surveys have been made by advertisement agencies, cinema organisations and individuals. They have used different methods. So, naturally the figures differ. For example, the number of video parlours ranges between 50,000 and two lakhs, according to different estimates. Films are transferred to the tapes or cassettes illegally. Several "blue" (obscene or not in pod taste) films are also obtained in this manner. Cassettes are also obtained illegally, from Dubai and Hong Kong. The government amended the Cinematograph

Act. It was made illegal to screen or show films without a certificate from the Central Board of Film Certification. In spite of the amendment, the video business continued. It is rather difficult to catch hold of every video criminal. One reason why people gather in video restaurants and parlours is that cinema theatres are not enough even in towns and several cities. Villages have only mobile, make-shift cinema theatres. Video parlours cash in the hunger of the people for watching films. Another reason is that people do not have to stand for long in queues to buy tickets.

It is quite convenient to go to a parlour and buy a ticket easily. Also, the price of entry into the parlour is reasonable. For the parlour owners too, things seem convenient. They do not have to construct a theatre for showing films. They can screen films at their shop or in a room of their house. And the cost of the video is fast recovered. They can also rent out the video players at fairly high rates at night till the early hours of the morning or till they themselves will require it for their group of customers. The cassettes are not very costly for the businessmen.

One cassette costs anywhere between 100 and 150 rupees, depending on its quality. All sets of cassettes are today available from T-series and Gold to the National Film Development Corporation cassettes. The NFDC cassettes have foreign film prints too. The video owner uses one cassette several times. Many a times a film is copied from a copy. mat is why many video cassettes are poor in quality. Video has affected the film producers and theatre owners. People who can see a movie on video, have stopped going to the cinema theatre. Illegal screening of films on video without paying any royalty to the producer or distributor means a loss to the latter. That is why cinema producers, film-makers, distributors and exhibitors have joined hands to demand laws and action against illegal video operators.

Cable TV: Cable TV is another significant development. It has spread in a big way, especially during the 1990s. Cable was there earlier too, in metro cities like Bombay. Cable has been operating ill Bombay and other metros for almost ten years. But in the past two years cable TV has invaded much smaller cities. Cable TV is operated by linking the viewers' TV sets through cables to a common antenna. It is operated through a dish antenna and from a control room. The dish antenna, placed in a particular angle, can catch signals from broadcasting services like Doordarshan or foreign services like Star TV, CNN, BBC, MTV, Prime

Sports, Pakistan TV, etc. These broadcasts can be relayed through cable to individual customers of a cable TV operator. He also provides what is generally called "domestic service or TV".

In this service, he shows films or other programmes like Pakistani tele-plays, according to the demands of his customers. The Customers are charged installation fee to lay cables. After this they are charged a monthly fee. This fee, generally varies from ₹50 to 200 per month. The fee or the rent would depend on the cost of providing the service, quality of the service, number of channels made available to customers and the customers' capacity to pay. Cable TV is fast becoming popular. By paying, say, one hundred rupees a month you can get five to eight or even more channels. On the top of it you also get one or two movies in the domestic service provided by the operator. And these movies the customers call get on demand.

Video and cable TV are now increasingly being used by political parties, especially during elections. Industrialists, businessmen and professionals like doctors, architects and consultants have also started using these media. Several video news magazines like India Today's Newstrack, Stardust's Starbuzz and former Union Minister, Harmohan Dhawan's Third Eye give a round-up of recent news. These magazines probe subjects which are not taken up by Doordarshan. Their coverage and comments tend to be bolder and deeper. Sometimes, of course, they can indulge in what is called "yellow" journalism (cheap, sentimental).

Effectiveness of Doordarshan: Our TV, like all TV services abroad, offers a wide variety of programmes. These programmes are generally divided into general audience and special audience broadcasts. In the first category are included programmes of general interest like news, current affairs, films, light music, film songs, chitrahaar, tele-plays, serials, soap operas. In the second category are included broadcasts for particular sections of the population. For example, youth programmes, women's broadcasts, children's films and other children's telecasts, quiz shows, interviews, discussions, documentaries on particular subjects, features, docu-features, sports, educational TV (ETV), Countrywide classroom, classical music, western music, etc. We have also now Intext Service, which was introduced in Delhi in 1985. It now broadcasts information on airlines, transport, railway services, stock exchange, cultural engagements, tourist services, current affairs, sports.

This information is made available from the Second Channel of Delhi Kendra. Our TV has made some contribution no doubt but there is much left to be desired. It has provided entertainment to the viewers. It has brought films in their drawing regions. It has served the farmers by informing them of new methods and techniques of agriculture, horticulture, poultry and village industries. It has also tried to spread awareness about our great epics, about women's condition and role, about political processes like elections. It has made people aware of what is happening beyond India. ETV (educational TV) and HETV (Higher Education) have also imparted education to school, college and university students in an informal way.

But our TV has not been able to do several other important thing It has not been impartial and fearless in reporting political developments. Its current affairs programmes could have been an. important platform for political education for the general public. It has also not been as efficient as required in reporting the national and international news - in respect of neither speed nor quality of analysis. It is too much dependent on news agencies. After all it is a medium of immediacy, of "here and now".

Q8. Write a detailed not on the film industry of India.

Ans. The cinema of India consists of films produced in the nation of India. Cinema is immensely popular in India. Every year more than 1800 films get produced in various languages in India. Mumbai, Chennai, Kolkata, Hyderabad, Thiruvananthapuram-Kochi, Bangalore, Bhubaneshwar-Cuttack and Guwahati are the major centres of film production in India. As of 2013, India ranked first in terms of annual film output, followed by Nigeria, Hollywood and China. In 2012, India produced 1,602 feature films. The Indian film industry reached overall revenues of $1.86 billion (93 billion) in 2011. In 2015, India had a total box office gross of US$2.1 billion, the third largest in the world. In 2011, Indian cinema sold over 3.5 billion tickets worldwide, 900,000 more than Hollywood.

The overall revenue of Indian cinema reached US$1.3 billion in 2000. The industry is segmented by language. The Hindi language film industry is known as Bollywood, the largest sector, representing 43 per cent of box office revenue. The combined revenue of the Tamil and Telugu film industries represent 36 per cent. The South

Indian film industry encompasses five film cultures: Tamil, Telugu, Malayalam, Kannada and Tulu. Another prominent film culture is Bengali cinema, which was largely associated with the parallel cinema movement, in contrast to the masala films more prominent in Bollywood and Southern films at the time.

Indian cinema is a global enterprise. Its films have a following throughout Southern Asia and across Europe, North America, Asia, the Greater Middle East, Eastern Africa, China and elsewhere, reaching in over 90 countries. Biopics including *Dangal* became transnational blockbusters grossing over $300 million worldwide. Millions of Indians overseas watch Indian films, accounting for some 12 per cent of revenues. Music rights alone account for 4–5 per cent of net revenues.

Global enterprises such as Universal Pictures, 20th Century Fox, Sony Pictures, Walt Disney Pictures and Warner Bros. invested in the industry along with Indian enterprises such as AVM Productions, Prasad's Group, Sun Pictures, Geetha Arts, Zee, UTV, Suresh Productions, Eros International, Ayngaran International, Pyramid Saimira, Aascar Films and Adlabs. By 2003 as many as 30 film production companies had been listed in the National Stock Exchange of India (NSE).

The Beginning: The first important step in the motion picture industry was the invention of kinetoscope by Edison. It was a peephole box through which one person at a time could peep or see. The box contained a spool of pictures. The pictures were photographed on the new flexible film invented by George Eastman. The spool of pictures was revolved and it created the illusion of motion for the person peeping through the hole of the kinetoscope. Such a "magic" was first shown by a phonograph parlour at Broadway, New York, on April 14, 1894.

Lumiere Brothers (Louis and Auguste) in France combined Edison's kinetoscope with a new projection machine. Now there was no need of the peephole. The Frenchmen invaded the US in 1896 with their improved machine. This forced Edison to improve his own kinetoscope. He combined it with a superior projector invented by Armat in USA. It could project a series of photographs of moving pictures to not just one man but to a whole group of people. The machine or device made by Edison was called vitascope. Vitascope was born on April 13, 1896, just two years after the birth of kinetoscope, and, with vitascope started the glittering career of the motion picture industry. There is no motion in the pictures:

they only give the illusion of motion to viewers. The pictures or photographs on the film do not move. They are static. Advantage is taken of the principle of "persistence of vision".

The principle is: if a series of pictures is passed before the eye, the image of one picture stays in the eye and seems to merge with the image of the succeeding picture. When pictures are rotated very fast by the film projector, they can give the illusion of continuous motion. That is the magic of the film.

Film Comes to India: The first film to be ever shown in India was screened at Watson's Hotel, Bombay. The date was July 7, 1896, the magic was made possible through the cinematograph of Lumiere Brothers. The event was advertised in "The Times of India". The new invention was called "the marvel of the century" and "wonder of the world". The brief items shown were "The Sea Bath", "Arrival of a Train" and "Ladies and Soldiers on the Wheels". These and other short films were also shown at the Novelty Theatre in Bombay.

In January 8, 1897, followed a large number of imported movie shows at the Gaiety Theatre, Bombay. These shows included short films like Mr. Gladstone's Funeral, Death of Nelson, Call on London Fir Brigade, etc. The foreign film-makers also made films in India. Some of them were Our Great Empire, Great Imambara Palace, A Train Arriving at Bombay Station, Poona Races, A Dancing Scene from the Flower of Persia and A Panorama of Indian Scenes and Processions.

The Silent Era: The first Indian to make short films (shorts) was a Maharashtrain H.S. Bhatvadekar. He imported a British camera in 1897. He already had a projector. He filmed a fight between two wrestlers and a man training a monkey. He then bought a Lumiere camera and projector to make more films. He first exhibited his films in 1899.

F.B. Thanawalla showed his shorts like splendid New Views of Bombay and Taboot Procession in 1900. In the same year, Hiralal Sen in Calcutta filmed pieces from several Bengali plays. In 1902, J.F. Madan in Calcutta launched his "bioscope" showings in a tent. Around 1900, the imported films were 60 to 75 feet in length (about one minute). The length increased with time. By 1905, it was possible to have a film of 30 to 40 minutes duration. That duration was considered enough for a feature film. Bhatvadekar filmed the Coronation Durbar for Edward VII in 1903.

By 1905, films were being imported mainly from France, but also from the USA, Britain, Germany and Italy. Movie theatres, popularly called Picture Palaces, were coming up in all the important cities of India. J.F. Madan's company alone had a chain of more than 30 such Palaces. Many foreign films had the stage actors playing in them.

The first attempt to make a film with a dramatic story and treatment was made by Torney. He made Pundalik with the help of N.G. Chitre. Pundalik, released in 1912, was the dramatised story of the Maharashtrain saint. It immediately became very popular. Patankar made Savitri and An Episode from Ramayan.

Around this time, Dadasaheb Phalke appeared on the cinema scene. That was the most fortunate thing that happened to Indian cinema. He was a scholar and a fine printer and was full of creative imagination. He saw a foreign film Life of Christ in Bombay. There-and then, he decided to make films on subjects close to the heart of people.

Phalke travelled to England to get equipments and the required technical knowledge. He faced financial difficulties like others who were trying to make films. Others gave up but Phalke had determination. He had the will and he found the way. He is rightly called the Father of Indian Cinema. His first film was Raja Harishchandra, in 1913. This film appeared exactly one year after Pundalik. It had 4 reels or a length of about 3700 feet.

The whole effort of Phalke was "Swadeshi" or Indian. The film won immediate and wide popularity. This film is considered the first true Indian feature film. No lady came forward to play Taramati, the wife of the Raja. Phalke got a stage boy, Salunke, to play Taramati. The same year, Phalke made another mythological film Bhasmasur Mohini. Now, he was able to get two women to play the female roles in his second film. He could get four actresses to perform in his third film Satyavan Savitri in 1914. Then came the First World War.

Film production decreased in France, Germany and England. It became a problem to import equipment. Its cost also increased very much. In spite of all this, Phalke came out with Lanka Dahan which was a great success. Because of a shortage of finances, he invited Hindustan Cinema Film Company to become, his partner.

He now made two very successful film Krishna Janma and Kalia Mardan (Killing of the Serpent). In both these films Phalke's daughter,

Mandakini, played the little Krishna and became a star overnight. These two films were made in 1918 and 1919. J.F. Madan came out with Satyawadi Raja Harishchandra in Calcutta in 1919. That was Bengal's first silent film. In Madras, the same year, Natraj Mudaliar made KeechakaVadham. This was another mythological film. Its story was from Mahabharata. In Bombay, Patankar Friends made Exile of Shri Rama. Suchet Singh made Shankuntala and brought an American actress, Dorothy Kingdom, to play the main role.

One interesting thing during this period of film screening was an effort to add song and speech to films. It could not be introduced in the film itself. So, bands were arranged on the stage in front of the cinema screen. Songs were sung and sometimes speeches were made to make the silent film more understandable and interesting. From 1913 to 1931 was the era of the silent cinema in India. About 1300 films were made during this period. Some important developments in this period were the passing of the Indian Cinematograph Act in 1918 and Gandhi's call for non-violent non-cooperation in 1920. The Act set up a system for licensing and censorship. Gandhi's call reminded the film-makers of their responsibility towards society.

By 1923, there were about 150 cinema halls in India. But bold film-makers, who broke away from the old, accepted, traditional beliefs, weie not yet welcome. For example, Ganguly who showed a Hindu-Muslim romance in Razia Begum, was ordered to leave Hyderabad within 24 hours. In 1923, J.F. Madan, a pioneer of Indian cinema, died.

In 1924, in Bombay, Chandulal Shah made Gun Sundari (Why Husbands Go Astray). This film, sometimes, is called the first social film. Himanshu Rai made The Light of Asia in 1925. This was an Indo-German production. It was the first attempt at international co-production.

At this time, America dominated the Indian film scene. It had the highest share of the foreign films shown in India. And, we must note that foreign films made 85 per cent of the total films shown in India. Only 15 per cent films at this time were Indian.

The Talkie: By 1928, some countries in the West had developed the sound film. It also came to be called a talkie. The first talkie shown in India was Universal's Melody of Love at Calcutta, in 1928. Exhibitors of Bombay, Sidhwas, also screened brief talkies from England. Each of these contained several brief coverage of events.

In 1930, came the first attempt to make an Indian talkie programme. It contained a Khadi exhibition with Gandhi, C.F. Andrews, etc. speaking and a dance by Sulochana. The first talkie feature film came in 1931. It was Ardeshir Irani's Alam Ara with Zubeida, Prithviraj Kapoor and Master Vithal in the cast. Prabhat Film Co. was founded in 1929 at Kolhapur, Maharasl~lra. New theatres wasorganised at Calcutta by B.N. Sircar in 1930. Both these film companies played a great role in the development of Indian cinema. In the year in which the first Indian talkie feature film Alam Ara appeared (1931), 22 more films in Hindi (rather Hindustani) were also made. Three films were made in Bengali and one each in Tamil and Telugu.

By 1933, seventy five films had been made in Hindi. The first attempt at producing a film in colour was made in 1032 by Madan Theatres. The company took its film Bilwa Mangal abroad for processing. Prabhat Films also took their film Sairandhri to Germany for colour prints. Both the films were not high-grade success in colour. The first Indian attempt at colour in the country again came from Ardeshir Irani. He made Kisan Kanya in 1937. In the real sense, of course, colour film came only in the fifties with Mehboob's Aan, Sohrab Modi's Jhansi Ki Rani and Shantaram's Jhanak Jhanak Payal Baje.

Besides the films mentioned above, some other outstanding films till the beginning of the second world war were: Typist Girl (1918) of Chandulal shah, Shiraz (1926) and Himanshu Rai's A Throw of Dice (1929) and Karma (1'134). He made Devika Rani, the heroine of most of his films, immortal. Ay0dby8chit Raja (1932), Sant Tukaram (1936), Amar Jyoti (1936), Duniya Na Mane na Admi, all of Shantaram- Toofan Mail (1932) and Jai Bharat (1936): the first film on HinduMuslim unity, of Wadia Brothers. Chandidas (1932). Devdas (1936) and Mukti of New Theatres, Calcutta. Gangavataran (The Descent of Gangs) in 1937 was the last film of Phalke, known as the father of Indian cinema Madras United Artists Corporation in 1938 started making, films in Tamil, Telugu and Malayalam, and also in Hindi.

A great film Shakuntala was made by Shantaram in 1943. Pukar and Sikander of Sohrab Modi in early forti&were.huge successes. Shantaram also made Dr. Kotnis Ki Amar Kahani in 1945. Mehboob's successful films of the forties included Aurat, Roti and Sister, from the south Chandrakh was a super-spectacle in Hindi. Influence of major Indian studios started decreasing in the forties. Independent ' productions were increasing. The "star" system began in which heroes and heroines attracted public more than the studio name. Along with it, came "formula" films in which the 'themes and their treatment were repeated with a fixed dosage of song and dances. For the first time, "black" money too entered the films. These three - characteristics can still be found. Himansu Rai died in 1940 and Phalke in 1944. Dharti Ke Lal of KA. Abbas, in 1949, became the first feature film to be shown in Moscow. Shakuntala was shown in the USA in 1947. In 1943, the showing of newsreels of "Indian News Parade" and documentaries of Information Films of India, was made compulsory in Cinema theatres. This was mainly a measure to promote war effort.

After the world war was over, both Indian News Parade and Information Films of India were dissolved in 1946. On the pattern of the latter, the Films Division of the Government of India was established in 1948. Calcutta Film Society was formed by Satyajit Ray and Chidananda Das Gupta in 1947. That started the Film Society Movement which gradually spread to other parts of the country. In 1949, a Film Inquiry Committee was set up to give its recommendations on the various aspects of Indian cinema.

The Seventies and After: In 1971, India was producing the largest number of films in the world. Calcutta'71, (1971) was an example of the film taking notice of the current politics. This film was made by Mirnal Sen. Garam Hawa of M.S. Sathyu WIS funded by the Film Finance Corporation and won several awards. Ankur in 1974 was the first film of Shyam Benegal and was a great success. The new wave cinema (or parallel or alternative or "the other" or art cinema) which started with Bhuvan Shome was carried further by its creator, Mrinal Sen and others like Benegal, Sathyu, Basu Chatterji and others. Rajnigandha of Basu Chatterji was a very successful film of this "wave" in 1974. That very year, the International Film Festival of India became an annual feature.

Raj Kapoor made Bobby in 1973. This film on teenage love became very popular. A great spectacle Sholay (1975) was shot in 70 mm. Amjad Khan, a heartless dangerous dacoit, became a star overnight. The film set a new trend in multi-star films, spectacular locations and scenes and violence. Side by side films with offbeat, uncommon theme and treatment like Mahesh Bhatt's Janma and Daddy were also produced. In the late eighties and early eighties, 8 new trend of love between the very young started as in film such as Main Ne Pyar Kiya, Ashiqi - and Love Story. New young artists acted as heroes and heroines. Commercial cinema has the lion's share in the number of films. The producers have an eye on profits, so they try to 'provide entertainment, even when entertainment means an escape from reality. The type of cinema has all sorts of "masala". It has well-known actors, dances, music, fights, melodrama in story and dialogues. Heroes and heroines are all "white", they can do no wrong. Villains are all "black", they can have no virtue. Commercial cinema works on success "formulas". Dharam Veer, Parvarish, Amar Akbar Anthony, Shehanshah, etc. belong to this type of cinema. Art cinema, referred to, above, became popular in the seventies. It continued beyond the seventies too but in a smaller way. It started with Bhuvan Shome of Mrinal Sen in 1969.

The Film Finance Corporation played an important role in giving a boost to this cinema. Besides Satyajit Ray, whose film always have been artistic, some other names in art or new wave cinema are: Mrinal Sen, Sathyu, Basu Chatterji, Shyam Benegal, Avtar Kumar, Kumar Shahani, Karanth and Ritwick Ghatak.

Art cinema films are low-budget and do not have real life. Their treatment is artistic and away from the formula. But, generally, the criticism of art or alternative cinema is that not many people see it. So, it hardly covers its cost.

Cinema, the critics argue, should be a medium of mass communication. It should entertain the common man, the masses. So, we have "middle" cinema. It is a sort of compromise between the commercial and the art cinema. It should show taste and art but be a financial success too. Benegal's Jumn, Govid Nihalani's Aakrosh (or TV serial on Partition "Tamas"), Saeed Mirza's Albert Pinto Ko Gussa Kyu Aata hai. Mehta's Mirch Masala, Mahesh Bhatt's Daddy an some examples of -middle cinema.

Government Organisations: Documentary films are mainly in the public sector. They are certainly produced in the private sector but only in a very small number. Documentaries are largely produced by the Films Division of the Government of India. FDI also produces newsreels, also called news magazines. The Division was set up in 1948.

- **Films Division:** Besides documentaries and news magazine, FDI produces 16 mm short films for rural audience in regional languages. It also produces cartoon films and educational films for various ministries and departments of the government. I The Division's films ire shown by Doordarshan and cinema theatres whose audience is about 10 to 12 crores weekly. They are shown by Field Publicity units of the I Central and the State governments as well as by educational institutions, industrial houses, social and cultural organisations, filmsocitie s, etc. These films are also screened abroad through out embassies. In 1990, 152 documentaries and 28 news magazines. were produced. Several films of the Division have won national and international _awards. The Division has also organised festivals of its documentary films in various state capitals. That is a way to reach out to a large number of people, educational institutions, etc. The Division also organised its first International Film Festival of Short and Documentary Films in 1990, in Bombay.

- **NFDC:** Another organisation set up by the government for the promotion of good cinema is the National Film Development Corporation (NFDC). It came into existence after the amalgamation of the earlier Film Finance Corporation and Indian Motion Picture Export Corporation in-1980. It has provided 'financial and other essential services to talented film-makers. Its effort is to see an integrated growth of Indian Cinema. NFDC promotes low-budget but high value films. It also produces films if good scripts are available and well-known directors are directing. It started a programme of co-productions with the extremely successful Gandhi. This fist co-production was directed by Richard Attenborough and won 8 Oscars and many other top World awards. NFDC also participated in the production of Salaam Bombay which won 13 awards in various international film festivals. The corporation has an agreement with Doordarshan too to produce good films and tele-films jointly. Such productions are telecast from national and regional networks. NFDC provides finance for cinema theatres. It imports foreign films and distributes them all over India. It also exports Indian films. It markets good quality legal video cassettes to video libraries. It has also started

NFDC Video Classics scheme which provides classic file from all over the world.

- **Directorate of Film Festivals:** The Directorate of Film Festivals was set up in 1973. Its aim was to promote good cinema through organising International Film Festivals in India. It promotes Indian films in India and abroad through International Film Festivals held in the various parts of the world. It organises film weeks and National Film Awards. The Indian International Film Festival is held every year. It is organised. at various film centres in the country by rotation.
- **FTII:** The Film and Television Institute of India (FTII) was set up in 1961 at Pune. Its aim was to give training to young, talented people in the art of film-making. It also provides in-service training in television to the Doordarshan personnel. Originally it was only a film training institute. Later training in TV production was added. Earlier, a course on film acting existed but it has been discontinued. Now training is given in film photography, direction, sound recording and engineering and film editing. The Institute regularly enters student-films in National and International Film Festivals.
- **Children's Film Society:** The Children's Film Society, India (CFSI) was established in 1955. It is an autonomous body and its objective is to promote Films for children and young people. It produces, acquires and distributes films with healthy entertainment for children and young peoples. Its head office is at Bombay and regional offices at Delhi, Madras and Calcutta. Till 1990, the Society produced and acquired 283 films out of which 89 were feature films and 194 short films. It aim is to, reach both urban and rural young generation. It organises International Children's Film Festivals in India. The Society participates in important International Film Festivals abroad. Recently, the Society started bringing films on video to reach, out a larger number of young people. It also makes and acquires cartoon films. It obtains time on Doordarshan Network to screen its films. The Society has made a great contribution to the promotion of the Children's Film Movement.

Q9. What do you mean by Traditional Folk Media?

Ans. Traditional folk media is a term used to denote 'people's performances'. This term refers to the performing arts which can be described as the cultural symbols of the people. Folk dance, rural drama and musical variety of the village people, all come under traditional media. Traditional folk media is not just confined to dance and music, but also includes art and crafts. Traditional folk media originated as a consequence of people's need to express themselves. These performing arts pulsate with life and slowly change through the flux of time. In India folk performance is a composite art. It is a total art created by the fusion of elements from music, dance, pantomime, versification, epic ballad recitation, religion and festival peasantry. It absorbs ceremonials, rituals, beliefs and of course the social system.

According to veteran folk media scholar Balwant Garhgi "Folk media represents the people in their natural habitat, with all their contradictions and multifarious activities. It gives a glimpse of their style of speech, music, dance, dress and wisdom. It contains a rich store of mythological heroes, medieval romances, chivalric tales, social customs, beliefs, and legends. In order to understand the colourful diversity and unity of India, it is important to see the folk theatre in its natural settings."

Rural India is a treasure trove of folk art, theatre, music, dance, art and craft. The folk art forms satisfy our innate need for self expression. The traditional forms preserve and disseminate the tradition and culture of our forefathers infusing life into them. Every region has its own folk art from that is immensely popular and relevant in that area and Assam is no exception.

Some of the most popular traditional folk media of Assam include Ojapali, Mobile theatre, Bhaona, Sattriya dance, Loka Geet, Bor Geet, Bon Geet, Bihu. Puppetry and street theatre are also quite popular. Again there are several types of variations of a single art from. Bhaona for instance is a classical form which is performed within strict norms in the naamghars. On the other hand in parts of lower Assam, there are Dhuliya Bhaona and Khuliya Bhaona which are free from the rigidity of the classical Bhaona and are very flexible. Similarly the Bihu is performed with slight variations by the Assamese, the Misings, the Bodos, the Karbis, etc.

Being ancient forms of art, the folk media is very close to the hearts of the people. Traditional media holds universal appeal. Its understanding is direct and at the personal level. Traditional folk performances are uniformly popular, irrespective of the educational, social and financial standing of any community. Various researchers have established the importance of traditional folk media in development communication. Traditionally, folk media were primarily used for entertainment, social communication and persuasive communication. Now, there are efforts to involve folk media for conveying development messages. In the past few decades traditional folk media have been increasingly recognised as viable tools to impart development messages, both as live performances and also in a form integrated with electronic mass media.

Q10. Write a short note on the following:

(a) Limitations of mass media

Ans. In our country, the print medium has not breached the rural millions to the desired extent due to illiteracy. But the print medium, through cartoons, caricatures, symbols, emblems and photographs, does convey meaning to the masses, though not to the extent that the printed word can. Radio, on the other hand, has made inroads into the distant rural homes in developing countries, but perhaps it is more a box of entertainment than of information, let alone education. Even the Farm Forum Programme which involves community listening, discussion and feedback to the source, covers only a handful of people, who often do not work in the fields and so are not knowledgeable of the ground realities. of agriculture. The radio is a one-way-track to the villager, bringing messages from an unknown and unfamiliar source. To the rural illiterate, "to see is to believe" and so, the sound medium is urbane and impersonal to him. Television has made its presence felt in most of the developing countries though there is a limitation of coverage. When harnessed with imagination, the medium is expected to revolutionise the living style of the rural inhabitants with new and tested inputs of information in agriculture, education and health. An audio-visual medium like TV proves too glamourous to the rural ignorant. The message sought to be conveyed gets overwhelmed by the glamour. The unsophisticated rural viewer finds more of entertainment than information in the software, Also, the medium is far too expensive for the rural poor. The film medium enjoys immense popularity and has been influencing rural masses in changing over to the urban life-style. Films are packed with action. Yet the medium has remained static about ever-changing themes like population control.

(b) Strength of Folk media

Ans. It is against this backdrop that the traditional folk media have come into the limelight in developing countries like India. Since these arts are woven into the social and cultural fabric of the rural society, their role in educating the non-school population assumes significance. At one level, they give expression to people's lifestyle and values through the spoken word, songs, plays and spontaneous choreography, and at another level, they act as persuasive channels of communication. They have lived and grown with the rural people and so the rural masses, without any inhibition, get involved in their game and emerge more relaxed and better informed. There are many advantages of traditional folk media to inform and educate the rural illiterate, including women. Field experiments have shown that the credibility of selected traditional folk media is very high in convincing and even motivating the rural individual. They are rich in variety, readily available and economically viable. They are relished by men and women of different age groups. They command the confidence of the rural masses as they are live. They are themes-carriers by nature, not simply as vehicles of communication but as games of recreating and sharing a common world of emotions, ideas and dreams. Above all, Traditional folk is in a face to face situation between the communicator and the receiver of the message, a situation which energises discussion that may lead to conviction and motivation. In a developing country like India, traditional folk media have been reckoned as successful mass-motivators. During the years preceding the advent of the sound and sight channels of mass media, the traditional folk media not only reflected the joys and sorrows of people but inspired the masses during the times of stress and strain. They played a significant role in the freedom movement in India. Since the country achieved independence, selected folk media have been effectively harnessed for communication of new "development messages". An integrated mass and traditional folk media approach has paid dividends in communication.

Q11. Explain the role of traditional folk media in communicating modern themes.

Or

Discuss the role of Folk media in communicating modern themes citing suitable examples. [Dec-2019, Q.No.-6]

Ans. Role During Freedom Struggle: Indians comprehended the communication potential of their rural performances as early as in the 1820s. The 'Lavani' and 'Geegee' songs of North Karnataka were used as effective channels of communication to motivate the masses to rise in revolt against the British, in the times of KitturChennamma. An ingenious British agent, however, employed the same medium to help quell the uprising with counter-arguments. However, the 'ballad', 'Katha-kirtan' and the rural drama with its jester continued to play a crucial role in motivating the masses to rise against the British in 1857. Nearer our times, in the 1940s, the Indian People's Theatre Association (IPTA), the cultural front of the Communist Party of India, trained and employed popular rural performers to carry to the villagers the messages of a different set of economic theories. The IPTA even earned an encouraging pat from Pandit Nehru for investing the traditional folk media with functional relevance. And, in Gandhiji's time, it is said that 'mass communication was achieved by non-mass media'. The six radio stations in the country were then under the control of the British, but the people's performances, charged with inflammatory messages, roused the Indian people during the freedom struggle, drowning the sound of the British-controlled radio. There could not have been clearer signals of the power of the people's performances.

Song and Drama Division: Not surprisingly, soon after achieving freedom, the National Government started a full-fledged Song and Drama Division in 1954, to identify, train and utilising the services of traditional folk performers to inform the rural masses about the planning and development programmes of the country. A decade later, the Amarnath Vidyalankar Committee, which was appointed to assess the communication potential of different information media, recorded that:

"From the point of view of its great appeal to the masses and its quality of touching the deepest emotions of the illiterate millions, the medium of song and drama is matchless".

UNESCO and MacBride Commission: The UNESCO picked the thread and made new efforts to find the most viable means of communications for rural millions in developing countries of Asia and Africa. It sponsored an international seminar in London in 1972, and a follow-up workshop in Delhi in 1974. The document prepared by the experts, practitioners and critics in London proved most significant in laying guidelines for utilising the traditional folk media for communication. It declared that "no communication strategy would be complete unless it included people's traditional media". Declaration confirmed the positive qualities of folk media and declared that they were indeed the most viable tools of communication in rural countries.

A little later, when the world stood invaded by mass media, the MacBride Commission attributed considerable credibility to popular art forms in modem communication strategy when it recorded that, "Even where modern media have penetrated isolated areas, the older forms maintain their validity, particularly when used to influence attitudes, instigate action and promote change ... practitioners of the traditional media use a subtle form of persuasion by presenting the required message in locally popular artistic forms. This cannot be rivalled by any other means of communication ... examples Abound when song, drama and dance group and the like we're used to promote campaigns against social evils such as alcoholism, burdensome dowries, discrimination against women and archaic taboos ..."

Efficacy for Development Communication: As against the urban-based mass media, the rural-based folk media are found to enjoy greater credibility with rural audiences. They much the new messages on vital themes like Family Welfare Plan in their performances in such a way that the people can easily understand and accept them. The London Seminar declared that "themes like family planning programme are intensely personal and have to fall back on motivational methods which touch traditional beliefs, customs and social structures ..." And so, the folk media are the answer. Selected traditional folk media have been effectively harnessed for development communication during the past five decades. When they were integrated with mass media, the result was even more rewarding. While mass media like radio, TV and film extend the sizes of the audiences for the folk media, the log file folk media in their turn enrich the content of mass media. ' Organised and systematic use of traditional folk media makes the motivational work more community based, for social, economic and cultural development.

A Word of Warning: A word of warning has been sounded by the London Seminar for mass media practitioners about the handling of the traditional folk performances for entertainment and communication. The-folk media are sensitive and need to be handled with care and consideration in the entire process of integration. It is desirable that the radio microphone and TV camera capture the 'message charged folk performances in their haunts so that the tradition and cultural ethos of the media is not lost. The stress and sophistication of studio management of folk performances have often ironed out the charm of the rural ruggedness and wild beauty of the folk performances to render them tailor-made, tame affairs.

Q12. How folk media can be used as social change?

Ans. Folk media is an effective means of communication in today's world since it not only helps connect people with their cultures but also revives the lost culture of the society. Folk media forms the language of expression for the local populace and gives them a chance to voice out their opinions on various issues.

Traditional folk performances like ritualistic dances, religious songs or mythology-based rural plays, though highly popular, have proved unsuitable to absorb and reflect new messages on population, health or hygiene. Communicators, therefore, have to test different categories of folk performances to identify the ones that are flexible enough to absorb development messages to meet contemporary needs. Flexibility is the most important factor which determines the viability of a folk medium for rural communication. The flexibility of a folk medium might reveal itself either in its form or theme or in both. The art of story-telling or the puppet offers unlimited flexibility for new messages both in their form and theme. Traditional rural theatre, on the other hand, associated with religious or classical themes have limited flexibility only in some of their characters in story-situations. A folk play, like the 'Bhavai' of Gujarat or 'Tullal' of Kerala, based on social and even contemporary themes, has unlimited flexibility for development messages.

Categories Based on Flexibility: Depending on the nature and extent of flexibility, the traditional folk media reveal themselves in three categories, namely, rigid, semi-rigid and non-rigid. This classification, however, does not imply watertight compartments. A particular folk medium may turn out to be rigid for a particular message (say family planning) but maybe semi-rigid or even non-rigid for another type. of the message (say eradication of illiteracy/untouchability). Rigid media are those that reject a new message summarily. these are ritualistic or intensely religious in form and theme. Their content is hard- and they are unchangeable, like the African and Indian ritual dances, songs based on religious scriptures or those in praise of gods and goddesses. 'Theyyam' of Kerala, 'Bootasthana' of Kamataka and 'Gondal' in praise of Amba Bhavani in Maharashtra, are an example of this category. Semi-traditional folk media are those that provide limited scope for the new message. Even while dealing with a classical theme, the medium would have in-built charade or situations which hold out flexibility. The rual drama with its jester, the Katha-Kirtan, and the temple-based, traditional Rod-puppets as examples of this category. Non-rigid media are those that absorb new messages without any reservation to reflect them effectively in the field. Many varieties d the ballad with social content, educational and functional songs, the string d glove puppets and group sessions of poetry recitation and story-telling are illustrations of this category.

Need for Balance between Entertainment and Information: When employed with discretion, the traditional folk media have proved rewarding as tools of communication both as LIVE performances and also when integrated with mass media. As they come from the people themselves, their appeal is personal and functional. They have seldom failed to entertain, inform and even introduce new ideas for change. -. Limitations of traditional folk media are revealed when the communicator, in his enthusiasm, 'overloads' them with messages of instructional nature. The folk performances demand a balance between entertainment and information in their content material. So the new messages need to be fitted in with due consideration to the innate quality and cultural ethos of the media. Traditional folk media should be considered as a pad of the social fabric of the community. While they could reinforce relevant social changes that are already occurring, folk performances should not be used for propaganda as they could become counter-productive.

Q13. How the efficiency of communication strategy can be increased?

Ans. For increasing the efficiency of a communication strategy to obtain the intended results, there are four methods as follows: (1) Multi-media approach, (2) Package plan, (3) Utilising rural structures and village functionaries, and (4) Objective evaluation of the strategy.

(1) Multi-Media Approach: While folk media create a face-to-face situation in the field and go a long way to convince the masses about the varied meaning of the message 'on a personal basis, with a personal touch, simultaneous support of mass media channels would be of great value. The multimedia approach holds glamour for the field, covers different aspects of the message and interacts with different sections of people simultaneously. Documentary films, printed material, phased broadcasts and telecasts, together with folk media, mutually support each other in the cause of effective motivational strategy. Multi-media approach demands careful planning and faultless co-ordination.

Folk media performances in-built into the multimedia package would surely establish a two-way communication channel. They would strive to dispel unfounded fears and misgivings in the field. The programme would also pave the way for the smooth functioning of extension service. The multi-media approach demands fool-proof planning and involves mote expenditure. But its benefits are multiple for each medium makes up for the deficiency of the other, and all together make communication proficient and productive.

(2) The Package Plan: The package plan is an integrated time-bound work-programme which eliminates time-lag between communication, extension and service and brings to fruition the efforts of the communicator. Time-gaps between (i) communication and extension, and (ii) extension and service are often responsible for the failure of a goal-set communication strategy. Hence, the gaps should be plugged.

(3) Utilising Rural Structure and Village Functionaries: It is borne out by experience that mass media channels of sound and sight do bring awareness to the people of a development theme, and traditional folk media succeed in reinforcing it with information and education by a personal approach. However, motivation for action could be energised by change-agents who are inter-personal communicators. One should look for such change-agents in. the rural situation itself and identify the motivators in village teachers, priests, goldsmiths, blacksmiths, barbers, tailors, toddy-sellers and carpenters, apart from the village mid-wife and doctor. The village postman is a potential change-agent when motivated and harnessed for development. The service of the traditional folk artists will draw good results with such village-based functionaries.

(4) Objective Evaluation of the Strategy: A need for scientific research on the role of folk media in communication is essential, but until such studies are undertaken and results made available, the communicator would base his planning and action on information obtained through local observers, experienced informants and the artists themselves'. With the feedback material so collected, it should be possible for the communicator to identify attitudes 'that need to be changed to create the necessary social and psychological climate' in the field for people to receive the needed message. The programme package should then be suitably altered to incorporate the required messages. Evaluation studies may tend to become quantitative rather than qualitative in terms of achievement. They may prove to be general assessments of the impact of all types of media and not of folk media in particular. Hence' the recommendation of communication experts that 'evaluation of the quality and impact of the use of folk media should be ensured since quantitative evaluation may in itself be inadequate.

Q14. State the new communication technologies.

Ans. Communications technology, also known as information technology, refers to all equipment and programs that are used to process and communicate information. Professionals in the communication technology field specialise in the development, installation, and service of these hardware and software systems.

Writing, printing and electronic media like radio and television are examples of traditional technologies which are essentially one-way in nature. Therefore, their interactive capabilities are very limited. Besides, this limited interactivity occurs after a considerable delay. For example, a newspaper which depends on the traditional technology bf print can be said to be interactive to the extent that it publishes readers letters in its 'letters to the editor' column. Similarly, a radio station too is interactive in that it broadcasts programmings which carry responses to audience queries. We can, therefore, say that interactivity is at best a marginal property of traditional communication media. In the new communication technologies, on the other hand, interactivity is the main property. The use of computers in one form or the other, as an integral part of their system, is what enables thrilled to be interactive.

Computer Networks: The idea of interlinking and communicating with the aid of computers was as old as the mainframe computers of the

1970s. Owing to their prohibitive price, the mainframes came to be owned only by mega-establishments like governments, big business houses, universities, etc. Individuals could not afford them for personal use. At the same time, the high cost of the mainframes required their owners to find ways and means to maximise their utilisation to make them cost-effective. The networking of computers, it was found, allowed simultaneous access to a single mainframe by any number of users. Naturally, this development suited owners and users alike. Computer networks thus emerged as a kind of public utility to help users communicate with a central computing facility such as a database, and retrieve information too. In the decades that followed, computer technology advanced by leaps and bounds. This resulted in the invention of much smaller computers that displayed greater capabilities at just a fraction of the price. At present, the use of computer networks for various specialised and general purposes has become quite common, even in the less developed parts of the world. In our own country, computer networks are widely used by the public sector - organisations, big business houses, government department, etc., for their day-to-day transactions. Indian Airlines, Indian Railways and a few state undertakings own computer networks dedicated to managing their operations.

Such real-time flow of information enables planners and other decision-makers at the headquarters to decide on appropriate policies, taking into consideration the latest statistics. In the absence of such computer networking in the past, it is said that vital decisions at the national level had to be taken with the help of data which were at least a decade old! Apart from helping administrators, NICNET is also said to be regularly used for other application like an exchange of expert medical advice by specialists to doctors working in remote areas. On a global scale, the INTERNET is the largest computer network which permeated almost all parts of the world. Composed of thousands of interconnected networks initially in the united states. INTERNET can offer you an immense range of information services such as electronic mail, file transfer, databases and multimedia. INTERNET also provides connectivity to mobile receivers through a wireless broadcasting service operating on satellite links. Computer networks have several advantages over interpersonal communication. A synchronicity, that is flexibility inherent in the system to enable information exchange without the need for the sender and the recipient to be present simultaneously, is one such advantage. However, it also suffers from various drawbacks like the lack of human touch. Communication engineers constantly endeavor to improve the so-called 'user-friendliness' of the system concerned by approximating it to impersonal interaction.

Teleconferencing: Teleconferencing is a means by which individuals or groups located at different places call exchange data, speech, visual materials like graphs or diagrams, or loving pictures of themselves and any other relevant information. Teleconferencing is made possible by the integration of computers and communication in such a manner as to form a holistic system which call work in real-time. Depending on all particular application, scope and complexity involved, teleconferencing can be classified under the following types:

- **Computer Conferencing:** In this case, only computer data can be exchanged among multiple locations. Real-time interaction among the location is possible, but only to the extent of computer data. The physical linkages among the several computers can be in the form of telephone wires or through wireless means as in the case of microwave or satellite.
- **Audio Conferencing:** In this, the participants can talk to one another as if in a face-to-face situation. Facilities are provided for anyone location to talk to any other or all of them simultaneously. Also, audio teleconferences also enable an exchange of computer data on the same physical link Audio conferencing enables real-time exchange of information without losing the human touch.
- **Audio Graphic Conferencing:** This is a more advanced form of audio conferencing. teleconferencing in which, in addition to audio and computer data, still graphics like drawings, maps can also be exchanged. Further refinements in technology enable even slow-scan video pictures to as exchanged as a part of audio teleconferencing system The same pair of teleconferencing wires would suffice to carry all the above by 'Band-width Compression' techniques which are technically known as JSDN (Integrated Services Data Network).

  This is the highest form of teleconferencing in which a two-way exchange of moving pictures is possible without any restriction, in addition to audio and data. The telecommunication links required for such a conferencing system prove to be very costly because moving pictures need very wide bandwidths. Hence, a lower version of video teleconferencing which is called 'one-way video and two-way audio' is gaining currency. In the latter case, the main location (typically the headquarters of an organisation) will have facilities for sending audio as well as a video which are received by all the remote locations. But the remote locations will have facilities for sending only audio and not video. In other words, while the remote locations can receive both - pictures and voices - they will be able to respond only through voice. Teleconferencing of this kind has been widely experimented with by many organisations in India using satellite links. Already, Teleconferencing is an accepted form of technology in advanced countries, especially for business communications. It is only a matter of time before this technology comes popular in countries such as ours because the necessary infrastructure like telephone links and satellite are already available.

Teletext: Teletext is a form of broadcast technology using which several 'pages' of textual information (say, latest weather reports, stock exchange figures, airlines train reservations, etc.) can be transmitted on an already existing television channel. The Teletext information is encoded in the so-called 'vertical blanking interval' of the television screen which is invisible in the normal course of television viewing. However, when activated by a Teletext 'decoder' at the receiving end, the television screen starts displaying the-Teletext information instead of the normal TV programme. Facilities exist in Teletext to enable viewers to choose a particular page of Teletext containing relevant information which serves their needs and recall that particular page. Thus, a business man wanting to know the latest trend in the stock exchange can press his decoder for the particular page containing stock market news, and get the display on' his TV screen instantly. He will be able to view that page as long as he wishes, or he can turn over to some other page or revert to the national TV programmes as per his wish. TV stations equipped with a Teletext service, normally update the information in regular intervals, say every half an hour, for the benefit of the viewers. About 300 Teletext pages (a page means one TV frame containing information) can be accommodated per TV channel and a collection of these pages goes by the name of 'Teletext magazine'. The pages of a Teletext magazine can incorporate illustrations like graphs, bar charts, etc., in addition to simple text. The Delhi Station of Doordarshan provides a Teletext service on the second channel; access to it is possible with the help of a decoder. The magazine contains specific pages earmarked for national and international news, travel information, sports, local announcements, weather reports, etc. A few main pages of the magazine are also put out in the 'picture mode', i.e. on the main channel itself for the benefit of those not equipped with decoders. It is possible to extend this service to other Doordarshan stations for the benefit of viewers all over the country: Teletext is a simple technology which can be used to advantage for public communication. The advantages inherent in broadcast media such as instant and widespread teach, to an unlimited clientele, are applicable to teletext as well.

Radiotext: Better known by the term 'Radio data systems' (RDS), Radio text is a technology similar to Teletext but with the important difference that it works in conjunction with FM Radio (frequency Modulation) while Teletext works on television.

While conventional radio broadcasts on medium wave and shortwave bands have the advantage of larger service areas for a given radio station, the severe congestion of radio stations in these bands in recent years has forced the use of higher frequency bands for radio transmission. Use of these higher frequency bands as in the case of the FM Radio, however, would mean restricting the reach of a radio station essentially to the line of sight range which is about 30 km radius. FM stations are ideal as local radio stations, as they can offer programmes of local community interest, high fidelity music, local news, etc., to the public. Radio text is to be seen as a value-added service on FM Radio. This technology essentially consists of transmitting data and other textual material piggy-back on the FM camera so that the listeners/viewers who are equipped with a radio text 'decoder' can extract this signal from an ongoing FM transmission and watch the same on a computer screen which forms a part of the radio text receiving system. Facilities are available in a decoder to select either the radio text or the normal FM transmission at will. Also, the listeners or viewers, as in the case of Teletext, will be able to select the particular page of information of their interest and hold on to it for any length of time. Audio signals of speech quality (i.e. of restricted bandwidth) can also form part of a radio text signal. This would mean that institutions like Open Universities can transmit their Audio lessons or radio text, while simultaneously transmitting portions of their print material.

Videotex: Videotex (please note the absence of 't' at the end of the word) is another form of interactive communication technology which is in wide usage in several advanced countries. While the Teletext operates on television and radio text on FM radio, videotex dorks with the help of the public telephone network. The home computer, telephone connection and the domestic TV set/computer screen form integral components of a videotex system. Customers provided with videotex facilities can make use of it for such varied applications as electronic shopping, access to databases, tele-banking, or exchanging messages with friends.

As videotex is essentially interactive it has much more to offer than Teletext or radio text in terms of selective information exchange and retrieval. However, a well developed and reliable telephone network is essential for operating a videotex service. For this reason, as of now, videotex services are popular only in advanced countries. With gradual improvements taking place by way of digital telephone exchanges and replacement of conventional telephone wires with optical fibres, the reliability as well as the capacity of telephone systems everywhere are bound to increase in due course. Value-added services like the videotex too are expected to gain in popularity alongside such developments.

Interactive Cable Distribution Systems: Dissemination of television programmes via cable to a community of households started in the '50s. To begin with, the advantages of cable distribution was seen as improving the reception conditions of television in isolated mountainous- regions. Later on, TV signals received via satellite were put out on cable distribution systems, thus offering many more TV channels for the viewers. With this, the popularity and spread of cable distribution systems grew dramatically. Concurrently with the distribution of satellite channels, facilities like 'pay-TV' in which individual viewers have the choice of receiving programmes of their preference at a price, have also been introduced. In other words, cable systems have been endowed with interactive properties. Advancements in digital technology and fibre optics have resulted in further improved versions of cable distribution.

For example, viewers in advanced countries can now make use of the cable for receiving programmes of their choice at the press of a button. The selected programme is then downloaded by the cable company onto the viewer's terminal as a compressed 'digital packet' in a matter of seconds. The programme is then held in the electronic memory of the receiving terminal which can be viewed straight away or sometimes at leisure. The asynchronicity of interactive cable distribution systems is a unique advantage in the gamut of new communication technologies.

Communication Satellites: Transnational television, i.e. transmission of television programmes from one country too, another, became a reality with the development of Communication Satellites. These satellites are stationed in an orbit above the earth's equator at a height of about 36,000 km. called the geostationary orbit. All satellites parked in the geostationary orbit have a period of rotation equal to 24 hours and hence, appear stationary to an observer on the earth. Besides, the great distance of the orbit also offers the advantage for the satellite to 'see' as much as one-third of the earth's surface thus enabling it to cover such a vast area. Communication Satellites are owned by various individual nations as well as collectively by groups of nations to cater to several applications like broadcasting, television and telecommunications. INTELSAT (International Telecommunications Satellite Consortium) is an international body consisting of more than 90 member countries of which India is one. The satellites commissioned by INTELSAT cater to, the collective needs of the member countries as per a mutually agreed tariff structure. Ground terminals (these are known as earth stations) for receiving sending signals from/to the satellites are located in several places in the member countries. In India, two such earth stations have been established for the INTELSAT network - one near Pune and the other near Dehradun. Most of the international telecommunications traffic and exchange with other countries of live coverage of events takes place via the INTELSAT network. India is credited with taking several major initiatives in the field of satellite communications. The famous SITE experiment (Satellite Instructional Television Experiment) during 1975-76, in which about 2400 remote villages in the country were served with television programmes via satellite, is a case in point. The experiment has proved the efficacy of satellite communications as a cost-effective means for countrywide dissemination of educational and developmental TV programmes. Gradually, our country has developed its satellite system, INSAT (Indian National Satellite System).

INSAT is a multi-purpose satellite service catering to telecommunications, radio and TV transmission and weather forecasting. The second generation of INSAT satellites which are currently in operation has a larger number of transporters which can be used for further expansion of satellite communications. In particular, regional telecasting can be extended in all language zones and new services like teleconferencing introduced. Mushrooming of satellite-based transnational television in recent years is a cause for concern as well as hope. The sudden spurt in the availability of satellite channels all over the country from across our borders would mean a potential threat to our national broadcast media. The virtual absence of any legal mechanisms to check or control these transmissions of external origin can jeopardise our priorities in the communication sector and divert the attention of the populace away from the important information on developmental activities. On the other hand (, the competitive presence of eternal channels call to motivate the local broadcasters to become more professional and quality conscious. Direct Broadcast Satellites '(DBS) are specially designed for broadcast applications so that the signals transmitted from them can be directly received by home receivers equipped with a small dish antenna (typically half a metre diameter) and an interfacing unit. Use of such satellites obviates the need for land-based retransmitting stations (called LPTs). DBS are in extensive use in Europe, the USA and Japan.

Q15. Compare the new communication technologies.

Ans. The comparison of new communication technologies is as follows:

- **Interactivity:** While interactivity is a property in which the new communication technologies, as a rule, excel over the traditional ones, some of them are much more interactive than others. Teleconferencing and video teleconferencing can be cited as the most interactive while, Teletext or radio text can be placed at the other end of the interactivity scale. Even in traditional communication media, the ordinary telephone is a very good interactive device. The strength of the new technologies in this regard is that their interactivity is much more extensive and is not necessarily limited to just two individuals as in the case of telephone.

- **Asynchronocity:** The term asynchronocity refers to that property of the medium whereby the simultaneous presence of all the participants in a communication exercise is not compulsory. For example, in a computer network, facilities like "store & forward" enables the message to be retrieved at a convenient time other than the one at which the message has been sent. Thus, while real-time exchange of communications is possible through such a technology, it offers the added flexibility of asynchronocity. The degree of asynchronocity varies from one technology to the other. It can be said to be the highest where only computers are required to interact without live human intervention, as in the case of Electronic Mail, or computer data are the only kind of teleconferencing. It is least in a two-way video teleconferencing.
- **Demassification:** Traditional media like press, radio or television are instances of 'one-to-many' kind of communications. Therefore, they are unsuitable where the communication needs are more individualised. Demassification refers to the extent to which a given technology can lend itself to such individualised communication. The normal telephone system is an ideal example of a technology endowed with a high degree of demassification. New communication technologies in general possess this characteristic while at the same time enabling communication among large groups or individuals dispersed over large areas. In other words, new communication technologies are the reverse of traditional technologies. Teleconferencing or computer communication are high in their demassification while Teletext is at the lower end of the demassification ladder.

Q16. What are the social issues?

Ans. In the Third World Countries, the new communication technologies haven't penetrated sufficiently. So, the social issues being faced are as follows:

- As the new technologies are relatively costlier and knowledge-intensive, they will be adopted only by the higher echelons of society at first, who can afford them. Thus, ironically, communication gaps would widen among several sections of society because of the new communication technologies. This phenomenon is, of course, not unique for new technologies. When television was introduced, a similar thing has happened as only the rich could embrace this medium in the beginning. As the ownership of TV sets gradually increased, the initial imbalances too have become less pronounced. A similar situation is expected in the case of new technologies. Despite initial imbalances, however, overall information flow in the society is bound to go up.

- What happens by way of information imbalance within a society is also true of situations among countries at large. Advanced countries which are already information-rich tend to become richer, thereby widening the information gap between countries. This may lead to an unfavourable situation for the Third World countries which are already at the receiving end of the technological supremacy of the First World.
- Information overload is likely to happen, which in turn poses problems of coping with selective retrieval of the required information, from heaps of randomly accumulated information. Here again, the new technologies themselves are likely to come to our rescue, as special computer software which may enable users to obtain such selective display of information as is relevant to them.
- Unemployment may abound in certain sectors as the new technologies would eliminate or render surplus certain traditional jobs and occupations. Some new jobs and new occupations may be created in their place, but not in numbers sufficient enough to compensate for the loss of traditional jobs. Displacement of jobs may be felt more acutely during the introductory phase of the new technologies, than when the technologies in question get integrated fully into society.
- The universal presence of computers and easy access to. them via networks is likely to raise problems concerning privacy and security of communications. Use of special passwords and the like are of course obvious protection, but they too have their

limitation. Clever use of special software may also enable computer miscreants/hackers to break the secret passwords and get at the classified information straight away.

- Greater use of the new technologies may enable the organisations concerned to become more decentralised in their decision-making and other functions. Here again, an exact opposite may be possible as the new technologies permit much tighter monitoring on the movements and performances of subordinate staff thereby bringing about a 'Big-Brother' kind of centralised control. Much depends on the way the managements want to use the new technologies.
- It is feared the gender-inequality will increase. Though unfounded, the apprehension is prevalent that boys rather than girls will adapt themselves faster and more easily to things like computer programming, due to their supposedly inherent superiority in mathematical skills. This is of course a debatable point. However, in the initial stages of adoption of the new technologies, social pressures may be generated bemuse of gender inequalities. The book you can believe most–GPH book.

4 OWNERSHIP PATTERNS, ORGANISATIONAL STRUCTURES AND MANAGEMENT OF MASS MEDIA IN INDIA

INTRODUCTION

This chapter concerns the ownership, organizational structure and management of mass media in India. After that, it goes on to news agencies and feature agencies. News agencies form a major part of the print media, and are in fact the mainstay, without which many newspapers would find it difficult to function. It Also Discusses the organisational structure of the principal government media organizations in India and the role that the government plays in the film industry through its various institutions. At last, the educational media- first, AIR'S school Broadcasts and than ETV.

Q1. Write a short note on the following:

(a) Changing nature of newspaper management

Ans. On January 29, 1780, the first ever newspaper made it's appearance in India known as the Bengal Gazette by James Augustus Hickey. An employee of the East India Company, James Augustus Hicky was himself the founder- editor, printer and promoter of his newspaper. He did not need any elaborate organisational magazines are giant enterprises. Besides a colossal investment running into lakhs of rupees, hundreds of workers, with different kinds of skills and specialisations, are necessary. A mammoth infrastructure, ingenious planning, imaginative designing and creative production are essential to bringing out newspapers and magazines which millions of readers would wish to read and enjoy every day, day after day. The owners and managers have, over some time, adopted certain unique practices to make the newspaper enterprise economically viable and profitable. These relate to the areas of newspaper economics and management and the areas of newspaper production and distribution. The economic and management aspects include advertising, circulation and sales promotion. The structure of newspaper ownership is relevant to 'the issues of public interest and editorial freedom. Usually, the nature of editorial policies and business operations vary according to the patterns of newspaper ownership. The development of newspaper ownership patterns has passed through numerous stages, and all though it has been influenced by the business environment in India.

(b) Newspaper ownership patterns in India

Ans. The media that exists in our Country is heavily influenced by the ownership form it takes. There are a number of factors – such as content distribution, profits, etc. There exist some very basic ownership Patterns.

Types of Ownership Patterns According to the 1990 Report of the Registrar of Newspapers of India (RNI), Ministry of Information and Broadcasting, Government of India, the latest newspaper ownership pattern in the country is as follows:

Ownership Pattern of Newspapers, 1990

Form of Ownership	No. of Newspapers
Individual	18,873
Society/Association	3,875
Firm/partnership	1,237

Joint Stock Company	1,199
Government Central/State	673
Others	1,197
Total	27,054

It can be seen from this list that the number of newspapers concentrated in the individual, ownership is the largest, followed by societies/associations. In the newspaper industry, though the type of ownership is important, even more, significant is the influence that a newspaper unit commands. The influence that a newspaper wields in society, can be gauged to quite an extent from its paid circulation, advertising volume and revenue.

Distinctive Features of Ownership Patterns According to the Registrar of Newspapers' annual report cited above, the joint-stock companies own only 1199 newspapers, but their share is the highest in the overall circulation, followed by ownerships of individuals and firms partnerships. Here, it will be appropriate to note as to what a particular type of ownership stands for. A single individual owner means one who generally owns 100 per cent of the newspaper company's stock, and runs it as a private enterprise. For example, The Hindustan Times, New Delhi, is owned by K.K. Birla and The Telegraph, Calcutta, is owned by Avik Sarkar. Or, there can be a partnership of a small group of individuals holding stock in the company, i.e., The Hindu, Madras. Similarly, a joint-stock company is big commercial organisations such as Bennett Coleman and Company, publishers of The Times of India and several other publications. A trust is a non-profit organisation which runs a newspaper such as The Tribune of Chandigarh or The Lok Sevak of Calcutta.

(c) Press commission's recommendation on ownership patterns

Ans. The second Press Commission which was appointed in 1978 gave its report in 1982. Among the various matters relating to the press which the Commission had examined were the issues of Ownership Patterns and Delinking and Diffusion of Ownership and Control. In the Abstract of Recommendation, the Commission noted: "It appears to us that a very significant part of the press in the country in general, and a major portion of all-important daily Press in particular, is controlled by persons having strong links with other business or industries." The Commission noted that the Press is the most vital instrument in our country for educating the citizens in matters of public importance so that they may form an independent judgement to play their role as the ultimate governors of the country. The Commission observed that "the joint-stock company is the predominant type of ownership of newspapers in our country. It means generally the dominance of a few shareholders.

The pattern of editorial working follows the pattern of ownership. When an industrialist owns a paper, it is subsidiary to some other industrial, business or commercial interest". The Commission recommended as follows: "We think that in the interest of the public it is necessary to insulate the Press from the dominating influence of other businesses. We propose the enactment of a law in the interest of the general public making it mandatory for persons carrying on the business of publishing a newspaper to sever their connections with other businesses to the extent indicated hereinafter by us." Among the many details that followed, the most significant point was that the Commission's suggestion that in the first instance this proposed legislation "should be enforced in the case of all persons who are in a position of controlling the publication of one or more daily newspapers with the same or different titles, in one or more languages, the circulation of which, taken singly or cumulatively, exceeds one lakh copies per day". The book you can believe most–GPH book.

Q2. Explain the organisational structure of a newspaper.

Ans. The newspaper proprietors structure their organisations in a particular manner so that all the essential functions of the newspaper are performed most efficiently. Some of the most important and common functions of a newspaper enterprise, according to Professor Herbert Lee Williams, include:

- Decision- making
- Organising
- Staffing
- Planning
- Controlling
- Communicating and Co-ordination
- Directing Innovation

In a modern newspaper unit of medium size, generally, the organisational structure is divided into five distinct wings/divisions/sections/departments. These are:

- Editorial department
- Dealing with news and views;
- Printing and production department;
- The business department which includes sections for advertising,
- Circulation, billing, collection, etc;
- Computers, engineering and equipment store;
- Personnel, sales promotion and public relations.

In some organisations, engineering and equipment sections are merged with printing and production departments.

The Editorial Department: The editorial department of a newspaper organisation is its heart and soul. The entire business of a successful newspaper depends on the effective, efficient and prompt operations in this department. As stated earlier, the functions of a newspaper's editorial department are extremely crucial and significant.

The editorial department of a newspaper magazine collects, receives, processes and finalises the news and all other writings relating to news for publication in the newspapers magazines. The news is collected, received and solicited by a newspaper from all parts of the world as well as from all concerns of the country.

For collecting the news efficiently and promptly and making it fit for presentation to the readers in a readable, attractive and digestible form, the editorial department of a newspaper has to take the entire responsibility. The editorial department is the life-sustaining force and be-all and end-all of a newspaper establishment. The three main operations of the editorial department are carried on as follows:

- **Newsroom:** Editing and processing the news on the editing desk.
- **News gathering**: Making arrangements for gathering news from the city where the paper is located, other parts of the country and other countries. Prominent news categories include political; economic; financial and business; sports; crime; social; educational; cultural; health and environment. All this news may come from Parliament/Assembly, stock markets, chambers of commerce, labour organisations, courts, hospitals, universities, police, social and cultural organisations and so on.

Anything happening anywhere in any part of the globe in which the readers could be perceived to be interesting needs to be covered in newspapers.

- **Views and Opinions**: Every newspapers magazine has one or more editorial pages which reflect the policy of the organisation. The means that every newspaper has its own opinion on all serious national and international issues. Opinions have to be in conformity with the newspaper's policy which is determined by the proprietor owner. The chief editor or editor as the head of the editorial department has to ensure that opinions expressed in editorials are in line with the publication's policy. The editorial page or section carries material such as editorials, special articles, letters to the editor, special columns and cartoons.

News Editing: In the newsroom, the news editor is the boss. He makes sure that the editorial desk operates smoothly, receives the news from news agencies, reporters, correspondents and other sources. He is assisted by a chief sub-editor, who, in turn, has four or five sub-editors to process the copy (all news items received on the editorial desk are collectively called copy, not copies). It is this desk which finalises many of the pages of each newspaper issue. Generally, there are three shifts of the editorial desk 9.30 a.m. to 3.00 p.m., 3.00 p.m. to 9.00 p.m. and 9.00 p.m. to 3.00 a.m. As there are several editions of a newspaper in 24 hours to serve the readers in different cities towns, far and near, where the newspaper/magazines are sold, the publication of these editions is timed, taking into consideration the modes of transporting copies of the papers to particular towns and cities. The newspaper/magazines copies are sent by air, rail, road, or even by specially requisitioned taxis so that the newspaper is served to the readers without loss of time. Since the news fall has no prescribed timings, the editorial desk has to be ever ready to publish the latest news in the next editions under preparation.

The Sports and Commerce Pages: The sports desk is looked after by the sports editor assisted by the sports reporters. Similarly, the commerce and business desk has a commerce and business editor who is responsible for the coverage of commodity markets, stocks, and share and bullion trends.

Foreign News: For the foreign news coverage, normally, the newspapers depend on international news agencies such as UPI, AP, Reuters and AFP and our own PTI and UNI. Some newspapers have their correspondents in world capitals where news fall is frequent. These are London, New York (UN headquarters), Washington, Paris, Moscow, Beirut, Nairobi, Hong Kong, Harare, Singapore, Islamabad, Kathmandu, etc.

The Editorial Page The editorial page is the editor's responsibility. The editor has a team of assistant editors, who are usually specialists in diverse areas of current affairs on which the newspaper has to comment and come out with editorial articles. These include economic matters: international issues- further divided into Asia, Africa, America and issues in the United Nations; national politics, and then several other subjects such as education, science and technology; women, children, other weaker sections of society; religion, community relations, etc. The editor and his assistants also receive letters from the readers, contributions from freelance writers and journalists. These are to be evaluated for use. It is the editor who has a final say in all these matters. It is also the editor who commissions special pieces from established and well-known writers and journalists.

Functionaries: Thus, you will see that we have indicated above the various wings/divisions/sections1 departments into which a newspaper magazine organisation is divided. Each department has to discharge its functions as sleekly as possible. The responsibility of the editorial department is to marshall all resources to produce a complete and satisfying newspaper/magazine issue. The functionaries in the editorial department are as follows:

- Editor/Chief Editor/Managing Editor
- Associate Editors
- Deputy Editors
- Senior Assistant Editors
- Assistant Editors
- Chief/News Editors
- Chief Sub-Editorials
- Chief of Political News Bureau
- Deputy Chief, Political News Bureau

- Diplomatic/Political Correspondent
- Special Correspondent/s
- Staff Correspondent/s
- State Bureau Chiefs
- City Editor/Chief Reporters
- Staff Reporters
- Stringers

The Business Department: The business department looks after the sale of space, that is, advertising, and the sale of printed copies, that is, circulation. The advertising section is concerned with the procurement of advertisements from diverse sources such as advertising agencies, business houses and small individual advertisers. The collection of advertising revenue is the job of the advertising section in the business department. Similarly, for the sale of the newspaper/magazine, the circulation section is charged with organising the network of hawkers selling agents at the station where the newspaper1 magazine is published and at another place where its copies, can be sold.

The business department has two important wings: Advertising, Circulation

The functionaries in these wings are as follows:

Advertising Manager

- Display Ad. Manager
- Classified Ad. manager
- Billing and collection
- Space-selling or marketing

Circulation Manager:

- transportation Manager
- Packing and Dispatch Manager
- postal subscription ad agency relations billing and collection
- print order
- circulation audit

Other Departments: Other departments have their respective jobs to perform. The print and production department organise composing, make-up, paste-up printing and production of the newspaper/magazine. The Promotion of sales and public relations activity for the unit is to be carried on regularly. This is done by the personnel in the sales promotion and public relations department of the newspaper establishment. The general structure of these wings/sections/departments is briefly detailed here. It should be remembered that the structure of these departments is not fully identical in any two newspaper organisations:

Printing and Production:

- press manager or
- mechanical superintendent
- composing supervisor (engineer)
- press supervisor
- paste-up supervisor
- process photographers
- platemakers
- press operators

Engineering, Equipment, Stores

- Manager of the computer operation
- Computer engineer
- Data processing supervisor
- Computer operators
- Programming managers
- Systems manager
- Store manager
- Purchase manager
- Store supervisor

Technological Changes: The technological changes in newspaper management and organisation are taking place at a fast rate. The newspaper establishments in India are somewhat slow in adopting these changes. But the newspaper management, organisation and structure in India are in for the revolutionary transformation. All newspapers are not alike and things are bound to vary between single and big newspapers. The Proprietors of small and medium-size newspapers in the country, generally tend to combine two or more of their departments and make the systems work effectively. The big newspapers such as The Hindustan Times, The Times of India. The Statesman, Indian Express, Deccan Herald, The Hindu, Ananda Bazar Patrika. Malayala Manorama, Nav

Bharat Times, Mathrubhumi, Eanadu, The Tribune and some others have evolved their system to organise sales, advertising and overall management.

Q3. Discuss the features of news agency.

Or

Describe the main features of a News agency. Explain how the functioning of a news agency differs from newspapers organisation.

[June-2019, Q.No.-5]

Ans. A news agency is an organisation that gathers news reports and sells them to subscribing news organisations, such as newspapers, magazines and radio and television broadcasters. A news agency may also be referred to as a wire service, newswire, or news service.

Although there are many news agencies around the world, four global news agencies, Agence France-Presse (AFP), Associated Press (AP), Reuters and United Press International (UPI) have offices in most countries of the world, cover all areas of information, and provide the majority of international news printed by the world's newspapers.

How is it Different from a Newspaper?: Firstly, the news agency does not publish any newspaper of its own. Whatever its reporters of writer/report, is transmitted to the newspapers and radio and television stations. It is then up to the newspaper to use the news item sent by one news agency or that sent by another news agency or use the report prepared by its reporter. In fact, at times, a newspaper may even prepare an item quoting some paragraphs from one agency, and some from another agency. The choice of what item to use will depend on which agency sends its copy faster and which agency has sent a better-written copy. Thus, there is a constant flow of news from the news agency 24 hours a day, whereas a newspaper 'goes to sleep' (the printing press) after midnight every night. There are two other significant differences. Every news agency report has to be attributed to a source, unlike a newspaper story. Furthermore, there will be no comments, editorialising or interpretation in a news agency report and it will be purely a factual report.

Ownership Pattern: These newspapers have established Boards of Directors, each headed by a Chairman, to make the policies of the respective news agencies. The Boards have representatives of prominent newspapers as well as public figures. As you will realise, the same newspapers may be on the Boards of both PTI and UNI. But do not forget that there is a constant professional competition between the two agencies and, therefore, the Boards may take decisions on how to keep ahead of the other agency. Naturally, it would not be appropriate to have the same person sitting on both Boards. Therefore, the newspapers assign different representatives on the Boards. For example, the Editor of "The Statesman" is on the F'TI Board, the newspaper's proprietor or some other nominee will be on the UNI Board. But apart from meeting four or five times in a year to decide on policy matters, the Boards do not interfere in the day-to-day functioning of the agencies.

Financial Structure: For this purpose, a teleprinter/computer is installed at the office of the subscriber. This is maintained by the agency, just like the telephone in your house is maintained by the Telephone Department. Thus, any repairs are carried out by technicians of the agency concerned. The newspapers and other subscribers pay a monthly subscription fee, plus rental charges for the computer/teleprinter, apart from the installation charges paid when the subscription was first taken. The rate of subscription is determined by specific criteria like the circulation of a newspaper, and it remains the same, irrespective of whether the newspaper uses the news items sent out by the agency or not. As we said earlier, the Government does not own the agencies. But like other subscribers, the Government-All India Radio, Doordarshan, various Ministers, Ministerial offices and other governmental departments-is also a subscriber. Ultimately, the Government is the largest subscriber.

The Organisational Structure: The Editorial Desk, which we loosely refer to as the Desk, is under the charge of a News Editor, while the reporting section is under the charge of a Chief of Bureau. The reporting staff is divided into two groups: the Reporters who deal with day-to-day reporting are under a Chief Reporter and the Correspondents who deal with Ministerial or Legislative reporting are under the Chief of Bureau. Thus, the Chief Reporter is also answerable to the Chief of Bureau. Apart from this, there are the transmission, technical, administration and account, from where it is immediately sent to the subscribers. Meanwhile, one or two reporters rush to the scene, and collect whatever facts they can get from eyewitnesses and police, and then either file the story by telephone or rushing back to give their stories. (All the reporters are expected to know how to type.)

Thus, within two or three minutes of the phone call by the caller, the first report would go out to the world. The other reports may also be on the wire within hours. The agencies have offices in all the state capitals and full-time or part-time (stringers) reporters in almost all the districts. They also have correspondents in many world capitals and at the United Nations. News agencies do not generally accept contributions from freelancers unless commissioned by the agency for a particular event. The news agencies are generally the first to get wind of a news break, be it disaster, announcement, or election result. Each agency takes pride in being the first to break the news to its subscribers; thus beating the other agency. For instance, PTI was the first to break the news of former Prime Minister, Rajiv Gandhi's assassination. Similarly, UNI was the first to report that Mr Premdasa of Sri Lanka had been killed in the blast in the island country. UNI also reported the magnitude of the earthquake of September 30, 1993, to the world about an hour before PTI. The news of the Sati by Roop Kanwar which shook the nation some years ago was also highlighted by the UNI. So fast is the functioning of the agencies that a news report on the bomb blast at the Youth Congress office in Delhi was on the teleprinters within fourteen minutes of its occurrence in September 1993.

Q4. Explain the growth of news agencies in India.

Ans. News agency is wholesaler of News The innovative idea of news service was derived from pigeon courier between two cities for multipurpose objectives. Newspapers all over the world depend exclusively to a large extent on news agencies for news flow Larger media level. It is traditional chronic dependence on international news from news wire.(News agencies circulate important national, international news event and engaged media houses in the process of to transmission latest news updates. Functions Of News Agency News agency provide news reports of current events to newspapers and others who subscribe to its service A news agency in a democratic society should provide complete, impartial, objective, accurate, countrywide and competitive news service free from slant, pressure of interference from any source or quarter. It has to guard against the danger of being dominated by any vested interests - economic, social, communal or political In India.

Foreign news in the Indian English daily newspapers exclusively depended on agencies like Reuters and A.P. houses do not have their own abroad news network & porous news network at domestic Indian News Agency Strengths:

- Accumulative corporate knowledge
- Local experience
- Local content.

Indian News Agency Weaknesses:

- Not up to date with Technology and equipment
- Marketing network are not strong
- Competition from international news agencies
- Competition from local portal
- Competition from commercial agencies.

India Attains Independence: State of Agencies: When India attained its independence from British rule on August 15, 1947, some vestiges of the British remained behind. The news agencies operating in the country at that time were either foreign agencies with offices in India or British-owned Indian agencies. The foreign agencies operating in India then, which are still reporting from India, include Reuter, the United Press International, the Agence France Presse, etc. The Associated Press came sometime later. This structure has no doubt changed and we will discuss that later. Also, there were India-based news agencies like the United Press of India and the Associated Press of India, both of which had owners who were only too willing to leave the country for their homeland at the time of Independence. They soon began winding up operations.

Formation of Various Indian Agencies: The Government of Independent India, under Pandit Jawaharlal Nehru, had begum encouraging Indians to start their Indian news agencies so that these would give a more balanced picture of the developmental activities going on at the time. Encouraged by the Government, some major newspapers joined together to form a trust, and the set op independent India's first news agency, the Press Trust of India (PTI) in 1949. It took over the business of the Associated Press of India, which was in the process of winding up. The API had been a subsidiary of the Reuters. The PTI functioned as the only agency for the next eleven years. It will surprise you to know that although both PTI and the United News of India (UNI) are professional rivals, the UNI ' owes its birth to PTI. Since PTI has little competition, its working was not considered good enough for the standard of a news agency. The PTI Board of Directors felt that something needed to be done to pull it out of its lethargy. One immediate solution was that another Indian agency should be set up to compete with the PTI. Thus the United News of India was formed in 1961 and registered under the Societies Act. Like PTI, the UNI was also lucky to inherit the assets of the United Press of India, then in the process of winding up. The PTI had headquarters in Bombay, though the main administration continued to be in Delhi, while UNI has its head office in Delhi. Earlier, in 1948, a Hindi news agency had come into being. Called the Hindustan Samachar, it was backed by some political and private groups. Later, in 1966, another Hindi agency, the Samachar Bharti, came into being. Although both agencies had limited subscribers confined to certain areas of the country, they functioned more or less on the same lines as of PTI and UNI. Another news agency, the Asia News International (ANI) came up in the late eighties but is yet to start all-India operations.

Emergency: The Era of Samachar: All the four agencies saw their ups and downs. The PTI, being the oldest, was more stable than the others. The Hindi agencies were never on very solid ground, financially, since their inception. The UNI started gaining its strength, since 1969. Several political events were happening in the mid-seventies, after the then Prime Minister, Mrs Indira Gandhi had signaled certain changes. Following the events that took place as a consequence of the Supreme Court judgement in an election petition against Mrs. Gandhi, the Prime Minister suddenly promulgated a National Emergency in the entire country on June 25, 1975. One of the stipulations of the Emergency was the imposition of press censorship in the entire country. For the agencies, this functioned in a very special way. A Censor Office was established in the Press Information Bureau-which is the publicity wing of the government -and the news agencies were directed to send all their copy (news items typed by reporters) to this office every hour. After the Censor Officers had gone through the news items and used their red pencil to cut out what should not go, the rest was sent back, to be used. From time to time, the Government also issued certain directives about what to report and what not to report. For example, the Government asked the news agencies to stop reporting cases relating to the Maintenance of Internal Security Act (MISA) pending in various High Courts or in the Supreme Court.

However, the Government felt that not all the agencies were following these directives, and the impression began to gain ground that my agency was less controlled than the other. Consequently; in a surprise action, the government decided to merge the news agencies into a single unit so that it would be easier to control. On February 16, 1976, orders were received by the agencies that all of them had ceased to exist and a new news agency called Samachar had been created. The surprise order said that the UNI and the two Hindi agencies would be shut down, and Samachar would operate from the building of the former PTI. The managerial and editing staff was also reorganised, and J the topmost posts were given to the staff of the PTI. The Hindi agencies, which were not doing well financially, welcomed this merger. However, the UNI staff felt let down. But the situation was accepted and the agency continued to Work as one, under a new regime. Naturally, parity was. brought in the wages of the staff, since the PTI salaries were higher than the salaries in the other agencies. For this purpose, the Government gave financial help on a tapering basis. Late in 1977, circumstances forced Mrs. Gandhi to order General Elections, and she was thrown out of power. The Janata Party, led by Mr. Morarji Desai, was swept to power. After the new government came to power, large sections of the staff of Samachar, mostly belonging to the former UNI, demonstrated with the Government. After much deliberation, in April 1978, the Government announced that Samachar would cease to exist from September 1978 and the former four news agencies would be brought to life again.

Growth of Language Wings: With the two existing Hindi agencies not being able to work efficiently to meet the demands of the newspapers, the UNI in 1982 launched UMVARTA, it's Hindi Wing. Since it was a wing of UNI, it worked initially only on translated stories. However, it gradually built up its staff for both editing and reporting. Naturally, the emergence of a new Hindi agency further damaged the existing Hindi agencies, since the staff came mostly from Samachar Bharti and Hindustan Samachar. A couple of years later, the PTI also started its Hindi wing, called PTI Bhasha. Today, both the Hindi wings are serving the majority of language newspapers in the country, and the Hindustan Samachar and Samachar Bharti, are virtually shut down, though they continue to work in pockets in the country. In May 1992, the UNI took one other step, by introducing the world's first Urdu News Service. Thus, for the first time in the world, Urdu news is being transmitted by teleprinter/computer using Arabic script.

Aligning the Non-Aligned: In the late seventies, the non-aligned countries, at one of their summits; discussed how the international news agencies and visual media, were damaging the understanding amongst peoples by misrepresenting facts. It was suggested, and commonly adopted by all, that the non-aligned countries should have their news agency. It was agreed that before such an agency could be set up, one national news agency would coordinate on behalf of each member country to present and disseminate news on behalf of a Non-aligned News poll. In India, this task is being performed on by the FTI on behalf of the Government. The PTI gets an annual grant from the Government for this purpose. Receiving the news from other newspaper member agencies and disseminating it to newspapers in the country, and to sending the news to other member news agencies is the basic aim.

Q5. What is the difference in the operations of news agencies and newspapers?

Ans. A newspaper has its own policy under its own specific management; however, news agency cannot form a specific policy or point of view. It does not generally publish news itself but supplies news to its subscribers, who, by sharing costs, obtain services they could not otherwise afford.

Basic Difference: It is financed by newspapers. Unlike newspapers which may be owned by an individual or a company, a news agency is owned by a trust jointly formed by, newspapers. Unlike newspapers which may be owned by an individual or a company, a news agency is owned by a trust jointly formed by newspapers. A news agency, ' furthermore, does not publish any newspaper of its own.

Differences in Working Apart from these basic differences, there are some other differences in working. These may be summed up as below:

- In the first place, the news agencies work round-the-clock. Whereas, a newspaper may "go to sleep" (go for printing) after midnight or soon afterward, the news agencies are SP ding and receiving news twenty-four hours a day. Thus, its sub-editors, and reporters, have to be alert all the time.
- For the news agencies, it is deadline every-minute. Since a newspaper goes to the press after midnight, a reporter knows that he has plenty of time to file his report. But a news agency reporter must file his report immediately, since he may have to

catch a newspaper deadline, in India or abroad, a radio or a television bulletin. And, since there is keen competition, each agency tries to outdo the other, as we have already seen.

- Accuracy and speed being very essential for a news agency, it becomes important that a news agency report should be crisp, precise, and to-the-point. News agencies apply the 'Inverted Triangle' principle. This means that the first paragraph gives the crux-the main gist-of a news story. The second paragraph will add more details and the third and subsequent paragraph will give details in order of diminishing importance. The aim is to answer the five Ws and the one H-what, where, when, who and why, and how in the first two or three paragraphs.
- Since there is no time for a news agency reporter to confirm or re-confirm facts, there must be an eye on accuracy. The newspaper reporter reports the morning, but h: per centthe whole day to correct any mistake. But a news agency reporter will not get another chance.
- Because a news agency's news is considered the last word, every news item must be attributed to a source. In other words, every news item has to be quoted by someone, unlike in a newspaper where a reporter can give his/her own version. Proper sourcing generally results in truthful reporting.
- A news agency is not serving the city in which it works, but the whole nation and beyond. Therefore, its news will not be purely from a local perspective. What is more, it will often ignore a purely localised event and will prefer to report something which will be of interest to readers elsewhere. However, every newspaper devotes lots of space to local news stories, reporting the events in great detail.
- A news agency generally avoids publicity of commercial units. Of course, this is only a general guideline, and the decision is taken on the merit of each situation. A newspaper of course may not mind publicising an individual.
- A news agency always gives its news without any comment or personal opinion. This is unlike a newspaper which may be permitted not only to give a news item without a source, but

also to put in reasonable comments. Objectivity is the buzz word for news agencies.

Q6. Explain the government's print media and related media organisations and what are the government-run film media organisations.

Or

Write a short note on 'Press Information Bureau' and 'Central Board of Film Certification'. [June-2019, Q.No.-7 (a) (b)]

Or

Critically ananlyse the role and functions of 'Central Board of Film Certification'and 'Film Division' and 'Directorate of Film Festivals'.

[Dec-2019, Q.No.- 8 (a) (b)]

Ans. Government's Print Media and Related Media Organisations:

(1) Press Information Bureau: The Press Information Bureau (PIB) is the central agency of the Government of India for the dissemination of information on government policies, decisions; programmes, initiatives and activities. It puts out this information to daily newspapers, periodicals, news agencies and All India Radio and Doordarshan.

The PIB has its headquarters in Delhi. The Bureau in Delhi consists of information officers attached to different ministries and departments of the Government of India. A publicity officer liases with newspaper correspondents on behalf of the particular ministry or department by providing background information on official decisions and announcements.

The same officer provides feedback to the ministry or department of the Government of India regarding press relations and nature and extent of publicity measures to be adopted. Also, the PIB evaluates public reaction and accordingly renders advice to the Government of India on its information policy. The PIB is specifically concerned with the accreditation to the government of correspondents, camerapersons, technicians and other media personnel. The PIB also organises conducted tours of press personnel to places currently in the news. It facilitates the exchange of delegations of journalists through Cultural Exchange Programmes. Besides, the PIB provides a pictorial service which makes possible photo coverage of government activities. The PIB operates from its 37 field units. Two of these field units are information centres, eight are regional offices and 27 are branch offices, some attached to information centres.

(2) Publications Division: The Publications Division is the largest publishing house in the public sector. It is the media unit of Ministry of Information and Broadcasting. From 1941 to 1943 the present Publications Division was part of the Home Department and was known as the Foreign Branch of the Bureau of Public Information. In 1943, it was transferred to the Department of Information and Broadcasting and renamed the Publications Division in December 1944. The Publications Division has various wings to oversee the production of print material. These are the Editorial Wing, Production and Art Wing, Business Wing, Administration Wing and Employment News Wing. The last-mentioned Employment News Wing brings out the weekly Employment News in English and Rozgar Samachar in Hindi. The Publications Division seeks to provide information on every subject of national importance through the journals, books and albums that it publishes, It also acts as an agency that facilitates national integration and stimulates widespread interest in Indian culture. The Publications Division publishes some twenty journals, 'Kurukshetra' a monthly journal published in Hindi and English, has its focus on the areas of rural reconstruction and cooperation. Other notable publications include Aajkal, Bal Bharati, Yojana, India a Reference Annual, Mass Media in India. The quarterly newsletter of The Publications Division is called Samachar.

(3) Office of the Registrar of Newspapers for India: The Office of the Registrar of Newspapers for India was started on 1st July 1956. The Registrar of Newspapers for India (RNI), popularly known as the Press Registrar, heads this office. The office of the RNI maintains a record of the registered newspapers and periodicals in all languages of the country. It publishes annually the Press in India, volumes of which contain detailed information about the press, including circulation figures of the various newspapers and magazines, language-wise. The RNI decides the Newsprint Allocation Policy and revises it whenever necessary.

Research and Reference Division As its name indicates, the Research and Reference Division is an agency that conducts research and provides reference information on a variety of subjects. The Ministry of Information and Broadcasting and its constituent media units utilise the information services of the Research and Reference Division. Compilation work is carried out by the documentation and catalogue section of the Library.

There is a separate wing that specifically collects and maintains newspaper clippings. Accredited media personnel have access to the library maintained by the Research and Reference Division. India: A Reference Annual is published every year by the division. The National Documentation Centre on Mass Communication, set up as a part of the Division in 1976, documents and indexes news items and information about the mass media also compiles and edits the book Mass Media in India annually, which is an update on events and progress made by the government media in the previous year.

(4) Photo Division: The Photo Division comes under the administrative purview of the Ministry of Information and Broadcasting. It documents the socio-economic progress and cultural activities of the country through photographs. It houses an entire range of photographic negatives that have immense archive value. The positive photographic prints of major events in the news are distributed to the media through the Press Information Bureau. Periodic advanced training in photography is conducted for photographers of the state governments and those from Commonwealth countries. With the head office in New Delhi, the Photo Division Maintains three regional offices at Bombay, Calcutta and Madras. It also has a photo unit at Guwahati.

(5) Press Council of India: The Press Council of India is a quasi-judicial body, constituted by an Act of Parliament. It has 28 members headed by a Chairman. The Chairman of the Council has traditionally been a sitting or retired judge of the Supreme Court. While twenty members are press personnel five are members of Parliament and one each nominated by the University Grants Commission, Sahitya Academy and Bar Council of India. It hears complaints by the press and against the Press regarding freedom of the press. It suggests guidelines on the ethical standards to be maintained by the press.

(6) National Library: The National Library was established in 1948 under the Imperial Library Act, 1948. It is situated in Belvedere Estate, Calcutta. It has more than twenty lakh volumes in its custody. This number excludes the maps, manuscripts, Official Documents and books received as gifts or in exchange schemes. The National Library is a subordinate department under the Ministry of Human Resources,

Development, Department of Culture, Government of India. The special feature of this Library is that it organises exhibitions, lectures and seminars at the national and international levels. It is headed by a Director in addition to a Librarian.

Government-Run Film Media Organisations

(1) Films Division: The Films Division was established in 1948. It produces and distributes documentaries, news magazines, 16 mm featurettes, cartoon films and educational films for the different departments of the Government of India. These Films are produced in each of the major regional languages. The Films Division has its headquarters in New Delhi, and regional production centres in Bangalore and Calcutta. The Division has its branch offices in various regions of India. The films produced by Films division are released for viewing in cinema halls across the country.

(2) Central Board of Film Certification: The Central Board of Film Certification was established in 1952 under the Cinematograph Act, 1952. The Board has its headquarters at Bombay, besides-a regional office there. Its other regional offices are located at Bangalore, Calcutta, Cuttack, Hyderabad, Madras, New Delhi and Thiruvananthapuram. The Board certifies all Indian and foreign films - feature, short and long films-prior to their exhibition. Advisory panels assist the regional offices in the examination of films for their certification. Some of the most eminent people from various walks of life are invited to be on these panels. The Board, constituted by the government, is headed by a chairperson who is assisted by non-official members numbering anywhere between 12 and 25. The principles enshrined in the Cinematograph Act, 1952 and cinematograph (certification) rule, 1983 serve to guide the members of the Board in their work. Provision has been made to allow a challenge of any decision of the Board. For this, one needs to file an appeal with the Film Certification Appellate Tribunal (FCAT). The FCAT has been functioning from March 1984. The Tribunal has its headquarters in New Delhi.

(3) National Film Archive of India: The National Film Archive of India (NFAI) was established in 1964. It has its headquarters in Pune with three regional offices at Bangalore, Calcutta and Thiruvananthapuram. The archive is a media unit of the Ministry of Information and Broadcasting. It is the work of the NFAI to preserve films, audio and video footage. This it does in addition to documentation and research on films in Indian and even some foreign languages. The archive plays a pivotal role in sensitising the film viewing public to the nuances of film-making. It organises short courses on film-making. It also organises screening of films to audiences in select cities.

(4) National Film Development Corporation: The National Film Development Corporation (NFDC) was established in 1980 with the stated objective of promoting good cinema. It produces and finances films, oversees matters concerning export to Indian films, import of foreign films and their distribution, import of relevant technology and the production and distribution of recorded video cassettes. The NFDC provides financial support for the construction of cinema halls under its Theatre Financing Scheme. The NFDC has made inroads into the programming of small screen. The metro and other channels on Doordarshan telecast several serials produced or financed by the NFDC.

(5) Directorate of Film Festivals: The Directorate of Film Festivals was set up in 1973 under the Ministry of Information and Broadcasting. Its stated objective is to promote good cinema and Indian films. It organises national and international film festivals in India. The Directorate gives away the National Film Awards. Under the Cultural Exchange Programme (CEP), the Directorate arranges film weeks for the people in India. Similarly, it holds Indian film weeks abroad. The Directorate ceased to be an agency of the Ministry of Information and Broadcasting in July 1981, when it was transferred to the National Film Development Corporation. But in July 1988, the Directorate of Film Festivals was shifted back to the Ministry of Information and Broadcasting.

(6) National Centre of Films for Children and Young People: Earlier called the Children's Film Society, India (CFSI), it was established in 1955. It produces and distributes films which essentially provide " clean and healthy entertainment" for children and young people. Befitting this objective, the Centre finances films for children.

Q7. State the government owned electronic media.

Ans. State media, state-controlled media or state-owned media is media for mass communication that is under financial and/or editorial control of a country's government, directly or indirectly. These news outlets may be the sole media outlet or may exist in competition with corporate and non-corporate media.

State media is not to be confused with public-sector media (state-funded), which is "funded directly or indirectly by the state or government but over which the state does not have tight editorial control.

All India Radio: Broadcasting came under the control of the Government of India, in 1930 after the liquidation of the Indian Broadcasting Company. It was called the Indian Broadcasting Service. The same Network was renamed 'All India Radio' in 1936 and came to be known as 'Akashvani' from 1957, A.I.R.'s present network comprises 151 station & excluding the national channel, the integrated North-East Service and the External Service. Of these, 28 stations have a separate channel for commercial broadcasting, apart from the primary channel broadcast in the regional languages. Also, there are three commercial broadcasting centres at Chandigarh, Karrpur and Vadodara. A.I.R. covers 96.2 per cent of the population. The News Services Division, located at A.I.R.'s headquarters in Delhi, compiles and broadcasts news bulletins in English and all major Indian languages. The Division also undertakes preparation of newsreels, talks and various kinds of informational programmes which are broadcast on the national network. The Audience Research Unit carries out extensive listener research on A.I.R.'s programs. The data so collected is made available to A.I.R.'s programme planners. The Planning and Development Unit oversees the planning of the programmes. The Transcription and Programme Exchange Service facilitates the exchange of programmes between radio stations. It also transcribes speeches of important personages from different walks of life. The recorded speeches are preserved in the Archives maintained by the Transcription and Programme Exchange Service. The Central Monitoring Services of A.I.R. monitor broadcasts of foreign radio stations in various languages. The External Services Division offers the General Oversees Services and the Urdu Service. The output of the External Services Division's broadcasts goes on the shortwave. The Division brings out the programme journal called India Calling. The National Channel of radio was commissioned on 18 May 1988.

Doordarshan: Doordarshan, as on 25 February 1993 reached 82.4 per cent of the population through a network of 542 transmitters - 66 high power transmitters and other low power transmitters. There are 22 programme production centres. Also, Central Production Centre (CPC), with two large studios equipped with modern and sophisticated facilities, is in operation in Delhi since 1988. CPC undertakes production of the ballet, tele-films, serials, and various special programmes. The administrative set up is headed by the Director-General of Doordarshan. The Director-General is assisted by Deputy Director Generals. Then there are programme producers and others. Doordarshan has a national service (8.30 p.m. to 11.30 p.m.) and a regional service (5.00 p.m. to 8.30 p.m.). There are also morning and afternoon transmissions. Doordarshan introduced the second channel in Delhi in September 1985, and in course of time Bombay, Calcutta and Madras got the second channel. The Audience Research Unit of Doordarshan conducts surveys to assess the needs and the reactions of the audience. It evaluates the data so collected and makes suggestions to improve the programming on Doordarshan: The Doordarshan Audience Research Television Ratings (DARTR) are made public from time to time.

Autonomy for the Electronic Media: In 1964, a high power committee headed by Mr Ashok K. Chanda was appointed to look into the working of the various media units in the Ministry. The committee categorically stated that in the Indian context a creative medium like broadcasting couldn't flourish under a regiment of departmental rules and regulations. It is only by an institutional change that AIR can be liberated from the present rigid financial and administrative procedures of the government. For efficiency and economy, the committee stressed the need for decentralisation. The committee recommended for AIR the corporate form which would provide it with the freedom to evolve its methods of recruitment and devise a financial and accounting system appropriate to its creative activity. It said the Corporation should be set up by an Act of Parliament. It further suggested the separation of television from radio and wanted the formation of an Independent Television Corporation. The Government did not accept the recommendation for autonomous Corporation. The separation of AIR and Doordarshan, however, was brought about on April 1, 1976. In 1977, the Janata Government, in pursuance of its declared policy to free AIR and Doordarshan from government control, appointed a Working Group, headed by B.G. Verghese, to recommend the future set-up. This group suggested the setting up of an autonomous national trust-Akash Bharati or National Broadcast Trust. It did not want two separate corporations for Akashvani and Doordarshan but suggested a highly decentralised four-tier broadcasting organisation at Central, Zonal, Regional and Local levels. So far autonomous status for the electronic media has not been realised.

Q8. Explain government publicity organisations.

Ans. Directorate of Advertising and Visual Publicity: The Directorate of Advertising and Visual Publicity came into being in. 1955 and is an important agency under the Ministry of Information and Broadcasting for providing publicity to the Government of India. It has its headquarters in Delhi and Regional Offices in Bangalore and Guwahati. Its work is further facilitated by two regional distribution centres at Calcutta and Madras with assistance from some 35 field exhibition units. The Directorate includes an Exhibition Wing, Mass Mailing Wing, Outdoor Publicity Wing, Research Wing, Distribution Wing and Language Wing in addition to the Audio Visual Publicity Cell. Each of these sections contributes to the preparation and distribution of multi-media campaigns, print publicity, press advertising, exhibitions and audio visual publicity.

Directorate of Field Publicity: The Directorate of Field Publicity was established in 1953 under the title 'Five Year Plans Publicity Organisation'. This unit was renamed Directorate of Field Publicity in 1959: It has been constituted under the Ministry of Information and Broadcasting. The Directorate carries out its work through Field Publicity Units and Regional Offices. The Directorate organises contests, exhibitions and programmes which invite public participation even as they publicise information for and about the government. These activities are then evaluated by the Directorate of Field Publicity and suggestions placed before the government for necessary follow-up. The Directorate, therefore, may be said to be an interactive medium for the government.

Song and Drama Division: At the time of its inception in 1954, this Division was attached to A.I.R. From 1960, the Division is a separate unit of the Information and Broadcasting Ministry.

The Division functions with 44 departmental troops, besides 700 registered parties of performers on its panel. The Sound and Light Wing of the Division was established in 1976 in Delhi. A similar unit was installed in Bangalore by 1981. The Armed Forces Entertainment Wing came into being earlier in 1967. The performances of the Border Publicity Schemes of the Wing are popular among the villagers staying near India's international boundaries.

Q9. Write a detailed note on the Indian film industry.

[Dec-2019, Q.No.-5 (b)]

Or

Write a short note on Documentary Films. [June-2019, Q.No.-10 (d)]

Ans. How A Film is Made and Distributed: Film-making Process in India only those producing "Serious Cinema" in India usually follow the film-making process described above. For the mainstream cinema, the film industry has evolved its own process, necessitated by the shape the cinema itself has taken, with the emphasis on stars and the important place that music and dance occupy. The idea for a film often starts with a producer who starts by signing up a hero and a heroine. He then gets a scriptwriter to weave together a series of incidents involving these stars, interspersed with plenty of songs and dances. Simultaneously, a music director composes the music for the lyrics specially written for the film, and the producer's attempt is always to get the leading singers to sing the songs. Often, the songs are recorded first, and on the basis of the music and the stars who have been signed up the producer tries to interest financiers in funding the film. Somewhere along the way, the producer also chooses a director and a cameraman and pays them both a signing amount. Usually, these amounts are paid in cash; 'black' money is the basis of the film industry with huge, undeclared amounts changing hands. The money for shooting and completing a big-budget film with major stars, music directors and singers, seldom comes in all at once. The film also cannot be shot in one stretch as the stars can rarely give more than a few days at a time to one production, since they work in several films at the same time. Therefore, the normal pattern is to shoot a few scenes with atleast one song and dance sequence to start with. These scenes are edited and shown to the distributors and exhibitors in addition to the financiers.

Distribution of Films: Films are normally sold all over India in "territories". A distributor may buy just a single territory; a film can thus be sold to several different distributors covering the entire country. The distributor then negotiates with the exhibitors, who own theatres or chains of theatres. Although the manner and sequence of making a film may differ for 'commercial' and 'art films', the distribution pattern is the same. If a distributor is not interested in a film, it is extremely difficult to exhibit it. Since India has only big movie theatres, the distributor and the exhibitor can choose the kind of film they wish to show. Inevitably, and understandably, they will choose the kind of film that is likely to earn the largest amount by bringing in the greatest number of spectators. It is the serious cinema, designed for more intimate viewing, that suffers under such a system. Unlike most other countries, we still do not have the small cineplexes; which, in fact, is the pattern all over the world. Audiences, too, come b expect a certain kind of film to be shown in a certain kind of theatre. If expectations are belied, the reaction is usually hostile. Many people involved in the world of cinema are now demanding that the government bring in changes and encourage smaller theatres to be established.

The Role of the Government

Censorship: The Central Board of Film Certification has its head office at Bombay with a chairman and five members appointed by the government.

The non-official members are selected on the basis of their standing in the arts and their demonstrated interest in the cinema. When a film is completed, it is sent to the censor board to obtain a certificate without which it cannot be shown publicly. The censorship office then invites a minimum of three persons, from the board to view the film and pass judgement on it, in writing, on the spot. There are three categories of certificates: "V' for general release, "A" for adults above the age of 18 only, "UA" for children accompanied by adults. Usually, even when the film is clearly designed for adults, film producers prefer to pet a "U" certificate to bring in larger audiences. If the producer is not satisfied with a censorship decision, he can appeal against it to the Appellate Tribunal in Delhi. The decision of the Tribunal, which also has a chairman and five members appointed for a period of three years is final.

Government Institutions

- **National Awards:** The first of the positive steps the government took, to help the films develop as a form of artistic endeavour, was the establishment of the national awards in 1954. These are presented by the President of India. Since then, the number of awards for directors, producers, actors and actresses, technicians, art directors, music computers and lyric writers, has grown considerably, and now the presentation of the awards is followed by a national film festival showing the award-winning films. The films are judged by an independent jury nominated by the government. A recent addition to the awards is one for the film critics and one for the authors.

- **The Film Finance Corporation (FFC)/National Film Development Corporation (NFDC)**: In 1961, the government set up the Film Finance Corporation to give loans for low budget films. It was the start of a policy to assist in the emergence of an artistic rather than purely commercial cinema. In the early years, the FFC had an honourary chairman and a very small office. As its role became more significant, this grew in size until 1982, when the Film Finance Corporation was amalgamated with the Motion Picture Export Corporation, to become the National Film Development Corporation (NFDC). For several years, the NFDC was the key organisation in the Indian Cinema. It used to give loan usually to Film Institute Graduates. It then started producing films itself, giving the director a flat fee. It promoted Indian cinema all over the world and gave a great impetus to the art cinema. It held annual script competitions to discover new talent, financed the films of even established directors like Satyajit Ray and Mrinal Sen. It was with FFCWDC funding that the directors like Mani Kaul, Kumar Shahani, Ketan Mehta, Saeed Mirza, Adoor Gopalakrishnan were able to make first films and establish themselves. The works of these directors, and many more who accompanied them or followed in their footsteps, began to dominate the list of the national award winners. These films were also shown on the television and slowly led to awareness in the public, that there was another kind of cinema possible. The NFDC itself receives its funding through different means. Originally, entirely funded by the government, its activities and sources of funding were expanded. All films imported into the country had to be cleared by an NFDC-appointed committee, and the importers had to pay a large canalisation fee to it. With this and the international and national sale of the films it produced, the NFDC carried on its promotional and financing activities. in the present altered conditions, the import of films has been liberalised and the NFDC no longer obtains a canalisation fee. This had led to considerable financial difficulties and the future of the NFDC seems uncertain.

- **State Film Development Corporation:** Almost all the states have established the State Film Development Corporations, but only a few of them have proved to be really effective. The Kerala State Film Development Corporation has helped film-makers in many ways through financing their films and showing them at the theatres they have built. In Calcutta, the Nandan Film Complex has become the hub of film activity in the city with its two theatres, library, cafeteria and large grounds. They hold regular film shows and special weeks of films from other countries. It has nurtured an interest in the cinema that Bengal has always shown. In Bhopal, the Madhya Pradesh Film Corporation together with Bharat Bhavan, has financed films, published books and literary journals, and organised several seminars on the cinema. For some years, it proved a heaven for the more seriously inclined film-makers. The State Film Development Corporation, set up in Chandigarh, has been directly responsible for the emergence of viable Punjabi Cinema.
- **The National Film Archive**: Another institution to be established by the government was the National Film Archive of India (NFAI). with premises in Pune, in 1960. The Archive began to collect film classics wherever possible, cleaned, restored and preserved them. Slowly, its scope also expanded, and it began to add world classics and great contemporary films to its collection. The possibility of seeing great cinema and doing film research in the library of the Archive encouraged incipient filmmakers and writers to take the cinema seriously as a great art form. Each year, the NFAI holds a one-month Film Appreciation Course in Pune in conjunction with the Film Institute. It is an intensive course designed for those with more than a passing interest in the cinema. Many film society members, or those interested in starting film societies, budding writers, critics, actors and actresses, have taken this course. It has proved to be so valuable and the admission to it so much in demand, that the NFAI has designed a shorter, more compact,

ten-day course. This course is conducted all over the country in collaboration with various institutions. It has led to a spread of film culture and a deeper understanding of the cinema. Also, the NFAI gives research grants and fellowships and has agreed with a publishing company to publish books and monographs on the Indian cinema.

- **The Film Institute:** Film and Television Institute of India Within two years of the founding of the National Film Archive, the Film Institute of India was created on the premises of the old Prabhat Film Studio in Pune, situated next door to the Film Archive. The courses were designed on the Lines of the great French Film School in Paris. The students received? thorough grounding not only in technique but also in the history and aesthetics of the cinema. With the Film Archive next door, they can see the great cinema of the world at the two screenings held every evening in the institute's auditorium. Initially, the Film Institute also included courses in acting. Among its earliest acting students were Shabana Azmi, Shatrughan Sinha, Om Puri and Naseeruddin Shah. The first graduates in film direction went into the mainstream cinema, but when funding through the FFC became possible, they chose to make their films. Mani Kaul's Uski Roti made with an FFC Loan in 1969, Kumar Shahani's Maya Darpan in 1972, Adoor Gopala krishnan's Swayamvaram in 1972. It was the start of the New Wave in the Indian Cinema. In 1982, with the expansion of Doordarshan and the need for training in television, the Film Institute was expanded to include training in television as well. The film and television sections are quite separate although on the same campus, and the name of the institute has been changed to the Film and Television Institute of India (FTII).
- **Directorate of Film Festivals:** The first International Film Festival was held in India, in 1952, and it travelled from Delhi to Bombay and Calcutta. Some of the great contemporary films from all over the world were shown at this festival, which was attended by many internationally celebrated actors and directors. It was a phenomenal success and its impact was felt for many years. However, organising an international film

festival is a complicated and expensive exercise, and it was not repeated until 1965, at which time it was held only in Delhi. After that, international film festivals were held sporadically for the next few years until, in 1972, a permanent Directorate of Film Festivals (DFF) was established under the Ministry of Information and Broadcasting to hold an annual festival.

It was also decided that a competitive festival in Delhi with an international jury would alternate with a non-competitive festival to be held in a different city. The competitive festival in Delhi became known as the International Film Festival of India (IFFI) and the non-competitive one as Filmotsav. The standard set by the festival was very high, and it was so well organised that it quickly became one of the six A-grade festivals in the world.

The Ministry decided to give the DFF greater autonomy by placing it under the direct charge of the NFDC. However, with the office of the DFF in Delhi and the NFDC in Bombay, conflicts did arise, and, in 1989, the Ministry took back the DFF. That same year, given the mounting criticism that the IFFI did not attract the best-of-the year's production to its international competitive section, the Ministry decided to do away with the competition section-altogether and to hold the Festival in a different city each year rather than alternating it with Delhi. The elimination of the competition led to a fall in the prestige and importance of the Festival in international terms, although, for the Indian audiences, it remains a unique opportunity for seeing the best of the new world cinema.

For international critics and Festival Directors, the most important aspect of India's festival is the section devoted to the serious Indian cinema called the Indian Panorama. Films for this section are also selected by an eminent Indian jury and the DFF pays for them to be subtitled in time for the Festival. The Panorama has become an important showcase for the Indian cinema, and participation in it carries prestige as well as a guarantee of international exposure with the possibility of invitation for participation in other international festivals.

Documentary Film

The Films Division: Recognising the power of the cinematic image to transmit messages, the British colonial government established the Information Films of India to persuade the Indians to join in Britain's war effort. Perceiving this organisation as a propaganda instrument of colonial powers, the newly independent national government wound it up immediately after independence. However, recognising the need to present information and even news. the government re-established it as the Films Division to "inform Indians about India". An ambitious programme was put into practice. Documentary films were made not only about development projects and achievements, but a series of films were produced about national figures, both political and cultural. This was in addition to a weekly news review. These documentary films and news reviews were required to be shown in the theatres preceding the Feature Film. The theatre owners had to pay a fee to the Films Division and this became its major source of funding. With the advent of the television and the mounting resentment of the theatre owners at having to pay for and screen a short film that the audiences were growing increasingly impatient with, the ruling was withdrawn. In any case, with the daily news on the television and an even more widespread communications means at its disposal, the government no longer had to rely on the screening of the documentary and informational films in the theatres. The Films Division, however, continues to function out of its head office in Bombay with branches in most major cities, producing short films of either technical use such as agriculture, or films of lasting cultural value. Many of its technical films have won international awards. Films Division has several directors and technicians on its payroll, but a large number of films are made by independent directors under contract. Many well-known feature film directors have made documentaries for the Films Division. Among them are directors such as Goutam Ghosh, Buddhadeb Dasgupta, Kumar Shahani, Mani Kaul, Adoor Gopalakrishnan and the late G. Aravindan. The documentary film is being increasingly recognised worldwide as a significant form of expression in itself. Many young filmmakers start out making shorts and documentaries; several prefer to stay within this field as they find it satisfies their desire to use the cinema as a weapon of protest, or of creating awareness of issues they are concerned with. There are film festivals all over the world, showing only documentary and short films.

With India being perhaps the largest producer or documentary films in addition to being the biggest films producing country in the world, the Films Division felt the need to have an international festival in Bombay exclusively, for short films.

The Bombay International Film Festival for Documentary, Animation and Short Films: In 1990, the first Bombay International Film Festival was held, organised by the Films Division. Despite lack of experience in this field, it was remarkably well-received for its organisation, the wide variety of films it showed, the international participation, the excellent competition section with an international jury and the warmth and sincerity of its approach. The second festival was held two years later, in February 1992. and it is now a regular event, which will be held every two years in Bombay.

The Independent Short Film-makers: As an independent filmmaker, established or just starting, it is not always a simple matter to get a Films Division contract to make a film of one's choice clung directors started looking around for alternate sources of funding. They found it in different governments department such as the Department of Tourism, the Ministry of Social Welfare, Ministry of External Affairs, etc. Industrialists and business houses also want films about their achievements and their public-spirited enterprise. Others are prepared to be persuaded to finance films as a measure of cultural support. The film-making base is being expanded, but the problem of distribution remains. An all-India distribution can only be obtained if the film is acquired by the Films Division, or by Doordarshan. Many young filmmakers, driven by the need to make a statement of protest or anger, found their own resources to make films on topics as controversial as the blinding in Bhagalpur or deaths from the explosion in Bhopal. Anand Patwardhan, for instance, started out with making an anti-Emergency film, "Prisoners of Conscience", in Canada where he was then living and studying. Returning home he made films like "Bombay, HamaraSheher", a biting indictment of the way the city is run. His latest film is "Ram Ke Naam", a one-hour film shot in Ayodhya. Uma Segal, after graduating from the FTII, made "Shelter" about the homeless in Bombay. Meera Dewan in Delhi has taken up women's causes, making films on issues like dowry deaths. Nikita Vachani obtained Doordarshan funding for a film on a woman supposedly possessed by spirits "Eyes of Stone". All short films, however, are not about social or political protest. Many have used the form for aesthetically satisfying work. Rina Mohan's "Kamalabai" is on the life of famous Marathi actress of the thirties; Soudhamini's "Pitruchhaya" is a beautiful evocation of dance.

Problems of the Independent Short Film-maker: The main issue, even more, significant than funding, remains the one of distribution. If a film wins a national or an international award, it is automatically, and obligatorily, bought and shown by Doordarshan. But that is not the medium for which the films were necessary, made, and many of the technical and aesthetic qualities are lost on the small screen. The difficulty seems to be without a solution for the present.

Q10. Describe in brief the organisational set up of air and doordarshan.

Ans. The three major roles of radio and television are educating, informing and entertaining. The basic organisational structures are:

(1) Organisation at Headquarters: The annual budget of Akashvani (All India Radio) and Doordarshan comes, through the Ministry of Information and Broadcasting, from the consolidated fund of India, and is approved by Parliament. The organisational objectives, staffing-pattern and programme priorities of both the media; too are more or less the same. Earlier, Doordarshan used to function under the umbrella of All India Radio. But it was bifurcated on 1st April 1976 to work as a separate Department of the Ministry of Information and Broadcasting. The Director-General is the 'Head of the Department' in case of both Akashvani and Doordarshan. The staff, in both the cases, can be divided under four different streams or disciplines: 'Programme', 'Technical' (Engineering), 'Administration' (including Finance) and 'Audience Research'. Additional Director-Generals lead the 'Programme' and 'Administration' teams. On the Technical side, the Engineer-in-Chief holds the number one position. The senior-most officer in Audience-Research is called the Director of Audience Research.

- **Programme:** Deputy Director-Generals/Controllers (or Directors, in AIR) of Programme Deputy and Assistant Controllers (or Directors) of Programme/Programme Executives or Producers, etc.
- **Engineering:** Chief-engineers1Directors of Engineering/Deputy and Assistant Directors of Engineering, etc.

- **Administration:** Deputy Director-Generals/Directors of Administration Deputy Directors of Administration/Section Officers, Office Assistants, etc.
- **Audience:** Deputy Directors/Audience Research
- **Research:** Officers/Researchers/investigators/Tabulators, etc.

(2) Organisation at Stations: The above is the structure at the headquarters of Doordarshan and Akashvani. At the operational centres, the 'Head of Office' happens to be the Director (called Station Director in AIR), who belongs to the 'Programme' cadre. In Akashvani, however, the 'Headship' at some smaller Kendras is rotated between the senior-most Officer in 'Programme' and 'Engineering' disciplines.

The Director/Station Director is assisted by Deputy Directors/ Assistant Station Directors of Programmes, Producers/Programme Executives and Production Assistants/Transmission Executives. In the Engineering cadre come Station Engineers, Assistant Engineers/ Engineering Assistants, etc. The Administration side at a kendra is led by Deputy Director of Administration or Senior Administrative Officer, assisted by Accountant, Head Clerk, Office Assistants, etc. The Deputy Director of Audience Research or the Audience Research Officer leads a team of Investigators and Tabulators. AIR and Doordarshan Kendras work under their respective Director-Generals.

Q11. What do you mean by Air school broadcast.

Ans. The educational programme conducted by AIR is called "School Broadcasts".

This service is entirely regional, with the regional language as the medium of instruction (through radio). Each programme is of 40 minutes duration, with a short introduction before the main "lesson" and a follow-up discussion after, According to a rough estimate, All India Radio needs about 7000 programmes to fill in the School Broadcast Schedules of different centres every year. Of course, some of these programmes may be 'repeats' of earlier lessons. Still, it is quite a mammoth production commitment. It may be recalled that it was as early as in 1927 that the idea of utilising radio as a means of education was mooted in India. In those days the Madras Corporation had its transmitter- he was followed by efforts in Calcutta in 1932. The response at both the places was encouraging and paved the way for the "School Broadcasts" to be an important and regular activity of All India Radio.

Objectives and Selection of Topics: An official Report of AIR defines the basic objectives of introducing School Broadcasts as follows: "To supplement the school curriculum, to support the class-teacher and to provide information to students in both the urban and rural areas in an absorbing and interesting manner." The selection of topics for AIR to produce is made in advance in consultation with the State Government's Education Department. The dates and time of broadcast of each lesson too are decided well ahead of the schedule. This facilitates their proper integration in the time-table of all registered schools. The remaining part of the syllabus is taken over by school teachers, as per the scheduled plans. In a majority of cases, the presenters of radio-lessons are drawn from the teaching community itself.

Constraint of School Broadcasting: The School Broadcasting Service has, however, been facing some serious constraints. Firstly, with the massive expansion of television during the last few years, AIR as a whole has gone down in popularity. Then, the new accent on 'entertainment' on the electronic media has proved to be a setback for educational programmes-both on radio and television. Further, the lack of availability of good video sets in schools and their maintenance have all through been a major handicap. Then, the low priority is generally given to school broadcasting by AIR in comparison to other "high-profile" programmes causes a dampening effect. This applies to finances, production facilities and development of staff. Lack of full involvement of classroom teachers and school authorities is yet another shortcoming, faced by this Service. It is unfortunate that only a few studies have thus far been conducted to provide the feedback on School Broadcasting. The one carried out by the Directorate of Audience Research of AIR a few years back observed: "The successful use of radio in education has various aspects. All aspects would require simultaneous attention for any significant contribution of the medium in improving the quality of education rather than tackling different aspects in a piecemeal manner."

Q12. Explain the concept of educational television.

Ans. Educational television is the use of television programs in the field of distance education. It may be in the form of individual television programs or dedicated specialty channels that is often associated with cable television in the United States as Public, educational, and government access (PEG) channel providers.

The Beginning: It would be useful to trace, in short, the development of Educational Television in India. Well, the story of Doordarshan can perhaps be said to be virtually the story of an experiment of 'Education through Television' (ETV). Technically, an ETV Service, known as 'School Television (STV), commenced in India only in 1961. But during the preceding years, it engaged itself in social education, especially a project loosely termed as 'Citizenship Through Television'. A summative evaluation of this experiment showed in the audience a positive gain in information. Thus, encouraged by the initial experience, the authorities introduced 'School Television' to assist the middle and higher secondary schools, run by the Delhi Administration. Prof. Paul Neurath in his Report on this Experiment observed: "Television is already proving itself as a useful aid to teaching the students to see more and better experiments. There is a slight over-all superiority of the results of the students in Television schools over those of students in non-TV schools."

A Wide Network Now: Today, most of the programme-originating mass media in India Kendras of Doordarshan run regular programmes, with a bearing on education, whether formal or informal or both. Television programmes are now regularly available at all levels, from primary class to University level. Besides Doordarshan, organisations like the Indira Gandhi National Open University (IGNOU), University Grants Commission (UGC), National Council of Education Research and Training (NCERT) and Education Departments of State Governments are fully involved today in the use of television as a medium of education. Doordarshan also put out programmes on 'adult education', from many a Centre. Meant for the illiterate adults, these are presented on varied topics and in varied formats. Programmes with a bearing on social, psychological and occupational problems of this particular segment of society are telecast. Then, there is a series dealing with vocational guidance. The basic aim is to bridge, to the maximum extent possible, the gap created in their life by their failure to have gone to schools in earlier years. The most successful of Doordarshan's efforts in the field of 'adult education' has been Bombay Doordarshan Kendra's 'Gyandeep'. Telecast in Marathi, 'Gyandeep' has been widely acknowledged as an effective instrument for education. The erstwhile Upgrah Doordarshan Kendra, Delhi, also used to telecast a series of programmes, 'Andhere Se Ujale Mein'. Subsequently, Delhi Doordarshan Kendra started (under the same title) a regular programme for an adult audience. It was based on the pattern of 'Gyandeep'. But it could not achieve the same success as was gained by its Bombay predecessor.

TV's Potential as a Medium of Education: Education has today become a gigantic enterprise not only for developing countries like India but also for advanced nations of the world. Referring to the role of television, Anand Mitra, in his book Television and Popular Culture in India, has made an interesting observation which is reproduced below: "The logic of the development of the genre of the educational programme is intimately connected with the rationale for the introduction of television technology in India primarily as a medium that would be able to solve the problem of setting-up schools in remote areas. Television was conceived as a 'tool' that would become the centre around which an entire instructional institution would develop."

The availability of new technology these days has enormously facilitated man's fight against illiteracy. But in the case of India, the Joshi Working Group has recorded its lack of satisfaction with Doordarshan's efforts and achievements. The Group went to the extent of saying that "participation of Doordarshan in the battle against illiteracy and for educational development has hardly begun". Nonetheless, the Group did admit: "Thanks to the literary type of programmes shown on TV, the problem of literacy was brought home to the public in all its sharpness". In any case, it would be difficult to deny that television has the potential to give a new impetus to the spread of education in the country. Based on the experience of several countries considerable importance is being attached to television as a major source of mass education.

A UNESCO document thus emphasises the importance of television for education:

"While sound radio is so much cheaper, television has the advantage of providing a synthesis of all the available learning aids. It mutes virtually all other techniques including the flexible language of the film. There is also the value of the medium for the tele guidance of teachers and instructors in new methods."

Television can teach everything-the simplest and the most complicated things. It can go beyond the confines of schools. It can benefit men and women, rich and poor, literates and illiterates, city-dwellers and village folk. All those receiving TV signals have an equal right over the programmes. Modem technology can undoubtedly "revolutionise the teaching-learning process" in respect of both formal education and informal education. And, also, the distance education system.

Different Genre of ETV: The first educational service, or say, School Television Service(STV), introduced at Delhi, continues to be syllabus based. In other words, while Doordarshan takes up some selected topics from the prescribed syllabus for a television presentation, others are covered by classroom teachers. These telecasts are coordinated with school authorities and are integrated into the school time-table. It ensures that TV lessons come in a planned manner and a sequence falling in line with the general run of school-schedules. On the contrary, educational programmes, produced in a general way, are called 'enrichment' type. The term signifies that the subject chosen for telegenic treatment may not be exactly according to the syllabus. But it is certainly relevant to the syllabus of interest to the audience concerned. The 'enrichment' programmes aim at serving two essential objectives. Firstly, to familiarise students with the essential input of the subject proper. Secondly, to innovate and invigourate the presentation, bringing some 'fresh air' and avoiding a pedantic or pedestrian approach because of the rigidities of the syllabus. Education is a very comprehensive term. It goes much beyond the usual definitions or 'operational jackets' of 'Primary', 'Middle', 'Higher Secondary' or 'University' classes. Likewise, its wide scope exceeds the limits of 'formal' or 'non-formal', 'distance' or 'continuing' learning. Moreover, education and information are closely related terms. It is difficult to put them in two distinct water-tight compartments. Today's unprecedented information explosion has opened the flood-gates of knowledge. This is being justifiably attributed to 'education' which the vast television exposure has provided to different people.

Q13. What do you mean by ETV?

Ans. The word ETV means Educational television, the use of television in education.

Producer: The "Captain of the Ship" In this 'triple-relationship', TV is represented by the producer and the presenter involved in a particular programme. Surprisingly, the producer takes over as the dominant partner, or to use a TV jargon, becomes the 'captain of the team'. It is because he or she gives the show the necessary lead, direction and finish. The producer is involved right from the germination of an 'idea' to the final production and telecast, perhaps even beyond that. Naturally, the producer has to have a thorough awareness and appreciation, of the capability, requirements and problems or other partners. To quote from a study:

"the producer has a triple role. Knowing the facilities of the medium, he can bring to bear on it his professional knowledge, so that the telecourse uses as many resources as is possible within the available limit of time or money. Secondly, the producer is the counterpart of the teacher, his immediate echo, his critic, his stimulator and guide. Thirdly, he controls the cameras during the actual programmes".

A producer's responsibilities can broadly be summed up in three categories, (1) Planning and preparation; (2) Actual production in the studio and post-production; (3) Post-production activities like feedback; incorporating the audience reactions/suggestions into next production.

With television being essentially a visual medium, a producer of ETV programme has to pay a great deal of attention to the visualisation of show. In the selection of visuals too, the producer deserves to have the final word say this because it is not always the visuals that make an impact, but how these are used by the Producer. An example of a still photograph, illustrating an aeroplane being grounded after a bird-hit. Instead of running several feet of film or using half a dozen photographs, showing the spot hit by the bird, he might choose to take a close-up of that particular spot as the starting point for the camera and then can slowly zoom out to show the whole of the grounded plane. This might suggest that a hit by a small creature could be disastrous even to a big aircraft and several men on the flight. After the selection and preparation of visuals for the programme, the producer has to attend to various other production requirements before getting into the studio. These include scripting (or giving it a final shape) for the production; sound and sound effects; graphics, illustrations and charts; and above all, live experiments, especially in case of scientific or technical subjects.

Presenter: The Teacher: The presenter of a programme is the main link between the producer and the student. A good, effective presentation can cover up many a production deficiency. His pleasant personality, easy, articulate, convincing and conversational style of presentation, and a good knowledge of the medium and the subject are some of the attributes of a good presenter. What one wears, how one sits and walks and talks, even the minutest of such details, contribute to the success or the failure of a programme. For, a TV lens does not lie. The best and the worst of its subject is brought to the viewer in its truest form. The basic requirements of a TV presenter are different from those of an expert. The latter may be an authority in his field, but may not turn out to be as good in presenting a programme. Similarly, a successful TV presenter may not be an outstanding 'expert' but his physical charm and professional ability as a communicator may help him carry conviction with viewers. Naturally, for one, would opt for the latter for my TV show. The unusual glamour, associated with a TV presenter, makes a classroom teacher sore about ETV presentations. All the world over, wherever ETV started, the teaching community reacted the same way. They found in television a formidable rival, determined to oust them from their classes. If a TV show turns out to be good, the classroom teacher is jealous. And, in case it flops, he is critical. The indifference and apathy of the classroom: teacher towards television is not a happy or healthy trend. Television should be taken only as an 'aid' to the teacher. This may be one of the many tools (like a blackboard), available to him for carrying out his duties fully and faithfully. In fact, the key to the success of an ETV programme lies in how far and for how long it can hold the interest of the student-viewers. At the same time, it should be able to 'sell' properly the teaching points aimed at. It largely depends on the creativity, professional skills and personal involvement of the presenter-teacher as well as the producer. Also, the classroom teacher must ensure a congenial atmosphere and viewing conditions at the receiving end. Dr Palmer in his book entitled, Television (Edited by Bary G. Cole), made an interesting observation: "TV informs and instructs in its way as much as others do (But) TV has a much greater educational influence than all the formal establishments devoted to education."

The Taught: Lastly, the taught. The poor fellow, as pointed out earlier, is at the 'receiving end'. And the one who is reticent and reluctant to offer dissenting views or to argue is considered bright and well-behaved. Whether TV or teacher, no one generally is interested in assessing the needs-much less the likes or dislikes of their pupil. The level of understanding of all those exposed to television (or to the teacher) also differs widely. TV does not afford an opportunity to ask for repetition or clarifications. Moreover, in the initial steps of exposure, television is more of 'fun' for the young. They just remain glued to the set during this spell and may in the process, often miss the vital 'cue' involved in a lesson As the familiarity between the two develops, the television turns out to be an 'escape' from being taught.

A Team Effort: A comment made by Gerald Millerson in his book Effective TV production may be of relevance here: "Once we have overcome; the initial awkwardness of unfamiliarity, we tend to take TV technicalities for granted. TV direction appears deceptively simple. Our audience goes frustrated, confused and even reduced to laughter'. To make an Educational Television presentation a success, students of TV-classes have also to play their part. They should not forget that television offers to them an opportunity to have another even if not better perspective. And, certainly a more visually embellished show. Some subjects are indeed ideally suited to the television treatment; pot even the best of teachers normally can manage to do better. Television is a serious business, irrespective of whether it has educational inputs or those of entertainment. It becomes all the more serious if the subject matter happens to be a hard-core one, like an ETV lesson. Hence, all the three ETV partners must think and act together with single a common objective to make their show a success.

'Barriers' to ETV: Educational television suffers from certain limitations or ' barriers'. The gravest of them all is the element of 'anonymity', inherent in its very operation. It is strictly 'one-way' communication. The teacher-the taught contact, considered vital all over the world; is almost missing in case of television. No personal contact; no physical identification; no scope for repetition, clarification or elaboration. The gap between the 'sender' and the 'receiver' is too wide to be easily bridged. TV and teacher should prove to be more of companions than competitors. According to the Verghese Committee Report, "Radio and television are not teacher substitutes but teaching aids, another black-board or learning kit."

❑❑❑

5 JOURNALISM

INTRODUCTION

In this chapter, we will explore the importance of the English Press and discuss its contribution to our freedom struggle also considering the role of regional language journalism, as the regional language press is far ahead of the English press, both in the number of publications and their circulation, its impact has yet to be correctly analysed. The characteristics, categories, role and popularity index of magazines are presented. Discussing the principles of journalism and the role of journalists. In conclusion, talking about the various Professional and Statutory bodies related to mass media.

Q1. State the importance of the English Press in our society.

Ans. Generally, Standard English today does not depend on accent but rather on shared educational experience, mainly of the printed language. Present-day English is an immensely varied language, having absorbed material from many other tongues. It is spoken by more than 300 million native speakers, and between 400 and 800 million foreign users. It is the official language of air transport and shipping; the leading language of science, technology, computers, and commerce; and a major medium of education, publishing, and international negotiation. For this reason, scholars frequently refer to its latest phase as World English.

India, after becoming independent in 1947, was left with a colonial language, in this case English, as the language of government. It was thought that the end of the British Raj would mean the slow but sure demise of the English language in South Asia. This, of course, has not happened. The penetration of English in these societies is greater that it has ever been (Kachru 1994: 542). Compared to many other developing countries, the Indian Press flourished and depicted a large degree of freedom in its working. In 1950 there were 214 daily newspapers, with 44 in English and the rest in Indian languages. By 1990 the number of daily newspapers had grown to 2,856, with 209 in English and 2,647 in indigenous languages.

In 1965, when English was to cease being a principal language of the country, English newspapers numbered more than newspapers in any other language. They also claimed the largest share of the total circulation of all papers.

The English language newspapers deserve a strong mention in the story of India's struggle for freedom. And ever since Independence, they have acted as a beacon light for the regional language press by setting high standards of professionalism in reporting and packaging of their content. Since circulation is a good measure to gauge popularity, we may say that the English language newspapers are in great demand. Not so long ago they occupied the leading position in number and circulation, followed by the Hindi newspapers.

Important public matters that are discussed threadbare in the English Press eventually have a bearing on policy decisions .One can estimate the extent of their influence from instances when governments at the center, or in the states, have been either constituted or pulled down because of investigative reports appearing in the English press.

In general, the English newspapers' style of reporting is good and therefore they enjoy a high credibility. In addition, the people attach a lot of importance to these newspapers' capacity to impart education in the English language .All this has contributed to the wide readership of English newspapers.

The Growth of the English Press: English newspapers were published by Britishers in India, expressly to convey news from Britain and Europe to those residing here. The Christian missionaries were among the first to start newspapers in English. With a circulation of a few hundred copies per newspaper, the English press enjoyed popular support among the readers from the initial stages itself.

James Augustus Hickey, who takes the credit for having started the first English newspaper in British India, in the year 1780. The first English newspaper in India was also the first newspaper in India.

Q2. Describe the origin and growth of English Press in our country.

Ans. James Hickey, who takes the credit for having started the first English newspaper in British India, in the year 1780. The first English newspaper in India was also the first newspaper in India. Newspapers in India can broadly be classified into two groups - English newspapers and language newspapers. As the name indicates, English newspapers are published in English language, whereas language newspapers are published in different Indian languages. The Christian missionaries were among the first to start newspapers in English. With a circulation of a few hundred copies per newspaper, the English press enjoyed popular support among the reader from the initial stages itself.

Origin in British India: Newspapers of that time were in English, and the news only related to British activity in India. As the readers were also British, the local population was not the target. But the Company feared that these Indian papers could get to England and may defame the Company in England. English papers used to take nine months to reach India.

As East India Company spread its wing in southern peninsula, English language started to get newer pockets of influence. But it was still time for the first English book to capitalise. Late 17th century saw the coming of printing press in India but the publication were largely confined to either printing Bible or government decrees. Then came newspapers. It was in 1779 that the first English Newspaper named Hickey's Bengal Gazette was published in India, brought out by Hickey.

He later renamed it as the Oriental Calcutta General Advertiser. It appeared weekly, every Saturday. He attacked the East India Company vigourously through his paper. Finally, when he indulged in casting aspersions on the wife of the then Governor-General, Warren Hastings, he was forcefully deported on the Governor-General's orders. A prominent merchant by the name of James Silk Buckingham, was another pioneer of English newspapers in India. He started the Calcutta Journal as its proprietor editor. From October 2,1818 till November 9,1823 (the day it ceased publication), the paper enjoyed uncommon popularity as it carried items of local Indian interest and did not play favourites with any political party. However, on March 1, 1823, Buckingham was deported after Chief Secretary to the Government, John Adams announced his regulations on the free press by way of compulsory pre-publication licensing.

Bengal Harkaru, Friend of India and Bengal Herald were other newspapers that were quite popular in the beginning of the nineteenth century.

Bombay Herald was Bombay's first newspaper which was started in 1789. Madras Courier was the first newspaper to be published from Madras in 1785. The first regular venture of the natives in the field of English journalism was Reformer started by Prasunna Coomar Tagore and Bholanath Sen in 1831.

Contribution to India's Independence: In the nineteenth century, when just a few Indians were acquainted with the English language, some educated leaders ventured to publish English newspapers. Their efforts were twice successful, as these publications put across the majority viewpoint to the British rulers and also initiated British-influenced Indians into the freedom struggle.

Soon enough the fledgling press invited trouble in the form of severe government restrictions on the freedom of information and the right to criticise. Although licensing was not required, registration of newspapers was made compulsory in 1835 by Sir Charles Metcalfe, the interim Governor-General in Place of Lord William Bentinck. Licensing was reintroduced by an Act in 1857.

Leading members of the elite in society enthusiastically contributed their views to Indian-owned English newspapers. This in turn generated tremendous support for the nationalist movement. While the government clamped restrictions on the English and Vernacular Press, those papers which were owned by Anglo-Indians were exempted since they were not too critical of the British government.

The struggle for freedom gained momentum in the last few years of the nineteenth century, and this to a large extent was one of the views which appeared in English language newspapers. The English press responded to the call to fight for a free India. During the Civil Disobedience Movement, the Press (Emergency Powers) Act, 1931 was enforced. In spite of the constraints, the English papers continued to criticise the British government fearlessly. In general, all the English newspapers used forceful language and served to direct and organise the energies of the people who then moved nearer to their aim of self governance.

Post-Independence Role: The role of the English press in the 1950s was necessarily shaped in response to the immediate needs of development and modernisation. In a newly democratised country, the Indian press had the responsibility of educating the masses about the intricacies of the functioning of the administrative, legal and other departments of the government. All this the press had to do in addition to the task of promoting communal harmony the wake of the country's partition into Pakistan and India

The notable features of the newspapers at this time were:

- a marked increase in circulation,
- greater collection of advertisement revenue,
- modern equipment and expanded facilities of reporting from distant locations, and
- the appearance of features and columns with by-lines.

When India was at war with Pakistan (in 1965 and 1971) and China (in October, 1962), the English press did a commendable job of defending the country's sovereignty. The population 'boom' was another area that the mass media had to address head on. The English Press was not lagging on this front either. It was imperative, to contain the growth in population then, as it continues to be now, some three decades later.

The imposition of Emergency in 1975 by the government headed by Mrs. Indira Gandhi marked the beginning of the hard times. There were severe restrictions on the freedom of the press. The English Press was muzzled, especially the outspoken journalists and the papers they wrote for, during the two years of the Emergency.

Chain Publications, quite familiar on the Indian Press scene, have come to stay. By the 1980s, "chain" newspapers were a trademark of those publishers who notched remarkable circulation figures for their groups of papers and periodicals. The idea was to use the profits of any publication for the numerical expansion of the group. The general trend has been to view journalism as a profit making industry. There is an urgent need to change this attitude.

In the early years of the 1990s, the government's economic measures of liberalisation and integration of the country in the global economy are issues that have been receiving ample coverage in our English dailies. Besides, the disturbing trend of religious intolerance is constantly commented upon, in our English newspapers.

Q3. Describe the nature of ownership, with particular reference to the phenomenon of 'chain' publications.

Ans. Newspapers have long been viewed as economic enterprises with good monetary returns. Besides circulation revenue, advertising revenue is important in meeting cost of production and in making profits. Managerial skills are required to run the newspaper concerns efficiently, just as in any other business.

As for content, newspapers have contributed a great deal towards making the people more politically conscious. Further, no newspaper can claim to be neutral or apolitical.

The general trend which is apparent is one of increasing sophistication in the packaging and presentation of news. The news is segregated on the basis of the topic referred to. It is then printed on separate pages such as foreign, national, regional, local, sports, economy, edit page, etc. Neat and attractive get-up of the newspaper has been made possible by modern printing technology.

Ownership–The Phenomenon of Newspaper Chains: The Indian media market differs from those of developed countries in several ways. For one, India is a developing country and all segments of the media industry (including print and radio) are still growing unlike in developed countries. The media market in India remains highly fragmented, due to the large number of languages and the sheer size of the country. There are various types of media ownership. There are many media organisation in the country that are owned and controlled by a wide variety of entities including corporate bodies, societies and trusts and individuals. There were over 82,000 publications registered with the Registrar of Newspapers as on 31 March 2011.

There are different types of ownership of newspapers. These may be classified as newspapers owned by individuals, societies and associations, firms or partnerships. Joint stock companies, government (central/state), cooperative societies, educational institutions, international organisations, political parties, companies-public and private, etc. Common Ownership Units are among the more prominent types of ownership. The Office of the Registrar of Newspapers for India (RNI) defines the Common Ownership Unit (COU) as a newspaper establishment owning two or more news-interest newspapers of which at least one is a daily.

Leading examples of the common ownership Units are Bennett Coleman and Co. Ltd., Indian Express (Pvt.) Ltd., Ananda Bazar Patrika (Pvt.) Ltd., Hindustan Times & Allied Publications (Public Ltd.), Statesman (Public Ltd.), Kasturi& Sons (Public Ltd) Only the English dailies which these COUs publish are mentioned below:

Bennett Coleman & Co.	Times of India, Economics Times
Indian Express (Pvt.) Ltd.	Indian Express, Financial Express
Ananda Bazar Patrika	Ananda Bazar Patrika, Telegraph
Hindustan Times & Allied Publications	The Hindustan Times
Statesman Ltd.	Statesman
Kasturi & Sons	The Hindu

A 'Big unit' is defined by the RNI as a news-interest newspaper of a COU with a circulation of more than 50,000 copies. Given below is a list of some of the big units with their percentage share in the circulation of English dailies indicated alongside:

Bennett Coleman & Co.	18.8 per cent
Express Newspapers	14.3 per cent
Kasturi & Sons	9.0 per cent

Hindustan Times & Allied Publications	8.1 per cent
Blitz Publications	7.2 per cent
Statesman Ltd.	4.5 per cent
Ushodaya Publications	4.3 per cent
Tribune Trust	4.1 per cent
Ananda Bazar Patrika	4.1 per cent

In the context of industrialists venturing into printing of newspapers with a profit motive, some members of the commission pointed out the need to have journalists and their newspapers independent of any influence from the barons of industry. With this in mind, it was suggested that either the owners of newspapers who were involved with other business and industries, delink themselves from the latter, or else severe their connections with the press.

The Commission also took a serious view of the lack of 'diffusion' in the presentation of news. In a marketplace of ideas where every possible point of view must be projected, it is in the best interests of the readers to free the press "from the steamrolling of the commercial process so that it may mean maximum amount of freedom of expression for the maximum number of people".

The majority of newspapers are owned by Joint Stock Companies and provide views and analyses which benefit their other economic ventures. Thus, commercial interests operate and extend into the areas of newspaper content.

Q4. List the characteristics of the English Language Press in their content, style and presentation.

Ans. The characteristics of the English Language Press in their content, style and presentation are as follows:

- **Content of the English Newspapers:** English newspapers address key issues of the day, some in a particularly outspoken fashion. Specialised writing on subjects such as culture and arts, tourism, women, children, health science and technology, law, architecture, education, sports, the media, political analyses, etc., is the order of the day. Now, there are papers exclusively concerned with finance Financial Express and Economic Times are examples of this type.

  Despite the fact that there is a greater variety in the contents of newspapers to politics and politicians still seem to receive too much attention. For instance, occurrences of dowry death and rape receive prominent mention. There is a lack adequate effort on the part of newspapers to provide any constructive solutions the many social problems that are plaguing our society.

The style of writing in English newspapers has changed over the years. We do not have any more long verbatim reports of speeches. News reports are short and the writing is lively. The days of long editorials are also over. There is more and more stress on interpretative and investigative reporting. Analytical writings on many important issues are now available. A wide variety of features which are readable educative and entertaining are being published by most English newspapers.

While every edition of the newspaper, provides varied fare, the Sunday issues carry exclusive supplements devoted to review of books, the arts, the media, etc. Sunday newspapers are popular with the readers as much for their reading material as for their classified advertisements whether for accommodation, employment or matrimonials.

- **Presentation of Content in English Newspapers:** Newspaper designing has come a long way from the days when scanty or no particular attention was paid just by clubbing the news items into distinct categories. Every newspaper has a distinct personality of its own that sets it apart from other papers. It is important for the paper to retain its identity while at the same time come out with a fresh look everyday. Typography is an important factor in determining the appearance of the newspaper. Careful selection of the types for headlines and text is essential. Appropriate use of photographs, line drawings, graphs and other illustrations enlivens the text attention of the reader. Pocket cartoons are popular with the readers. For example, R. K. Laxman's 'You Said It' in The Times India delights readers daily.

  The front page is the most important in a newspaper. Items of greatest importance appear on this page. When an important news item is received, it has to be accommodated on the front page and as a consequence some of the items have to be shifted to an inside page. For this reason, the front page is one of the last to be made up. The design of the front page is important because it must be attractive enough to induce people to buy it off the newsstands.

- **Recommendations of the Second Press Commission:** Recommendations of the Commission to delink the press from industry and its call for greater diffusion of ideas in our society. The Commission made it clear that it views journalism not merely as an industry but as a public service and profession. It observed that public interest should be the criterion to regulate the news and views of the newspaper and not ownership, as is usually the case.

  The Second Press Commission desired that a National Development Commission (NDC) be constituted to promote the entire Indian press rather than just individual papers in select languages.

  One of the major recommendations of the second Press Commission was to specify a price-page schedule and a news-to-advertisement ration. The latter was fixed at 60:40 for big papers, 50:50 for medium and 40:60 for small newspapers. This was suggested in order to help 'promote competition and prevent monopoly of a few newspapers'. The Commission, viewing display advertising as a wasteful expenditure, called for curtailment of such advertising.

  The NDC was to extend financial assistance to small and medium newspapers. Besides, the NDC would appoint an autonomous corporation to oversee the fair and equitable distribution of both government and foreign advertisements.

Q5. Outline the development of the use of language in India.

Ans. India is the home to a huge variety of languages. India, a potpourri of different cultures, religions, and beliefs, is home to not just one or two languages but to an uncountable number of different lingual families. Languages belonging to the two major language families - Indo Aryan and Dravidian - are spoken by more than 90 per cent of the people of India. According to Ethnologue, India is considered the home to 398 languages out of which 11 have been reported extinct. The Indian languages of today have evolved from different language families, corresponding more or less to the different ethnic elements that have come into India from the pre-historic times. They may be classified into six groups as follows: (1) Negroid (2) Austric (3) Sino-Tibetan (4) Dravidian (5) Indo-Aryan and (6) Other Speeches.

We have distributed the language scenario of India into three parts these are as follows:

(1) History of The Indian Languages: The Indian language is hugely complicated and diverse and has been shaped, like most things in India, by years of cultural variety, regional differences, race, money, religion and war. The origins of the languages of India bring with them great stories and history which blends in with the wonder and mystery that so makes India so hard to define.

The Indo-Aryan branch of the Indo-European family came into India with the Aryans. It is the biggest of the language groups in India, accounting for about 74 per cent of the entire Indian population. The important languages in the group are; Western Punjabi, Sindhi, Eastern Punjabi, Hindi, Bihari, Rajasthanani, Gujarati, Marathi, Assamese, Bengali, Oriya, Pahari, Kashmiri and Sanskrit.

Hindi has produced two great literatures. Urdu and (High) Hindi. Both have the same grammar and the same basic vocabulary. They differ, however, in script and higher vocabulary. Urdu uses the Perso-Arabic script. Hindi uses the Nagari script and has a preference for purely Sanskrit words in contradiction to the numerous Arabic and Persian words borrowed by Urdu.

The Dravidian language was present in India centuries before the Indo-Aryan. The outstanding languages of the Dravidian groups are; (i) Telugu, the state language of Andhra Pradesh, numerically the biggest of the Dravidian languages, (ii) Tamil, the state language of Tamil Nadu, apparently the oldest and purest branch of the Dravidian family, (iii) Kannada, the state language of Karnataka, another ancient Dravidian language that has developed individually, (iv) Malayalam, the state language of Kerala, the smallest and the youngest of the Dravidian family.

(2) Status of the Indian Languages: With independence, the question of a common language naturally came up. The question was put to vote and Hindi won by the margin of a single vote-the casting vote of the President. Hindi, however, was only one of the many regional languages of India. The India National Congress had advocated the formation of linguistic provinces. The acceptance of this policy involved the statutory recognition of all the major regional languages.

The Constitution therefore recognised Hindi in Devanagari script as the official language of the union (Art. 343 et. seq.) and the regional languages as the official languages of the states concerned (Art. 345 et. seq.). Later, the 8th Schedule was added to the constitution; it listed all statutorily recognised regional languages. The Schedule originally contained 15 languages as follows: (i) Assamese (ii) Bengali (iii) Gujarati (iv) Hindi (v) Kannada (vi) Kashmiri (vii) Malayalam (viii) Marathi (ix) Oriya (x) Punjabi (xi) Sanskrit (xii) Tamil (xiii) Telugu (xiv) Urdu (xv) Sindhi. By the 77th Amendment to the Constitution Konkani, Manipuri and Nepali were added to the list in 1992.

(3) Constitutional Position: The Indian constitution, in 1950, declared Hindi in Devanagari script to be the official language of the union. Unless Parliament decided otherwise, the use of English for official purposes was to cease 15 years after the constitution came into effect, i.e., on 26 January 1965. The prospect of the changeover, however, led to much alarm in the non Hindi-speaking areas of India, especially Dravidian-speaking states whose languages were not related to Hindi at all. As a result, Parliament enacted the Official Languages Act, 1963, which provided for the continued use of English for official purposes along with Hindi, even after 1965. The current position is thus that the Union government continues to use English in addition to Hindi for its official purposes as a "subsidiary official language," but is also required to prepare and execute a programme to progressively increase its use of Hindi. The exact extent to which, and the areas in which, the Union government uses Hindi and English, respectively, is determined by the provisions of the Constitution, the Official Languages Act, 1963, the Official Languages Rules, 1976, and statutory instruments made by the Department of Official Language under these laws.

Q6. Comment over the development and growth of Regional language newspapers of India.

Or

Trace the growth and development of a Hindi or regional language newspaper of your choice. [June-2019, Q.No.-8]

Ans. Digdarshan was the first Indian language newspaper. It started in April 1818 by the Serampur missionaries William Carcy, Joshua

Marshman & William Ward. They soon started another journal in June of the same year & named it Samachar Darpan. The famous Raja Ram Mohan Roy also brought out periodicals in English, Bengali & Persian. Some of Roy's papers were SambadKaumadi, Brahmical Magazine, Mirat-ul-Akhbar, and Bangadoota& Bengal Herald.

Growth of newspapers in the major regional languages in India is as follows:

- **Assamese:** Amnodaya, a distinguished journal in the Assamese language was started in 1846 under the editorship of the Reverend Oliver. T. Cutter. The Assamese daily, Dainik Assamiya ceased publication in 1951 and a new Assmese daily, Natun Assamiya, under different ownership and management, was launched. Of weeklies and occasional publications, however, there have been several, of which mention may be made of Assamiya–the oldest Assamese language weekly of the state, and Deka Asom from Gauhati; Asom Sevak from Tezpur; Sramik from Dibrugarh and Janmabhumi from Jorhat.
- **Bengali:** In 1937, when Anand Bazar Patrika started the English Hindustan Standard, the Amrita Bazar Patrika brought out the Bengali Jugantar. During the war, the Amrita Bazar Patrika was started in English from Allahabad (1943) and since 1950 it has added the Hindi daily AmirtaPatrika from the same place.

  In 1939, two more dailies were started–the Bharat founded by Makhan Lal Sen, who had contributed substantially towards the establishment of Ananda Bazar Patrika, and Krishak, an organ of the Krishak Praja Party. In 1941, A. K. Fazlur Huq started publication of the daily Navajug in Bengali and five years later the official organ of the Communist Party of India, Swadhinata, came on the scene along with the Swaraj edited by Sri Satyendra Nath Mazumdar.

  Today, Ananda Bazar Patrika, and Jugantar are the most popular Bengali newspapers.
- **Gujarati:** The first Gujarati newspaper, Bombay Samachar began its long career in 1822, with a full-fledged printing press complete with types. Another paper which made an illustrious beginning was Jam-e-Jamshed, a Gujarati weekly, started by Pestonji Manak ji Moti wala in 1831. After 1850, the

development of Gujarati journalism was marked by the starting of a number of papers, many of which had a short life.

In 1943, Sri Amritlal Seth started in Bombay Janmabhoomi, a Gujarati daily which also has a large circulation. Yet another group consists of the daily Prabhat, the weekly Nav Saurashtra and the monthly Kumar, owned by Shri Kakalbhai Kothari. Surat has two leading dailies, Samachar, started in 1922 by Sri M. R. Vidyarthi and Gujarati, (1921) edited by Sri Ramanlal Chhotubhai Desai.

- **Kannada:** Journalism in Kannada started around 1870 almost in all the regions. Between 1880 and 1908, a number of newspapers in English and in Kannada made their appearance, prominent among them was Deshabhimani edited by B. Srinivasa lyengar. In 1908, the Mysore Legislative Council passed the Newspaper Regulation Act and soon after a Kannada weekly publication. Uryodaya Pakasika published a report which incurred the displeasure of the Government. Prompt action was taken and in protest, most of the newspapers of Mysore closed down.

  With the advent of Mahatma Gandhi, some prominent public men encouraged journals for the purpose of carrying on the freedom struggle. In 1947, two daily, papers, Vishal Karnataka and Navyug were started at Hubli and are still being published. Vishal Karnataka was started on August 9. 1947 by. Shri K. F. Patil and his friends, with Sri Patil Puttappa as its editor.

- **Malayalam:** Malayala Manorama of Kottayam, presently the leading daily of Kerala was founded 85 years ago by Kandathi Varghese Mappilai. Prominent literary and public figures of the time contributed freely to the columns of Manorama. Among them were Kerala Varma Valla Koyil Thampuran, Kunhikuttan Thanpuran, Sri Vallathol Narayana Menon, Ullor Achutha Menon and Murkoth Kumaran. In 1904, the founder-editor passed away and was succeeded by Sri K. C. Mammen Mappillai who maintained the high traditions built up by his predecessor till he passed away in December, 1953 at the age of 80. This is the largest circulated multiple edition daily in the country.

Special mention should be made of a fortnightly publication, Kayana Kaumudi started in 1905, which published news, views and a correspondence all in verse. It is now published as a literary magazine by Sri P. V. Krishna varrier from Kottakkal. The Narsni Deepika and Kerala Kesari edited by Ballath Kunjunni Achan and Yogakesheman edited by V. S. Nambudripad were well-known publications. Papers which stood for social justice were Deshabhimani edited by T. K. Madhavan, the Sahodaran edited by Ayyappan of Cochin and Mithavadhi of C. Krishnan of Calicut.

The struggle for independence brought into being a number of dailies in the 1920s. The most important of these is Mathrubhumi, it started as a tri-weekly in 1923 and is now published as a daily and a weekly (illustrated) and commands great popularity in Kerala.

- **Marathi:** Bal Shastri Jambhekkar started the first Anglo-Marathi paper, the Bombay Durpun, in 1832 as a fortnightly. A few months later it was converted into a weekly. Jambhekkar later brought out a monthly Marathi magazine, Dig Durshun (May 1840). In February, 1849, Dhyan Prakash of Poona came into existence under the editorship of KrishnajiTrimbak Ranade.

  The next Marathi daily to be published from Bombay was Rashtramat, edited by S. K. Damle and published by the Rashtramata Publishing Company Ltd.; It was the mouthpiece of the extremist party led by Bal Gangadhar Tilak.

  In 1923, Khadilkar started Navkal which is today the oldest marathi daily.

  Loksatta is the first Marathi daily to be published from Bombay after independence. It was started in 1948 by the Express Group with Sri T .VPargate as its first editor.

  The Poona-based Sakal was established in 1931 by Dr. N.B. Parulekar who graduated from the Columbia University, USA and was the first Indian to study journalism as a subject in the United States.

  The Maharashtra Times, was started in 1962 by the Times of India group.

- **Oriya:** Among the earliest Oriya newspapers, Asha and Samaj stand prominent. While Asha was published as a weekly by SashibhushanDutt, it was converted into daily in 1928. After a change in the proprietorship, it was closed down in 1951. But it is now being published as a weekly from Berhampur in the Ganjam district.

  Samaj was established by the veteran politician GopuBandhu Das in 1928 as a weekly newspaper. Later, in 1931, a daily was also started. A newspaper, Praja Tantra, was started under the guidance of Hare Krishna Mehtab, the noted Congressman, who later rose to such high political positions as the Union Minister and the Chief Minister of Orissa.

- **Punjabi:** The birth of Punjabi newspapers may be traced to the decade of the 1850s with the publication of English-Punjabi dictionary and the casting of the Gurmukhi type for the first time in 1854.

  Punjabi journalism entered a new phase with the Akali movement in 1920 when the first Akali paper was started. The division of Punjab dealt a heavy blow to Punjabi journalism in 1947. Lahore, the centre of Punjabi journalism, was lost to Pakistan. Many Gurmukhi papers and magazines were uprooted. Some of them rehabilitated themselves in a short time and others were started. Among the major Punjabi newspapers today are Ajit, Akali Patrika, Khalsa Sevak, Prakash, Newan Hindustan, Nawan Zamana. Among the periodicals, the largest circulated one is the monthly magazine, Preeth Lari, from Amritsar.

- **Tamil:** The first Tamil magazine was a monthly, **Tamil Patrika**, startedin 1831. The Progress of the Tamil press was accelerated in the last decade of the 19th century with the starting of **Swadesamitran** in 1882 founded by the great **G. Subramanya Aiyer**, who converted it into a daily in 1899. The next Tamil daily made its mark only in 1917 entitled **Desabhaktan**, but was forced to be closed down in 1926; that year **Tamil Nadu** under Varadarajulu Naidu started as a daily.

In 1936, the Indian Express group started **Dinamani,** a daily, in September, 1934. A. N. Sivaraman, its editor, spared no effort to make it a leading Tamil daily like **Swadesamitran.**

In Madurai, a Tamil daily known as **Dina Thanthi** was born in 1940. Within a short time simultaneous editions were brought out from Madras, Coimbatore, Salem and Tiruchirapalli.

Among the Tamil weeklies, it is Ananda Vikatan which achieved notable success Started in 1924.

But the largest circulated Tamil weekly is Kumudum, started in 1947, with a print order of over four lakhs.

- **Telugu:** The first newspaper in Telugu was Satyadoota, started in 1835. The renowned Andhra social reformer and literature, Kandkuri Veereshlingam Panthulu started Vivekavardhini in 1885 from Rajahmundry. The first competing journal to this was started by Kokkanti Venkatarathnam Danthulu; this was Andhrabhasa Sanjivini.

  In the beginning of the 20th century, Pinjal Subramanya Setty, started a Telugu daily called Samadarshini.

  An outstanding journalist in the Telugu language at that time was **Desodharaka** K. Nageswara Rao Panthulu. An enterprising young man, he migrated to Bombay where he built up a good business patenting a pain balm known as Amrutanjan.

  In the Telangana area, the first journal was Hitabodhini started in 1913, with Srinivasa Sharma as its editor. The most important journal was Golkonda Patrika promoted by Madapati Hanumantha Rao Panthulu.

  The inauguration of the State of Andhra Pradesh on October 1, 1953 gave a real fillip to the development of Telugu journalism. The following four daily newspapers were started in Andhra Pradesh after 1953: Andhra Janata edited by K.S. Subramanyam and published from Hyderabad, Andhra Bhoomi started in 1960 by K.R. Pattabhiram; Rajahmundry Samacharam edited by GandhamSeetharamayanjalu and published from Rajahmundry since 1956, and Vishalandhra started in Vijayawada in 1952, by K. R. Rajagopal Rao. Another prominent Telugu daily of recent years is Andhra Jyoti, started in 1960.

An exciting contribution to Telugu journalism has been, made by a businessman, Ch. Ramoji Rao, who launched Eenadu in 1974. It picked up circulation within no time and climbed to the top in just one decade.

- **Hindi:** The earliest Hindi newspaper was started in Calcutta in 1826. It was a weekly, Oodunt Martand; its editor was Jooghul Kishore Sookool. Banga Doot, sponsored, among others, by Raja Ram Mohan Roy and Dwaraka Prasad Thakore, appeared in 1829. The first Hindi daily, Samachar Subha Varshan, came out in 1854 with Shyam Sunder Sen as its editor.

  In 1920, Aaj was started in Banaras and it played a very notable part in the freedom struggle.

  In Patna, Desh, a weekly, was an influential journal and a mouthpiece of the Congress. It was founded by Babu Rajendra Prasad and his friends in 1920 and proved a valuable medium for nationalist propaganda.

  The Hindustan Times, started in 1936. The Nav Bharat Times of the Times of India group started in Delhi in 1950 and today it is the largest circulated Hindi daily.

  Aryavart, a daily, was started by the Indian Nation group of Bihar in 1940 and has wide circulation. Amrita Patrika of Allahabad is another daily well-known for its trenchant editorials. In Madhya Pradesh. Nav Bharat published from Jabalpur, Bhopal, Raipur and Indore is widely circulated and popular; its oldest edition is the one published from Nagpur in Vidarbha. Ravivar, a Hindi weekly of the Sunday group, has as much influence as its better known sister journal, Sunday . The Hindi Blitz (Bombay) has almost overtaken the circulation of the English edition.

- **Urdu:** The Urdu Press in India today is the fourth largest group numerically. Delhi's earliest Urdu newspapers, Fawaid-ul-Nazarin and Kiran-us-Sadai (1852) were edited by a Christian convert, Ram Chandra. In the 1860s, there were six Urdu papers published from Delhi and they were all owned by loyalists. The most enduring of these was Akmal-ul-Akbar published by Hakim Abdul Majid Khan. By the 1880s, there were more than 12 newspapers, many of them owned by those who were critical of the establishment.

A notable Urdu journal in the first decade of this century was Maulana Abdul Kalam Azad's Al-Hilal which came out from Calcutta in 1912. Al-Hilal marked a turning point in the history of Urdu journalism.

Q7. Discuss the role of the regional language newspapers and magazines in social awakening and development.

Ans. Contribution by Language Newspapers

- **Moulding Public Opinion:** Vernacular newspapers which were isolated during the freedom struggle are now wielding a lot of influence and are potent instruments of moulding public opinion. In the past, they were struggling to survive, but now they are thriving. Initially, they were organs of individual opinion. Now they are pre-occupied with political, economic and social issue of general interest. The language newspapers today are providing adequate coverage on all aspects of life.

  Through improved mechanical equipment, they are able to provide thicker and cheaper editions. There is more diversity in the contents of the Indian language newspapers today; besides, they also show greater responsibility in the collection and presentation of all reading material.

- **The Provincial Press:** With the advent of freedom and growth of democratic institutions, the regional and provincial press has assumed significance. From the financial angle the regional newspaper stands in the middle of the chain of which the metropolitan daily is the strongest link and the district newspaper is the weakest.

  A few of the small and independent language newspapers have attained affluence and are acting as the real link between the people and the government. In fact these papers, which command respect by virtue of their passion for truth and public service, are so effective that they act as opposition to the party in power. Undoubtedly, this is a great contribution of the Indian Press.

- **Location--Specific:** The Indian language newspapers have evolved their own pattern, guided by their own experience and responding to the demands of their readers. Local and regional news assumes importance for them more than national or international news. They normally do not miss any "spot news" of national or international significance which they get through the news agencies. But events and problems of the locality or the region are of special interest to them as they are not adequately treated in the metropolitan newspapers. The vernacular press has assumed leadership of the local community and is respected by their friend, philosopher and guide.

Indian language newspapers have ceaselessly tried to interpret the great heritage and culture of India. In this task, they have had the good-will and support of many great men from all walks of life. Thus, they have strengthened the basic unity of India. This is yet another contribution of language press.

Q8. Explain the concept of language newspapers and literacy.

Ans. The provision of universal and compulsory education for all children in the age group of 6–14 was a cherished national ideal and had been given overriding priority by incorporation as a Directive Policy in Article 45 of the Constitution, but it is still to be achieved more than half a century since the Constitution was adopted in 1949. Parliament has passed the Constitution 86th Amendment Act, 2002, to make elementary education a Fundamental Right for children in the age group of 6–14 years. In order to provide more funds for education, an educationacess of 2 per cent has been imposed on all direct and indirect central taxes through the Finance (No. 2) Act, 2004.

In 2000–01, there were 60,840 pre-primary and pre-basic schools, and 664,041 primary and junior basic schools. Total enrolment at the primary level has increased from 19,200,000 in 1950–51 to 109,800,000 in 2001–02. The number of high schools in 2000–01 was higher than the number of primary schools at the time of independence.

The literacy rate grew from 18.33 per cent in 1951, to 74.04 per cent in 2011. During the same period, the population grew from 361 million to 1,210 million.

Major advances in literacy rates have let to occur in the four big Hindi-speaking states where literacy is very low. Against an all-India literacy average of 52 per cent of the population over 7 years of age, Bihar stands at 39 per cent Madhya Pradesh 44 per cent, Rajasthan, 39 per cent and J. P. 42 per cent. Never-the-less these figures themselves represent a literate population of more than 10 million people in 1991. As per the figures of the Registrar of' Newspapers, the four states in 1988 had a circulation of about six million copies of daily newspapers in all languages. his gives a ratio of 55 copies of a daily per thousand literates. This approaches the Kerala ratio, but in Kerala, more than per cent of the population is literate given the large number of readers per newspaper (usually estimated between six and 12), this 1:20 ratio may represent the general pattern of newspaper consumption in a rural society.

Purchasing Power: Purchasing power appears to play only a small part in determining whether a person spends money on a newspaper. In 1993, the purchase of a daily newspaper represented an expense of between ₹50 and ₹60 months (most dailies sold at about ₹1.75). This totals to ₹600-700 a year or the equivalent of more than 100 kg of rice. In Kerala, the average per capita income in 1990 was estimated at ₹3,389. The cost of daily news as per thus represented 20 per cent of the average annual income. In Punjab, with the highest average per capita income of ₹7,081. the cost of a daily newspaper represented 10 per cent of annual income. In the 1980s, moreover, Kerala and Andhra Pradesh had roughly the same average per capita income (about ₹2,300). slightly below the national average. In absolute numbers. Andhra had about two million more literates than Kerala. Yet Malayalam dailies sold more than twice as many each day as Telugu dailies. Nationally Malayalam dailies in the late 1980's sold roughly 58 topics for every 1,000 Malayalam speaking population.

Technology and the Language Newspapers: One of the handicaps of the Indian newspaper industry in the 1970s was slow and antiquated printing technology and a poor road network in most regions. Language newspapers had to depend on hand composition of type and that was time consuming; it took unduly long to transport copies to other towns. The 1980s brought about a transformation in printing technology. Electronic technology and indigenous manufacture of offset presses have allowed printing centres to be set up in smaller towns as thereby reducing tile distance a newspaper has to be transposed. It would take seven hours to move a truckload of newspaper 300 miles in most parts of India. But using telephone lines, news copy can be sent by the facsimile process in a few minutes to distances of hundreds of miles. Indian newspaper publishers began using this in the 1980s.

Q9. Specify the reasons why magazines have become popular and why their circulation has gone up.

Or

Comment over the popularity of magazines.

Ans. The word magazine is derived from the Arabic word. Makhasin meaning warehouse or khazane, that is, a store-up.

Magazines and Journals; What are they: In India, we intermingle the terms magazines, journals and periodicals, although they have different connotations. The Week, India Today, Sarita, or Malayala Manorama Weekly, they are called by any of these names. The periodicity of these publications can be weekly, fortnightly, monthly, quarterly and half annually. Even annuals are included among the periodicals.

(1) Built-in Merits: Whatever be the term employed, these periodical publications contain some built-in merits. They are designed to be kept by the readers for a much longer time then daily newspapers. The magazines are centrally stitched and the publishers use more colours and variegated typographical and layout designs. They even point there magazines on better quality paper.

Compared to dailies, folders or pamphlets, magazines provide reading material of enduring interest and contain different shades of opinion.

Besides tantalising covers, the topics covered by the magazines vary from science to fiction, from current affairs to fine arts, and from social sciences to religion and philosophy. At the same time, they carry amusement of all sorts-- stories, pun, satire, humour, cartoons, comics and various other types of light reading material.

(2) TV of the Printed-Word Communication: For their visual appeals, titillating covers, pretty graphics and typographical variety, decorative boxes, drop letters, neatly cropped pictures, and other innovative devices are employed by the magazines to hold the attention of the readers. With catchy titles, cryptic captions, racy or feature style of writing, the focus is on current controversies. Besides, fun and frolic make magazines highly readable. They cater to the tastes of a wide variety of readers. For discerning eyes, they have much more to offer. For these reasons, some people call magazines the TV of the printed word.

(3) Are Magazines the 5th Estate?: The readership of magazines is by and large confined to somewhat influential, affluent and discriminating sections of the people. They cover important events, in-depth and investigative reports and sensational revelations. For these characteristics the magazines are called the 5th Estate in Japan and are proving to be that in India also.

Q10. List the emerging trends in magazine publishing.

Ans. The 1980s saw a boom in the publication of magazines in India, not only in English but in the major Indian languages as well. Indeed, nearly four out of every five Indian periodicals are in the Indian languages, and they have a circulation which is nearly three fourths of the total circulation. Hindi has the largest circulation (57.9 lakhs), with over 3,000 periodicals followed by English which has 2,670 periodicals with a circulation of over six million. Periodicals in Tamil, Malayalam, Gujarati, Bengali, Marathi, Urdu and Telugu too enjoy a fairly good circulation.

The magazine boom was perhaps set off by the launch of India Today in the mid-seventies, and the new-look Illustrated weekly of India under the editorship of Khushwant Singh. (India Today was initially targeted at Indians settled abroad, but having failed miserably to make an impression, changed gears to target its product at the upper and middle class at home). Its inspiration right from its red-border cover page to its mode of gathering and editing and 'packaging' news has been TIME–International. So it came as no surprise when in 1992, India today became the official agent of TIME magazine in India, collecting subscriptions and advertisements for it.

Riot of Colours at News Stands: We have seen many beautifully produced magazines at a stall or in a library; India Today, Frontline, The Illustrated Weekly of India, The Week, Reader's Digest, Sunday, Gentleman, Business India, Marg, Dharam Yug, Saptahik Hindustan, Chitra, Lekha, Sarita, Manohar Kahaniyan, etc.

Thanks to the new printing technologies and photocomposing, these magazines wear a bright look and create a riot of colour in window displays of book-sellers and news stands or even on the pavements where magazines are displayed for sale.

Black and White Toppers: India's two largest circulated magazines Malayala Manorama (over 11 lakh) and Malayalam, (over 8 lakh) both Malayalam weeklies, appear in black and white. Recently, Malayala Manorama has undergone a pleasant change by making its cover in colour. Malayala Manorama, which has won over a record number of readers in India and abroad, publishers articles on social and cultural subjects, light romantic pieces, two serial cartoon strips done by their staff cartoonists, poetry, literary columns and the most attractive feature is a serialised novel for which readers wait eagerly week after week. It also has a sports piece. Mangalam started comparatively later but is fast catching up; it also thrives on melodrama by serialising works of novelists.

Promotional Strategies: Promotional drives have been launched by almost all important groups of papers. Even India Today, a celebrated English fortnightly and a leading illustrated magazine, now carries a typically Indian promotional ad. "Take a pick of the world for a partner" through its classified matrimonial column.

For reasons of low literacy, lack of purchasing power and the widely common shared readership, no magazine in our country touches the seven figure mark in respect of either circulation or advertising revenue; seven figure circulation is a common feature in periodical journalism in the West. No single magazines here approaches anywhere near the aggregate sale figure of the multi-edition Reader's Digest. The Indian magazines have to go a long way to reach the production standards of the Life and the National Geographic of USA and Sunday of UK.

Role of a Good Magazine: A good or a bad periodical is basically a matter of opinion and individual taste. Broadly speaking, a good magazine must be the readers' forum. It should satisfy their needs as well as fancies. In a vast and multilingual country with ethnic variety, it should also fulfil the aspirations of each segment. For that, readers' surveys and preference polls are necessary so that the contents and design of the journals are close to the readers' hearts.

The other essential qualities of a good periodical, besides its slick production and titillating illustrations, are its liveliness, clarity, insight, probing investigative reports and individual character. It is heartening that some of the periodicals have attained standards comparable with the good western periodicals but the bulk of magazines and journals in the country still lag behind. Most of the magazines, as critics point out, seek to lure the readers by providing juicy and sexy stories, gossip columns, morbid sensationalism and exposures of the private life of VIPs or stars.

In India, Hindi magazines and journals which are the largest in number and carry the highest circulation. These magazines cover a variety of subjects and are widely recognised as potent in reach, power and influence in certain areas.

- **Accomplishments of Magazines:** Magazines fulfil the need for a medium of information, instruction and entertainment. They also interpret issues and policies. They have many accomplishments to their credit: During India's freedom struggle. opinion magazines like Gandhiji's Harijan played a vital role in moulding public opinion and mobilising it against the foreign rule. Magazines have helped strengthen social, religious and national bonds. They provide excellent entertainment at an affordable price.
- **A Composite Tapestry:** Cheap quality journalism exists in various regions and language belts and it co-exists with good journalism. One authority sums up well by saying that the Indian journalism presents a many-splendoured congregation varying from the good and the professional ones to the dirty rags, all set in the same tapestry. There are no professional organisations and professional journals of stature, actively and systematically engaged in promoting professional standards in the sphere of periodical journalism.

Q11. State the categories of periodicals.

Ans.A periodical is a type of publication that appears at regular, predictable, short intervals. They include such items as magazines, scholarly or professional journals, industry/trade journals, newspapers, and newsletters.

When doing research, it is important to understand the differences between popular/general interest magazines, scholarly/professional journals, and industry/trade journals.

News and current affairs journals constitute the India and Probe are the most-hearers of this group. Features of such periodicals, as witnessed in recent years, have been the emergence of investigative reporting, back grounding, incisive comments and team-based and interview-based reports, with collective pictorial and graphic support. Such quality reporting, however, is contained to only some top journals and is not a group virtue. Literacy and cultural magazines constitute the second largest group. The bulk of these magazines, particularly those with a large circulation, follow a formula of mixed contents In order to appeal to diverse tastes and thereby attract more readers. Mangalam and Malayala Manorama. Malayalam weeklies, Kummudam, a Tamil Weekly. Aajkal in Hindi and Urdu are examples of this group. Opinion periodicals are distinct from news magazines as also from journals of entertainment for leisure time reading. They are generally concerned with one or more themes of current interest. Seminar and Mainstream are illustrations of this category. Farm journals, as the name implies, deal with agricultural and other allied activities. Shetkari and Gramsevak belong to this group. The economic, financial and other trade journals are of recent origin but are coming up well. The Hindu Survey of Industry, Business India, Business World, Business Today, Vyapar Udyog represent this class. The growth of science journals, to which belong Vigyan Pragati as also the better selling Science Today, has not been quite satisfactory In terms of their number and quality. The number of women journals in India is not commensurate with the strength of the women population in the country. Vanitha, a Malayalam fortnightly from Kottayam, has the highest circulation in this category. Femina, an English periodical, is also gaining importance. In the group of children's journals, Chandamama and Indrajal comics are the leading examples. Bal Bharati, a government journal, is also popular. Most magazines in this section provide entertainment, short stories and some articles on current events and sports publishers try to lean on cheap circulation gimmicks instead of resorting to originality and creativity. Magazines and Periodicals The sports magazines had a low rate of expansion till recently. But now sports magazines have started improving with experts contributing columns and the journals giving quizzes, interviews and illustrations. Sports Star, an English weekly, is a leading example of this category.

Government Journals: Among the periodicals in India, 706 were brought out by the Government In 1992. Language-wise, the largest number of periodicals in the government sector appeared in English, followed by those in Hindi. The largest circulated government publication was Shraya (50,000), a bilingual bi-monthly of Canara Bank, Bangalore. The second largest one was Shrivir Patrika, a Hindi Weekly of Bikaner. As far as the contents are concerned, 139 periodicals were concerned with news and current affairs 65 journals dealt with social welfare and 55 with agriculture and animal husbandry. The government periodicals claimed a total circulation of 2.45 lakh copies, being less than 1 per cent of the total circulation of the Indian press.

Weak Links in the Periodical Press: The inadequacy of science and technology journals is obvious. They are necessary for a developing country like ours. The Press Commission felt that the number of science journal is inadequate. Besides, they lacked the technique and style to inculcate scientific temper among the people by telling them in a simple language as to how they could advance in certain hi-tech areas. Women in India constitute nearly half of the population. Press Commission study found that these journals address themselves to the urbanite or working women. Children constitute the future leaders of tomorrow. Stories abound in these journals but contributions on how our children should become enlightened, healthy and democratic citizens and forge ahead as world competitors in sports, technology and modern business are lacking. Cheap serials or comic stories borrowed from the West are allowed to fill in the columns of some of these magazines. Film journals which are read widely are full of gossip stories and rumour-mongering. They deal less with professional matters. There have been times which witnessed a direct confrontation between the film world and film journals. A study of the Press Commission revealed another interesting facet-that many juicy articles are written by the PR men in the payroll of film producers.

Emerging Trends: In recent years, interesting and encouraging trends in the field of periodical journalism have been witnessed. Some of the more significant ones are:

- Popular and widely circulated magazines branched out into regional languages and made a mark for themselves. Magazines like India Today, Femina, Stardust, Filmfare and others made their appearance in Hindi, Gujarati and other Indian languages. For example, India Today has five regional language editions including Hindi, Gujarati, Malayalam and others. These are largely independent publications with a separate staff for each language edition and have a definite regional slant.
- India Today, Stardust and a few others have made a mark by bringing out successfully international editions. In these editions, the editorial content is largely similar to the national editions, but advertising is different. The practice is in line with world-famous magazines trend of bringing out editions devoted to different continents. Time and Newsweek bring out

editions like Asia editions. Europe editions and so on. The motive is to earn more revenue from advertising.

- The emergence of city magazines is yet another interesting trend. Big cities like Bombay, Delhi, Calcutta and Pune have exclusive journals that focus attention on metro affairs, events, developments and problems. Bombay has Island, Delhi has First City and City Scan.

Q12. What do you mean by the coexistence of giants and dwarfs?

Ans. Giants and Dwarfs exist in Indian Periodicals: The giants are not only fatter in size but elegant to look at. By and large, they are well managed and are in sound financial health. Their printing is by the latest technologies like multi-colour offset. They have well-known columnists to contribute besides their staff. Occasionally, they bring out special numbers. Sometimes good local scoops also appear. By comparison, small and medium magazines have not been able to maintain professional standards. They lack trained journalists and an adequate number of reporters. This affects their newsgathering and reporting- standards. Most of them, therefore, lean heavily on fiction, gossip columns, detective stories, sensationalism, cheap humour, sexy pictures and western comic strips. Some political magazines find it more paying to write on factional fights and resort to who-on-whose-side kind of political analysis. Similarly, most of the tabloids, which thrive on explosive, critical, daring or expository reporting or titillating makeup, concentrate mostly on sex, scandals, inflated rhetoric's and fabricated juicy material. Some film magazines bank on film politics and rumour-mongering about the stars. They seek to thrive on pornography, both in pictures and script. A few journals carry humorous or otherwise light-hearted stuff but generally, these constituents appear as an appendix rather than an integral part. Some periodicals, of course, carry regular doses of contributed humour. Among them are Sunday, Mukta, The Illustrated Weekly of India, Eve's Weekly, DharamYug and Femina.

Giants Eat the Lion's Share: Advertising revenue is crucial for the periodical press. So a mad struggle is on to get a larger and larger piece of the cake. The sudden increase in advertisement revenue, especially on consumer goods, motivated the leading periodicals to improve their production standards and editorial contents.

The government has pursued a liberal advertising policy of offering special rates to Indian language newspapers and small newspapers. It has also extended to them newsprint facilities, a rebate from excise duties and so on but the big papers still have an upper hand. Lack of adequate newsprint continues to be one of the main problems for the small periodicals. The recently announced liberalisation policy regarding the import of newsprint will give an added advantage to big papers and rich units. The small magazines will have to trap the local or regional advertising and bank on contents which are dear to their segmented readers.

Q13. What are the circulation problems?

Ans. The chronic problems of small periodicals are income from advertising may keep a magazine going for some period but if circulation drops, for whatever reason, so would the advertiser's enthusiasm to buy space in it. As a bulk of the periodicals have low circulation, their financial viability constantly remains in doubt. Most of the small and tiny periodicals brought out from the mofussil areas survive from one publication to the next by sheer passion. The high price per copy, a large number of readers sharing the same copy, inadequate development of road transport in the interior parts of the country and unsatisfactory distribution facilities limit the circulation of magazines. Besides, illiteracy, poor purchasing power and low reading habits of the rural population are the broad-based reasons for low circulation.

Need for a Public Relations: Therapy Public relations and scientific promotion are new dimensions in the publishing trade though these are still in an infant stage in our country. The adoption of proper circulation drives can make the magazines more acceptable to potential readers and thus accomplish larger sales. The introduction of reader surveys can result in improved contents of the magazines and thus promote their commercial interest. The National Readership Surveys by the Indian Market Research Bureau and the Operation Research Group already cover the press, radio, television and film media to gauge the reading/listening/viewing habits and their socio-economic backgrounds. Many of these ventures are primarily for advertisers. Only a few newspapers and magazines independently conduct readership surveys to improve the contents, write style and design of their magazines. There are some irritants which require PR application. The editorial staff does not explain to the writers while soliciting an article, the nature, length, style and scope of the write-up and the type of illustrations to be used. Other flaws are delayed payments and replies, heavy editing without taking the author into confidence and blunt refusals. Most of the periodicals do not have even attractive readers columns where the readers could come out with their comments, suggestions and contributions. This is important for establishing a two way communication between the readers and producers of magazines. Poor payment in the case of articles perhaps explains the reluctance on the part of well-known writers to accept magazine assignments. They accept these assignments only when they do not have other lucrative assignments and mostly as a short-term arrangement. With literacy increasing steadily and the country making economic progress, both in rural and urban areas, there is a tremendous readership potential in India. Publishers can adopt ingenious promotion techniques. They-need not make loud claims, but resort to persuasive and credulous pleadings or appeals tied to the needs of the target readers. Here are some promotional devices which could be employed profitably:

- Promotion of sales on news-stalls, sales depots of other public places;
- Soliciting advance subscriptions by issuing appropriate direct mail literature;
- Simulation of the sale of advertising space;
- Building up of goodwill or corporate image;
- Promoting understanding of the contents of the publications;
- Making editorial contents more effective and problem solving;
- Seeking wider involvement of readers;
- Making advertisements more attractive and creative

Challenges from Other Media: Periodicals are exposed to competition from the electronic media, including video magazines. Satellite TV and cable TV pose quite a challenge. These media are captivating the mind and time of the people. To play its due role, the magazine publishers must make their magazines still more attractive, vibrant and satisfying. The squaring prices are no doubt a great hindrance but that makes, it all the more necessary for the magazines to step up their efforts to improve their quality, enhance their popularity and ensure adequate circulation and advertising support.

It is a professional obligation on the part of magazines to cater to the needs of diverse readership, from the elite to the common man, from the urbanites to ruralites, from people with deep interest in specialised areas to people with superficial interest in many areas.

Q14. Write a short note on the following:

(a) Principles of journalism

Ans. Journalistic ethics and standards comprise principles of ethics and good practice applicable to journalists. This subset of media ethics is known as journalism's professional "code of ethics" and the "canons of journalism". The basic codes and canons commonly appear in statements by professional journalism associations and individual print, broadcast, and online news organisations.

While various codes may have some differences, most share common elements including the principles of truthfulness, accuracy, objectivity, impartiality, fairness, and public accountability, as these apply to the acquisition of newsworthy information and its subsequent dissemination to the public.

Like many broader ethical systems, the ethics of journalism include the principle of "limitation of harm." This may involve the withholding of certain details from reports, such as the names of minor children, crime victims' names, or information not materially related to the news report where the release of such information might, for example, harm someone's reputation.

(b) Role of journalism

Ans. A reporter is a type of journalist who researches, writes and reports on information in order to present using sources. This may entail conducting interviews, information-gathering and/or writing articles. Reporters may split their time between working in a newsroom, or from home, and going out to witness events or interviewing people. Reporters may be assigned a specific beat or area of coverage.

Depending on context, the term journalist may include various types of editors, editorial-writers, columnists, and visual journalists, such as photojournalists (journalists who use the medium of photography).

According to Prof. John Hobenburg, a journalist should stick to the following four ideas:

- He should imbibe a never-ending search for the truth;

- He should be able to meet the needs of the changing times, instead of waiting to be overtaken by them;
- He should be able to perform services of some consequence and significance to mankind;
- He should maintain steadfast independence.

A journalist is an important unit of the democratic system in our country. He is supposed to gather facts, organise them and disseminate them to the masses. He also explains the significance of the facts and offers opinions on contemporary issues. He is expected to comment on matters of public interest in a fair, accurate, unbiased, sober, decent and responsible manner. A journalist must be cool, detached, even skeptical as he approaches his material. The right "attitude" is an important prerequisite for a successful journalist. He should have a high degree of skill in organising material and in using the language. He should not be lacking in confidence but should not be over-confident or overenthusiastic. He should avoid distortion in the news story in an effort to attain a striking effcct. "Attribution" or the "name of the source" is another thing which should not be overlooked. The best attribution is the name of the precise source. The next best is the name of the organisation, office or group, represented by the source as a spokesman. The least satisfactory, but sometimes the most necessary, IS some variation of the phrase, "informed source" if the origin of the news must be held in confidence.

(c) Responsibilities of journalism

Ans. Journalists educate the public about events and issues and how they affect their lives. They spend much of their time interviewing expert sources, searching public records and other sources for information, and sometimes visiting the scene where a crime or other newsworthy occurrence took place. After they've thoroughly researched the subject, they use what they uncovered to write an article or create a piece for radio, television or the internet.

- **Social:** The social responsibility of journalists is of paramount importance. It a now well recognised that "journalism is the mirror of society". The journalist acts as a spokesman of mankind. He must, therefore, provide a truthful, comprehensive, and intelligent account of the events in a context that gives meaning. Facts and opinions must be clearly differentiated by that effective sieve called "objectivity" The press must serve, as a forum for the exchange of comment and criticism. The journalist should act as an effective medium for two-way communication between readers and different organisations of society.

- **Legal:** Publication of baseless, graceless and manipulated material should be avoided at all costs to safeguard yourself and your organisation from the legal clutches. "Libel" or "defamation" is always a "live wire-on which a sensible journalist dreads to tread. He must be well aware of the various laws relating to the press such as Official Secret's Act, Copyright Act; he must always act within the limits of the law and never infringe them.
- **Professional:** Besides social and legal obligations, journalists have certain professional obligations to honour. The basic responsibility of a journalist is to disseminate information in all circumstances, sometimes normal and sometimes otherwise. The information provided helps the readers to make up their minds on vital issues; this may also have a role in shaping their attitudes. In unusual times, a journalist has to think fast and act fast and he must not lose his composure and his sense of objectivity. A journalist is expected to have his commitment to his profession. He must strictly adhere to the accepted professional norms. He has to know the limits within which to operate whether working as a reporter, sub-editor, editorial writer or whatever else, he must keep hi- biases at bay and should endeavour to be fair and balanced in the projection of news and views. Let news not be distorted, suppressed or exaggerated to suit anybody's personal interests- not his own, not his proprietor's, not of any business group, political party or government. Similarly, in the projection of views and comments, only the interests of readers at large, of the community and the country, should be taken into account. In modem times, the news is a business, a competitive business. At times, this profit making exercise results in hasty, biased, ambiguous and sensational reporting. A journalist must avoid such mis demeanour and keep his integrity intact. He must

never jump to premature and incorrect conclusions. The "opinion polls, much in vogue these days, are certainly an exercise in premature judgement and they do interfere in the electoral process". On contentious and sensitive issues, the professional responsibility of a good scribe is to pursue the event and report comprehensively but judiciously. "Follow up" is a very desirable attribute of a good journalist, and this should be put to use as often as possible.

Editor's Responsibilities: Here, we shall enumerate the responsibilities of Under the law, the editor has to assume responsibility for all matter published in the newspaper: news, views and advertisements. An eight-point Editor's Charter adopted by All India Newspaper Editors Conference (AINEC) in 1953. is still valid. It is as follow:

- The Editor shall enjoy complete freedom in respect of the implementation of the editorial policy and the staffing and conduct of the paper.
- The board of management of a newspaper shall prepare an annual budget of editorial expenses in consultation with the Editor, providing the normal expenditure, development programme. contingencies and discretionary grant.
- The Editor's decision shall be final in all matters concerning the editorial staff and the contents of the paper.
- The Editor shall have direct access to the Board or to the proprietor for the discussion of matters relating to his department.
- The Editor shall have the power to grant special increments in recognition of the special merit of a worker.
- The code of obligations for the Editor is to carry out the policy of the paper, to maintain high standards, to resist all pressures, to generate a cooperative spirit among members of the editorial department and to serve impartially the interest of society.
- As far as the editorial side of the newspaper is concerned, the Editor vis-a-vis the Government and the proprietor is to he left free in the discharge of his responsibility.

- In the event of disagreement between the board of management and the Editor leading to the Editor's resignation or removal, the Editor shall be entitled to six months' pay, gratuity and pay in lieu of the leave due to him at the time.

Q15. Explain the ethics of journalism.

Or

Define media ethics. Discuss the need and importance of media ethics in the present context with suitable examples.

[June-2019, Q.No.-9]

Ans. Journalistic ethics and standards comprise principles of ethics and good practice applicable to journalists. This subset of media ethics is known as journalism's professional "code of ethics" and the "canons of journalism". The basic codes and canons commonly appear in statements by professional journalism associations and individual print, broadcast, and online news organisations.

Journalists like other citizens are governed by all the laws of the land. In the profession of journalism, as in other professions, there is a sizeable area of activity which remains out of the domain of law and must be governed by a professional code of ethics. To carry his message effectively, and to maintain the credibility of his newspaper or magazine, a journalist has to disseminate news and views by established norms and traditions of the society. A free press, which is so essential for the functioning of democracy, postulates freedom from fear and violence which, in turn, postulates a strong government capable of coping adequately with the forces of terrorism and disorder. Today it is no secret that newsmen are being threatened and coerced and they are being even physically eliminated. Despite all the provocations and dangers, journalists must function strictly within the framework of ethical norms. Some of the well-accepted ethical norms are as follows:

- **Accuracy and Fairness:** A journalist must inform, and comment on matters of public interest, in a fair, accurate unbiased and decent manner. Inaccuracy and personal remarks should always be avoided.
- **Prepublication Verification:** Verification and checking of news before publication is all the more necessary where its publication, and the comments based thereon, can create complications.

- **Caution Against Defamatory Writings:** Newspapers should not publish anything which is per se defamatory or libellous against any individual or organisation unless, after due care and checking, they have sufficient reason to believe that it is true and that its publication will be for the public good.
- **Privacy:** intrusion or invasion on the privacy of individuals is not permissible unless outweighed by genuine overriding public interest. While publishing names or pictures of victims of sex crimes, great caution should be exercised.
- **Eschew Suggestive Guilt:** Newspapers should eschew suggestive guilt by association. They should not name or identify the family or relatives or associates of a person convicted or accused of a crime when they are innocent and a reference to them is not relevant to the matter reported.
- **Corrections:** When any factual error or mistake is detected or confirmed, the newspaper should publish the correction promptly, with due prominence and with an apology or expression of regret in a case of serious lapse. He should also give due weightage to the right of reply and the letters to the Editor.
- **Communal Reports:** Proper verification must be done before publishing reports regarding communal clashes or disputes. The report should not vitiate the situation. Instead, it should aim at soothing the ruffled feelings.
- **Sensational Headings:** Sensational headings should be avoided. Headlines should conform to the contents of news stories. They should be clear, unambiguous and authentic.
- **Eschew Vulgarity and Obscenity:** Obscene and vulgar items should be done away with as these offend the public's good taste. Also, never glorify violence.
- **Avoid Crass Commercialism:** To make profits, a newspaper should not throw the ethics and journalistic values to the winds. Instead, it should try to create a suitable equilibrium between objectivity and commercialism.
- **Avoid Caste, Religion or Community Disclosures:** In general, a newspaper should not identify a person with his caste, religion or community. It may be derogatory.

- **Respect Confidence:** If information is received from a source confidentially, the confidence should be respected.

Q16. Explain the codes of ethics.

Ans. While journalists in the United States and European countries have led the formulation and adoption of these standards, such codes can be found in news reporting organisations in most countries with freedom of the press. The written codes and practical standards vary somewhat from country to country and organisation to organisation, but there is substantial overlap between mainstream publications and societies. The International Federation of Journalists (IFJ) launched a global Ethical Journalism Initiative in 2008 aimed at strengthening awareness of these issues within professional bodies. In 2013 the Ethical Journalism Network was founded by former IFJ General Secretary Aidan White. This coalition of international and regional media associations and journalism support groups campaigns for ethics, good governance and self-regulation across all platforms of media.

The Chairman of the Press Council of India, Justice R.S. Sarkaria has also advocated the need for a code of ethics for journalists. In his view, the code of ethics is a statement of broad moral principles which will aid and guide the journalists, and which will help them in the process of self-appraisal and self-regulation. Several codes have been formulated from time to time, to guide journalists in their work. Press. being the conscience-keeper of the public must be safeguarded, and the codes are an exercise in this direction. In the present times, when several forces are up in arms for curbing the press freedom and are trying to malign the press, the codes have gained an added significance. It is in this spirit that different codes were framed. In 1968, the All-India Newspaper Editors' Conference (AINEC) formulated a code of ethics. Other codes such as the Parliamentary Code (1976) and the International Code (1991) were also proposed to give direction to the press. Though the Press Council is against cast-iron rules, it has formulated guidelines from time to time.

All-India Newspaper Editors' Conference (AINEC) Code 1968: In 1968 the All-India Newspaper Editors' Conference adopted a code of ethics for the press. It is a useful effort which retains its significance even in present times. It is as follows:

(1) A free press can flourish only in a free society. communalism is a threat to the fabric of our free society and the nation's solidarity.

(2) The press has a vital role to play in the consummation of the fundamental objectives enshrined in our Constitution, namely, democracy, secularism, national unity and integrity and the rule of law. The press must help promote unity and cohesion in the hearts and minds of the people and refrain from publishing material tending to excite communal passions or inflame communal hatred.

(3) To this end, the press should adhere to the following guidelines in reporting on communal incidents in the country:

(i) All editorial comments and other expressions of opinion, whether through articles. letters to the editor or in any other form should be restrained and free from scurrilous attacks against leaders or communities and there should be no incitement to violence.

(ii) Generalised allegations casting doubts and aspersions on the patriotism and loyalty of any community should be eschewed.

(iii) Likewise generalised charges and allegations against any community of unfair discrimination. amounting 10 inciting communal hatred and distrust.

(iv) Whereas truth should not he supposed. a deliberate slanting of news of communal incidents should be avoided.

(v) News of incidents involving loss of life lawlessness, arson, etc. should he described, reported and headlined with restraint in strict objective terms and should not be prominently displayed.

(vi) Items of news calculated to make for peace and Harmony and help in the restoration and maintenance of' law and order should be given precedence and precedence over other news.

(vii) The greatest caution should be exercised in the selection and publication of pictures, cartoons, poems, etc., so as to avoid arousing communal passions or hatred.

(viii) Names of communities should not be mentioned and the terms 'majority' and 'minority' communities are ordinarily used in the course of reports.

(ix) The source from which casualty figures are obtained should always be indicated.

(x) No facts or figures should be published without the fullest possible verification. However, if the publication of the facts or figures is likely to have the effect of arousing communal passions, those facts and figures may not be given.

Press Council Guidelines: The Press Council has laid down guidelines, which if faithfully observed by the media and the authorities, will go a long way in helping them perform their respective roles harmoniously in the troubling situations. These are as follows:

(1) Provocative and sensational headlines should be avoided;

(2) Headings must reflect and justify the matter printed under them;

(3) Figures of casualties given in headlines should preferably be on the lower side, in case of doubt about their exactness and where the numbers reported by various sources differ widely;

(4) Headlines containing allegations made in statements should either identify the personhood making the allegations or, at least, should carry quotation marks.

(5) Comments and value judgements in the presentation of news should be avoided;

(6) Presentation of news should not be motivated or guided by partisan feelings, nor should it appear to be so;

(7) Language employed in writing the news should be temperate and such as may foster the feeling of amity among communities and groups, and

(8) Corrections should be promptly published with due prominence and regrets expressed in serious cases.

Press Council Code on Communal Writings: Today, when communalism and other negative tendencies are posing a danger to the integrity and unity of the country, the Press Council has felt it pertinent to formulate a code of ethics on communal writing. In the present scenario when Ram Janambhoomi - Babri Masjid imbroglio is fast escalating and threatening the very fabric of the nation, this code has acquired even greater importance. It lags down what the press should avoid.

(1) Distortion or exaggeration of facts or incidents about communal matters or giving currency to unverified rumours, suspicions or inferences as if they were facts and basing their comments on them.

(2) Employment of intemperate or unrestrained language in the presentation of news or views, even as a piece of literary flourish or for rhetoric or emphasis.

(3) Encouraging or condoning violence even in the face of provocation as a means of obtaining a redress of grievances whether the same be genuine or not.

(4) While it is the legitimate function of the Press to draw attention to the genuine and legitimate grievances of any community to have the same redressed by all peaceful, legal and legitimate means it is improper and a breach of journalistic ethic, to invent grievances, or to exaggerate real grievances. as these tend to promote communal ill-feeling and accentuate discord.

(5) Scurrilous and untrue attacks on communities or individuals, particularly when this is accompanied by charges attributing misconduct to them as due to their being members of a particular community or caste.

(6) Falsely giving communal colour to incidents in which members of different communities happen to be involved.

(7) Emphasising matters that are apt to produce communal hatred or ill-will or fostering feelings of distrust between communities.

(8) Publishing alarming news which is in substance untrue or making provocative comments on such news or otherwise calculated to embitter relations between different communities or regional or linguistic groups.

(9) Exaggerating actual happenings to achieve sensationalism and publication of news which adversely affects communal harmony with banner headlines or in distinctive types.

(10) Making disrespectful, derogatory or insulting remarks on or regarding the different religions or faiths or their founders.

Parliament Code: Rajya Sabha, the Upper House of the Indian Parliament, adopted in 1976 a code of ethics for journalists and newspapers, in pursuance of its social and moral responsibility. The code is as follows:

(1) In the discharge of their duties, journalists shall attach full value to fundamental human and social rights, shall hold good faith and fair play in news reports and

(2) Journalists and newspapers shall highlight activities of the state and public, promote national unity, solidarity, integrity and economic and social progress.

(3) Journalists and newspapers shall avoid reports and comments which tend to promote tensions or are likely to lead to civil disorder, mutiny or rebellion. Violence must be condemned unequivocally.

(4) Journalists and newspapers shall ensure that information dissemination is factual. No fact shall be distorted nor information known to be false or not believed to be true, shall be published.

(5) No sensational report or tendentious report of a speculative nature shall be published. Any report or comments found to be inaccurate shall be rectified by publications.

(6) Confidence shall always be respected. Professional secrecy shall be preserved.

(7) Journalists shall not exploit their status for non-journalistic purposes or inquiries and shall not allow personal interests to influence professional conduct.

(8) there is nothing so unworthy as the acceptance or demand of a bribe or inducement for the exercise by a journalist of his power to give or deny publicity to news or comment.

(9) Journalists and newspapers shall not indulge in personal controversies in which no public interest is involved.

(10) Journalists arid newspapers shall not give currency to public rumours or gossip or even verifiable news affecting the private life of individuals.

(11) Newspapers shall refrain from publishing matter (including advertisements) which is obscene or is likely to encourage vice, crime and unlawful activities.

(12) Journalists and newspapers shall promote and project the national objectives of democracy, socialism and secularism.

(13) Journalists and newspapers shall refrain from giving tendentious treatment to news of disturbances involving caste, community, class, religion, region or language groupings and shall not publish details of the number or identity of groups involved in such disturbances except as officially authorised.

(14) Journalists and newspapers shall not publish information and comment detrimental to the interest of the sovereignty and integrity of India. the security of the State and friendly relations with foreign countries (newspapers include journals, magazines and periodicals).

International Code of Ethics: In 1991, at the Stockholm Symposium, an International Code of Ethics was drafted and adopted. It applies to everyone working for the press and other media. It is not a legal document and some countries may view some matters differently, according to their legal peculiarities and provisions. Various points in the code are as follows:

(1) The fundamental objective of a journalist is a fair, accurate and unbiased story.

(2) Unnamed sources should not be used unless the pursuit of truth will best be served by not naming the source.

(3) In general, the journalists have a moral obligation to protect confidential sources of information.

(4) Corrections or clarifications should 'be published for errors of fact promptly.

(5) Journalists should identify themselves, except in some exceptional cases.

(6) The use of any obscene or tasteless language should be limited to quoted material.

(7) In principle, journalists should avoid paying for information unless public interest is involved.

(8) Plagiarism, i.e. using some one's work without attribution, is a serious ethical breach, and it should be avoided.

(9) In general. the race of a Derson in the news should not be reported.

(10j) Except, in rare and justifiable circumstances, journalists should not tape anyone without that person's knowledge.

(11) Privacy of an individual should always be safeguarded except in some exceptional cases.

(12) Sex discrimination should not be done.

(13) Journalists should avoid offending individual and yet not compromise their reporting of the news.

(14) Journalists should distinguish clearly between comments, conjectures and facts.

(15) Children should not be identified in reported cases concerning offences.

(16) Living victims of sex crimes should not be identified in the news story.

(17) Journalists should judge no one unheard.

(18) Journalists should maintain the highest professional and ethical standards.

(19) Acts of violence should not be glorified.

(20) Publications of photographs showing mutilated bodies, bloody incidents and abhorrent scenes should be avoided.

Ombudsman: "Ombudsman" is an institution which took its birth in Sweden. The function of the Ombudsman is to establish and maintain smooth relations between the press and the people, between the press and the governments, various associations and political parties, public bodies, court and the Parliament. Some Newspapers in different parts of the world have appointed an Ombudsman to investigate readers' complaints and to survey the performance of newsmen in that organisation. Recently, a retired Chief Justice of India, P.N. Bhagawati has been appointed the Ombudsman of The Times of India.

Q17. Write a brief note on First Press Commission.

Ans. Press Council is a mechanism for the Press to regulate itself. This unique institution is rooted in the concept that in a democratic society the press needs at once to be free and responsible.

If the Press is to function effectively as the watchdog of public interest, it must have a secure freedom of expression, unfettered and unhindered by any authority, organised bodies or individuals. But, this claim to press freedom has legitimacy only if it is exercised with a due sense of responsibility. The Press must, therefore, scrupulously adhere to accepted norms of journalistic ethics and maintain high standards of professional conduct.

Where the norms are breached and the freedom is defiled by unprofessional conduct, a way must exist to check and control it. But, control by Government or official authorities may prove destructive of this freedom. Therefore, the best way is to let the peers of the profession, assisted by a few discerning laymen to regulate it through a properly structured representative impartial machinery. Hence, the Press Council.

The First Press Commission (1954) came across in some section of the Press, instances of yellow journalism of one type or another, scurrilous writing-often directed against communities or groups, sensationalism, bias in presentation of news and lack of responsibility in comment, indecency and vulgarity and personal attacks on individuals. The Commission, however, pointed out that the well-established newspapers had, on the whole. Maintained a high standard of journalism. They had avoided "cheap senstationalism and unwarranted intrusion into private lives." But it remarked that " whatever the law relating to the Press may be, there would still be a large quantum of objectionable journalism which, though not falling within the purview of the law, would still require to be checked." It was of the view that the best way of maintaining professional standards of journalism would be to bring into existence a body of of people principally connected with the industry whose responsibility it would be to arbitrate on doubtful points and to censure any one guilty of infraction of the code of journalistic ethics.

The Press Commission was asked "to inquire into the state of the Press in India, its present and future line of development and, in particular, to examine:

- the control, management and ownership, and financial structure of newspapers, large and small, the periodical press and news agencies and feature syndicates;
- the working of monopolies and chains and their effect on the presentation of accurate news and fair views;
- the effect of holding companies, distribution of advertisements and such other forms of external influence as may have a bearing on the development of healthy journalism;
- the method of recruitment, training, scales of remuneration, benefits and other conditions of employment of working journalists, settlement of disputes,affecting them and factors which influence the establishment and maintenance of high professional standards:
- the adequacy of newsprint supplies and its distribution among all classes of newspapers and the possibilities of promoting indigenous manufacture of newsprint and printing and composing machinery;
- machinery for (a) ensuring high standards of journalism and (b) liaison between Government and the Press; the functioning of press advisory committees.

The Commission also decided that their report contain a section on the history and development of journalism in 1ndia to serve as "background to the inquiry". Mr J. Natarajan, the then editor of The Tribune, Ambala (who had for some time served as a.member of the Press Commission) was entrusted with the task of preparing it.

The Commission did a work of lasting value and presented a clear picture of this important means of mass communication. The Commission was predominated by public element in its personnel. Thus, it was an inquiry on behalf of the people into the working of a significant sector of the democratic set-up. The Commission discussed the principles relating to the Press and the prevailing practices of the time; they considered whether any law required to repeal or amendment. The Commission was equipped with powers to take evidence from all sections of the industry and the public. The report of the Press Commission still serves as a guide not only on matters of principle but also on facts. The Press Commission recommended that the newspaper and periodical industry should be brought within the list of industries under the control of the Union Government. An Act should be passed to regulate the industry and should among other things, provide for the following:

- appointment of Press Registrars both at the Centre and in the States;
- collection of statistics of the newspaper industry;
- fixing by the Government from time to time of a price-page schedule;
- definition and punishment of the practices which are unfair or restrictive;
- laying down the manner in which the accounts of different enterprises should be maintained by a proprietor controlling more than one newspaper or publishing them from more than one centre;
- making the issue and publication of fraudulent advertisement punishable;
- making the new Industrial Relations legislation applicable to newspaper employees;
- prescribing the method of assessment and distribution of profits from the industry, including the payment of bonus to the employees;
- prescribing the terms of employment, including the notice period, minimum wage, leave, provident fund, gratuity, etc.;
- making it compulsory for newspapers to periodically a statement of ownership and control in the form prescribed;

- making provision for the Provident Fund Act to be applicable to the employees.

The Commission suggested new enactments for

- establishing a Press Council;
- bringing into existence a State Trading Corporation for dealing in newsprint and for furnishing finances for the operation of the Press Council;
- establishing a Public Corporation to take over the Press Trust of India; and
- defining the powers, privileges and immunities of legislatures.

Amending legislation would also be necessary in the case of

- the Press and Registration of Books Act;
- the Drugs and Magic Remedies (Objectionable Advertisements) Act;
- the Post Offices Act;
- the Indian Penal Code (repeat of Section 124 A, the addition of a new Section 121 B, amendment of Sections 153 A, 295 A and 499);
- the Criminal Procedure Code (amendment of Sections 99A, 198 and 202);
- the Sea Customs Act and
- the Indian Telegraph Act. With regard to the Press (Objectionable Matter) Act, four of the members said that they would like the Act to lapse after February 1956.

The rest of the members also recognised the essentially temporary nature of the Act and wanted the continuance of the Act after February 1956 dependent on

- the performance of the Press during the next two years and
- efficacy of the Press Council in exercising a restraining influence on the errant section of the Press.

The Government allowed the Act to lapse after February 1956. On "Freedom of the Press," the Commission said: "We think that the expression should be understood as meaning freedom to hold opinions, to receive and to impart information through the printed word, without any interference from any public authority. In a society where the rights of the individuals have to be harmonised with their duties towards society, all fundamental rights and their free play must be subject to restrictions. But the concept of freedom with responsibility should not be pushed to a point where the emphasis on responsibility becomes in effect the negation of freedom itself'. "'The provisions contained in Articles 19(2) of the Constitution are merely enabling provisions, and the ultimate sanction behind any legislation must be the will of the people. The Constitution merely lays down that certain fundamental principles may 1 not be disregarded in attempting to harmonise freedom of expression of an individual with the requirements of the public good. Apart from such safeguards as the Constitution has laid down, there are two other lines of defence against undue encroachment over the fundamental right of freedom of expression. One is the Legislature itself and the other is the High Courts and the Supreme Court. Although the Constitution invests the Legislatures with the power to place restrictions on the freedom of speech and expression for certain purposes, the power would, we trust, be exercised with discrimination and circumspection. I$any restrictions are placed by the Legislatures on the fundamental right, we have no doubt that the impartiality and broad and realistic outlook of the High Courts and Supreme Court will ensure that the power is not exercised by the Legislatures in an arbitrary or unreasonable manner. We, therefore, think that there is no case made out for going back to Article 19(2) of the Constitution as it stood before its amendment in 1951". On this issue, the Commission could not have unanimity. But the differences were within a narrow compass. "With regard to Article lb(2) of the Constitution, the majority recommended that there should be no change in the wordings of the three items that were added by the Constitution (Amendment) Act of 1951:

- in the interest of public order,
- friendly relations with foreign states;
- incitement of an offence. The others (four members) accept the necessity of
- above In respect of (i), they would prefer the wording "for the prevention of disorder" to the words "in I the interest of public order" which is not a substantial change. With regard to (ii), they would omit the clause altogether while the majority would, however, retain the words a: enabling provision".

Q18. What do you mean by press council of India?

Or

Critically analyse the role and function of 'Press Council of India'.

[June-2019, Q.No.-7 (a)]

Ans. The Press Council of India is a statutory, adjudicating organisation in India formed in 1966 by its parliament. It is the self-regulatory watchdog of the press, for the press and by the press, that operates under the Press Council Act of 1978. The Council has a chairman – traditionally, a retired Supreme Court judge, and 28 additional members of which 20 are members of media, nominated by the newspapers, television channels and other media outlets operating in India. In the 28 member council, 5 are members of the lower house (Lok Sabha) and upper house (Rajya Sabha) of the Indian parliament and three represent culture literary and legal field as nominees of Sahitya Academy, University Grant Commission and Bar Council of India.

Justice Chandramauli Kumar Prasad is Chairman of the Council as of 2015. He has been appointed for a second term. The predecessor was Justice MarkandeyKatju (2011 – 2014).

Composition: Under Section 5 of the Press Council Act, 1978, the Council shall comprise of 28 members, apart from the Chairman who is nominated by 8 Committee consisting of the Chairman of the Rajya Sabha, the Speaker of the Lok Sabha and a person elected by the members of the Council. As the Press Council exercises certain quasi-judicial functions, it is desirable that the Chairman should be a person with a judicial background. So far, all the Chairmen have been judges of the Supreme Court. Of the 28 members, 13 are working journalists, 6 from the management of newspapers, one each from news agencies, UniSmity Grants Commission, Bar Council of India and Sahitya Academy and 5 members of Parliament (3 from the Lok Sabha and 2 from the Rajya Sabha).

Powers and Functions: To preserve the freedom of the Press and to maintain and improve the standards of newspapers and news agencies, are the main objectives of the Press Council of India. Section 13 of the Act envisages various functions of the Council for attaining its objectives. The important tasks fo the Council are:

- to build up a code of conduct for newspapers, news agencies, and journalists in accordance with high professional standards;

- to help newspapers and news agencies to maintain their independence;
- to ensure on the part of newspapers, news agencies and journalists, the maintenance of high standards of public taste and foster a due sense of both the rights and responsibilities of citizenship;
- to encourage the growth of a sense of responsibility and public service among all those engaged in the profession of Journalism and also to promote a proper functional relationship among all classes of persons engaged in the production or publication of newspapers or in news agencies;
- to concern itself with developments such as concentration by other aspects of ownership of newspapers and news agencies which may affect the independence of the Press;
- to keep under review cases of assistance received by any newspaper or news agency in India from any foreign source.

The main function of the Council is to hold an inquiry on the receipt of a complaint made to it against a newspaper or a news agency if it has got a reason to believe that an offence against the standards of journalists ethics, or public interest or professional conduct has been committed. In the process of inquiry, principles of natural justice are strictly followed. For the purpose of holding an inquiry, the Council can exercise the same powers as are given to a Civil Court under the Civil Procedure Code in respect of following matters:

- summoning and enforcing the attendance of persons and examining them on oath;
- requiring the discovery and inspection of documents;
- receiving evidence on affidavits; It requisitioning any public record or copies thereof from any court or office;
- issuing commissions for the examination of witnesses or documents; and
- any other matter which may be prescribed.

Under Section 15(3) of the Act, every inquiry held by the Council shall be a judicial proceeding within the meaning of Section 193 and 228 of IPC. It has power to warn, admonish or censure the newspaper, the news agency, the editor or the journalist, as the case may be. The decision of the Council is final and cannot be questioned in any court of law. The Council is not a court of law. Its verdicts are not judicial pronouncements. It is not empowered to impose any punishment nor can it award damages, etc. It is clear that when a newspaper chooses to be recalcitrant, the Council is helpless. The public rebuke, that the Council administers along with the moral obligation of the offending newspaper to publish the Council's decisions, operate both as a penalty and as a deterrent.

Code of Journalistic: Conduct Section 13(2) (b) of the Act empowers the Council to build up a code of conduct for journalists, news agencies and newspapers in accordance with high professional standards. The Council is required to 'build-up' a code and not 'frame' one. "Such a code could be built up case by case over a period of time".

Q19. Write a short note on second press commission.

[Dec-2019, Q.No.-10 (d)]

Ans. The second Press Commission came barely 15 months after the first experience of government censorship that the Indian Press went through during Emergency, 1975-1977. After the emergency was lifted, the new government of India constituted the Second Press Commission on May 29, 1978. The Commission was set up under the chairmanship of Justice P.C. Goswami but he and his colleagues resigned in January 1980, with the formation of new government. The commission was reconstituted in April 1980 under the chairmanship of Justice K. K. Mathew.

The Janata Government in 1977 felt that a comprehensive inquiry was needed. The second Press Commission was appointed under Justice P. K. Goswami, with terms of reference about present constitutional guarantees and safeguarding of the freedom of the press, after the experience of the Emergency. Justice Goswami and his colleagues resigned when the Janata Government went out of office in 1979 and when Charan Singh's Government was formed, they were asked to carry on. Justice Goswami and his colleagues resigned again with the formation of a new Government after the elections of 1980.

The Commission was reconstituted with Justice Mathew as Chairman with fresh terms of reference. Of these, the main was the right to privacy and the role of the press and the responsibilities it should assume in developmental policies. The main thing that emerges from the report of the second Press Commission is that there has been an enormous growth of press since the first Press Commission was appointed and that the problems are the same. The solutions suggested are not basically, different.

The Indian press has grown considerably since the first Commission reported. Still, it is not adequate for .the needs of the people. This is the conclusion that emerges from the report of the second Press Commission, which combined the labours of the Goswami Commission and the Mathew Commission; it was published in 1982. The recommendations made by the Commission to reform the structure of the press are mainly the establishment of a Newspaper Development Commission to help. newspapers financially and in other ways and an autonomous corporation for distribution of Government advertisements fairly and equitably. Such distribution should apply also to private advertising.

Like the first Press Commission, the second Press Commission finds that-While the newspaper industry is largely owned by other industries, there is little orderliness in its structure or working. The first Commission felt handicapped by the lack of any authentic source of statistics. and so did the second Commission. The first Commission wanted that every newspaper, independent or a unit of a chain or group. should be constituted as a separate unit so that its profits and losses were ascertainable and both proprietor and employee knew where they stood.

The recommendation was addressed to management, and the Government agreed with it. But nothing has been done in this regard. The second Press Commission has repeated his recommendation. The Commission has recommended a measure of delinking and has found it to be constitutionally unobjectionable, after examining Supreme Court decisions, particularly in the Sakal (price-page) and Bennett Coleman (page-limit) cases. Four members of the Commission have written a minute of dissent, differing from the arguments and the recommendation of the majority. The Commission also recommends price-page schedule and news-to-advertisement ratio and examines in detail the Supreme Court judgement in the Sakal case and judicial pronouncements in other cases. It is held that even an amendment to the Constitution for this purpose will not destroy or damage the basic structure of the Constitution.

The Commission has also suggested changes in several other laws so that the area of freedom can be enlarged without the present restrictions, written or understood. It has sought to ease pressures on the press.

Q20. what do you mean by broadcasting council?

Ans. Indian Broadcasting Foundation also known as (IBF) is a unified representative body of the television broadcasters in India. The organisation was founded in the year 1999. Over 250 Indian television channels are associated with it. The organisation is credited as the spokesman of India Broadcasting Industry.

The Prasar Bharati Act, 1990 provides for the establishment of a Broadcasting Council It shall consist of:

- A President and ten other members to be appointed by the President of India from amongst persons of eminence in public life;
- Members of Parliament, of whom two from the House of People are to be nominated by the Speaker thereof and two from the Council of States are to be nominated by the Chairman thereof.

The President of the Broadcasting Council shall be a whole-time member and every other member shall be a part-time member and the President or the part-time member shall hold office as such, for a term of three years from the date on which he enters upon his office.

The Broadcasting Council may constitute a such number of Regional Councils as it may deem necessary to aid or assist the Council in the discharge of its functions. The President of the Broadcasting Council shall be entitled to such salary and allowances and shall be subject to such conditions of service in respect of leave, pension (if any), provident fund and other matters as may be prescribed, provided that the salary and allowances and the conditions of service shall not be varied to the disadvantage of the President of the Broadcasting Council after the appointment. The other members of the Broadcasting Council and the members of the Regional Councils constituted under subsection (4) shall be entitled to such allowances as may be prescribed. The Broadcasting Council shall receive and consider complaints from:

- any person or group of persons alleging that a certain programme or broadcast or the functioning of the Corporation in specific cases or in general is not by the objectives for which the Corporation is established;

- any person (other than an officer or employee of the Corporation) claiming himself to have been treated unjustly or unfairly in any manner (including unwarranted invasion of privacy, misrepresentation, distortion or lack of objectivity) in connection with any programme broadcast by the Corporation. A complaint under subsection (13 shall be made in such a manner and within such a period as may be specified by regulations. The Broadcasting Council shall follow such procedure as it thinks, fit for the disposal of complaints received by it.

If the complaint is found to be justified either wholly or in part. the Broadcasting Council shall advise the Executive Member to take appropriate action. If the Executive Member is unable to -accept the recommendation of the Broadcasting Council, he shall place such recommendation before the Board for its decision thereon. - If the Board is also unable to accept the recommendation of the Broadcasting Council it shall record its reasons thereof and inform the Broadcasting Council accordingly.

Q21. What is trade and professional bodies in journalism?

Ans. The main bodies are:

(1) Indian Newspaper Society: (INS) The INS is a representative body of newspapers and periodicals. It was founded in 1939 as Indian and Eastern Newspaper Society (IENS) to promote and safeguard members' business interests incidental to producing their publications to collect and communicate information on subjects of business interest to members and to hold periodical conferences of members to discuss and determine action on matters affecting the newspaper industry. It grants accreditation to advertising agencies which fulfil certain conditions. Since 1940, the IENS (which became INS in 1988) is publishing an annual Handbook containing advertisement rates, circulation and other data for all member publications and relevant information about the accredited agencies. In 1974 it set up a Research and Publications Divisions and started publishing journalism monthly, Indian Press in March; it died down in early 1980's. However, research pamphlets are published from time to time.

(2) Indian Languages Newspapers Association (ILNA): To serve special interests of language newspapers, ILNA was originally founded in 1941. This association of proprietors of newspapers and periodicals published in the Indian Languages has been registered under the Societies Act, 1860 and the Bombay Public Trust Act, 1950, in the year 1970. Any newspaper or periodical published in any of the Indian languages or an organisation or society of newspapers is eligible for membership. Language Press Bulletin is an official organ of the Association and is published monthly in English.

(3) All India Newspaper Editors Conference (AINEC): AINEC is an organisation of newspapers and periodicals as represented by their editors. Founded in 1940, it is chiefly concerned with the interests of the editorial section of the newspaper industry. Any newspaper or periodical published in India qualifies for membership. Those dissatisfied with the functioning of AINEC formed another organisation called Editors Guild "because of the AINEC, though an organisation of editors, is, in reality, a body representing proprietors". The opponents of Editors Guild call it "an organisation of rightist editors".

(4) Indian Federation of Working Journalists (IFWJ): The All India Convention of Journalists held in New Delhi in 1950, clinched the issue. in favour of journalists forming a trade union, thus hying the foundation for the establishment of the Indian Federation of Working Journalists in October 1950. Organisations of journalists had existed in Calcutta, Bombay and Madras for a long time before the New Delhi convention. However, given the nature of their profession, there were many among the journalists who strongly believed that journalists should not organise themselves on trade union lines The Commission's own view was that though working journalists should organise themselves on trade union lines, they should keep aloof from any political bodies or movements in the country, as a development of this type would be inconsistent with the objectivity in the matter of reporting or editing which is a pre-requisite for every genuine journalist.

It was also of the opinion that keeping in view, the number of people who sincerely believed in keeping out of trade unionism, on the score of the special characteristics of their profession, any attempt at "closed shop" (requirement of membership of the union for employment) would be opposed. The Commission further envisaged the possibility of two kinds of organisations co-existing and observed: "In England, there is the National Union of Journalists organised as a trade union which claims a membership of about 30 per cent of the journalists. But there is also the Institute of Journalists which is not incorporated as a trade union, but whose Salaries and Conditions Board, from which employers are excluded, is empowered, on behalf of the Institute, as a certified trade union, to negotiate and to conclude agreements. Although we ourselves look with favour on journalists organising themselves as a trade union, we do not see why the two kinds of organisations should not exist side by side". Hardly had the controversy on the issue of journalists organising themselves as a trade union died down, with the formation of the Indian Federation of Working Journalists. with 22 affiliating state units and membership of 1,500 in 1953, that the leadership of the Federation became sharply divided on the question of "dual membership".

This is related to the members of the I.F.W.J. holding dual membership of the All India Newspapers Editors Conference or pf the composite unions of non-journalists and journalists in individual newspaper establishments. unions composed of journalists and non-journalists, popularly known as composite unions, were in existence long before the formation of the I.F.W J. and there were several instances. as recorded by the Press Commission itself, when the composite unions had championed the cause of journalists in industrial adjudication but failed because industrial tribunals and high courts found that journalists were not covered by the definition of "workmen" under the Industrial Disputes Act, 1947, or the corresponding State Legislation. Since 1950, a large number of such composite unions had come into existence particularly in Delhi such as the Hindustan Times Employees Union, The Times of India and Allied Publications Employees Union, etc.

The argument of the opponents of dual membership was that a composite union would be dominated by non-journalists and since the general trade union movement in the country had political orientation, the result would be that journalists, willy nilly, would come to be used to serve political interests. As regards membership of the All-India Newspapers Editors Conference, the objection was on the ground that its membership was available only to newspapers. and not editors as such, and it was in effect an employers' organisation whose membership was incompatible with the membership of a trade union like IFWJ.

The subsequent developments have only reinforced the need for composite trade unions in the newspaper industry. The Working Journalists Act contemplated the setting-up of a statutory wage board only for journalists employed in the newspaper industry; but when the Central Government was constituting the second Wage Board for Journalists, it had to accede to the demand of the non-journalists for a wage board, though in the first instance it was non-statutory. The strike which continued for more than two months in the newspaper industry, for the implementation of the recommendations of the Wage Board for non-journalists, affected journalists and non-journalists dike, though the IFWJ had not joined the strike.

This was followed by the Government amending the law for constituting statutory Wage Boards for both journalists and non-journalists and since then, common presentations have been made on behalf of journalists and non-journalists before the third and fourth wage boards. Today the terms of employment of working journalists are taken care of, by the provisions of the Working Journalists Act. Experience has shown that in any struggle against the employers, there can be no success unless all the employees support the struggle. The All-India Newspaper Employees Federation which is the only all India Federation of composite and non-composite unions in newspaper establishments, therefore, needs to be broad-based and strengthened in order that it may more effectively discharge this responsibility. When the Indian Federation of Working Journalists was formed in 1950, it was intended to be an organisation not only for fighting for better working conditions for journalists but also for safeguarding their professional interests and the freedom of the Press. The objects of the Federation, among other things, were "to promote and maintain the highest standards of professional conduct and integrity; to strive for the freedom of the Press".

(6) National Union of Journalists (NUJ): (India) The NUJ was born on January 23, 1972. The resolution announcing the birth of NUJ (India) adopted at the convention said. "This national convention of journalists, recognising the strong feelings expressed by delegates from different I States on the need to have an all India organisation of journalists, free from political affiliations of any kind and dedicated to the promotion and safeguarding of professional and economic interests of journalists, resolves to form an all India body called the National Union of Journalists

(India). Founder President of the NUJ, Mr L. Meenakshisundaram, explained the formation of the new organisation in these ringing words:

"The major and the most important reason was that the federation of late had committed itself to a particular political ideology. That was an issue on which there could be no compromise. It cuts at the very root of the professional character of the organisation of working journalists. The last four years witnessed the phenomenon of outside elements, who have practically no stakes in the profession infiltrating into the journalist's movement. Rigged elections with bogus membership lists became the order of the day. A large number of members were either removed from the rolls or expelled without rhyme or reason in utter disregard of the provisions of the constitution. The leadership did, I not come forward to help all victimised journalists. On the other hand, they went out of the way to sabotage the interests of the aggrieved journalists on the sole ground/that they refused to toe the line of the coterie ."

Indian Journalists Union Bogus membership charges were hurled at each other by the two factions of IFWJ before another split in December. 1990. The new organisation that came up at Ranchi is called Indian Journalists Union. It's Secretary-General, Kalyan Chaudhuri said. "We cleared all obstacles and barriers in the way of our endeavour to renew the tradition created by the forerunners of IFWJ which was tarnished by a group of self seekers for the last few years."

Q22. Explain the advertising and public relation bodies.

Ans. Public relations (PR) is the practice of deliberately managing the release and spread of information between an individual or an organisation (such as a business, government agency, or a nonprofit organisation) and the public in order to affect the public perception. Public relations (PR) and publicity differ in that; PR is controlled internally, whereas publicity is not controlled and contributed by external parties. Public relations may include an organisation or individual gaining exposure to their audiences using topics of public interest and news items that do not require direct payment. This differentiates it from advertising as a form of marketing communications. Public relations aims to create or obtain coverage for clients for free, also known as 'earned media', rather than paying for marketing or advertising. But in the early 21st century, advertising is also a part of broader PR activities.

An example of good public relations would be generating an article featuring a client, rather than paying for the client to be advertised next to the article. The aim of public relations is to inform the public, prospective customers, investors, partners, employees, and other stakeholders, and ultimately persuade them to maintain a positive or favourable view about the organisation, its leadership, products, or political decisions. Public relations professionals typically work for PR and marketing firms, businesses and companies, government, and public officials as public information officers and nongovernmental organisations, and nonprofit organisations. Jobs central to public relations include account coordinator, account executive, account supervisor, and media relations manager.

Advertising Agencies Association of India (AAAI): The Advertising' Agencies Association of India, a representative body of the advertising agency profession, was established in 1945. Its membership is open to any organisation, firm or a company carrying on the advertising profession and having a permanent office within the territory of India. The Association introduced in May 1966 an official organ - Promotion to Cover developments pertaining to the advertising industry in India. With a view to promoting healthy competition and a high standard of advertising, the AAAI has adopted a code of standards of advertising practice which covers advertising ethics vis-a-vis the customer and the advertisers.

The Indian Society of Advertisers Ltd.: The Society was founded in July 1952 as an organisation of national advertisers in the country to promote. maintain and uphold sound ethical and economic principles of advertising. The Society periodically organises conferences and seminars on subjects relating to advertis~flg through various media. It publishes surveys and disseminates information useful to members It maintains a library of books and media material on advertising statistics, relevant Acts, rules and regulations. The Society awards the ISA-Khutau Gold Medal to a person or company for making an outstanding contribution in the field of advertising or public relations. The Executive Council runs the day to day administration through its Managing Committee.

Advertising Council of India: The Advertising Council of India was formed on August 20. 1959, as a voluntary association of advertisers, advertising agents, printers and newspapers. The Council is a synthesis of associations representative of companies-bound by the common desire to uphold the cause of advertising and improve its standards and protect the interests of the consumer in particular.

National Council of Advertising Agencies: A representative body of accredited advertising agencies was established in 1967. Its. membership is restricted to organisations, firms or companies that are carrying on advertising business in India, and are Indian-owned. It sponsored the First National Advertising Congress held at New Delhi in 1973.

Public Relations Society of India: The Public Relations Society of India was established in 1958 to promote the recognition of public relations as a profession and to formulate and interpret to the public the objectives and the potentialities of public relations as a function of the management. The Society functioned as an informal body till 1966 when it was registered under the Indian Societies Act with its headquarters in Bombay. The Society has now 13 Chapters namely, Hyderabad, Bangalore, Bombay, Calcutta, Delhi, Ahmedabad, Baroda+ Kerala, Madras, Vishakapatnam, Rajasthan, Bhopal and Chandigarh that organise seminars, lectures and conferences on public relations. Under the new constitution adopted in 1969, these Chapters depute representatives to serve on the National Council which guides and coordinates the plans and policies of the society.

Indian Council of PR Practitioners: The Indian Council of PR Practitioners was established in I983 to promote public relations as a profession. Membership is open to all in the PR profession and working in India. It seeks to maintain a code of practice for PR people in the profession. A quarterly Journal, PR-Today is its official organ.

Q23. State the training institutions of India.

Ans. There are several organisations that impart training in journalism and mass communication.

Press Institute of India (PII): The PII is a professional body of Indian Newspapers and Journals, set up in 1963. It holds professional workshops and seminars for editorial and managerial personnel at all levels; conducts research into press problems; awards fellowships; arranges an exchange of experience amongst newspapers, and organises the selection of Indian journalists for various foreign scholarships, etc. It is a centre for discussion of fundamental problems affecting the Indian Press. It publishes hooks relating to the mass media and a bi-monthly media journal Vidura. It also publishes DATA-INDIA, a weekly archive of developmental information about India. The PI1 edits and produces a feature news service on aspects of Indian developments called DEPTH news. There is no individual membership. Newspapers, periodicals and house journals in India qualify for membership which is corporate.

In 1990, another professional organisation, Research Insitute for Newspaper Development (RIND), was merged with PII. It provides information necessary about the press in India through its monthly bulletin RIND survey

Indian Institute of Mass Communication: The Indian Institue of Mass Communication is a centre for advanced training and research in communication. It is an autonomous society, receiving grant-in-aid from the Ministry of Information and Broadcasting. The Institute maintains a close liaison with professional organisations as also with other centres of learning. The major focus of the Institute has been on conducting orientation courses for officers of the Indian Information Service, conducting training programmes and communication research, holding seminars and workshops. The Institute's instructional courses cover print journalism, audio-visual aids, radio and television, oral communication, traditional media, advertising, campaign planning, public relation and communication research. Most of the foreign participants receive scholarships from the Government of India under the International Technical and Economic Cooperation Scheme, the Colombo Plan and under the Special Commonwealth African Assistance Programme. A few are sponsored under the bilateral cultural exchange programme or by the Commonwealth Secretariat.

QUESTION PAPERS

Introduction to Journalism and Mass Communication: JMC-001

December, 2017

Note: (i) Attempt any five questions. (ii) All questions carry equal marks.

Q1. Explain the process of communication with the help of Schramm's Model of Communication.

Ans. Refer to Chapter-1, Q.No.-11

Q2. Among various Sociological theories of mass communication which one do you consider most relevant in the present Indian context and why? Substantiate your answer.

Ans. Refer to Chapter-1, Q.No.-20

Q3. 'TV is a medium of immediacy'. Discuss the role and relevance of newspapers in the light of this statement in the Indian context.

Ans. Refer to Chapter-2, Q.No.-4 and Q.No.-8

Q4. Discuss the characteristics and elements of an effective media message with suitable examples.

Ans. Refer to Chapter-2, Q.No.-17

Q5. "Radio is an effective medium for development especially in the rural areas". Comment.

Ans. Refer to Chapter-2, Q.No.-7

Q6. Critically analyse the role of traditional folk media in communicating modern themes with suitable examples.

Ans. Refer to Chapter-3, Q.No.-9

Q7. Discuss the contribution of Indian press in India's national movement for freedom.

Ans. Raja Ram Mohan Roy was the founder of the nationalist press in India. Though a few papers had been started by others before him, his Sambad-Kaumudi in Bengali published in 1821, and Mirat-Ul-Akbar in Persian published in 1822, were the first publication in India with a distinct nationalist and democratic progressive orientation.

In 1822, FardaonjiMurzban, the pioneer of the Vernacular Press in Bombay, started Bombay Samachar (still in existence).

The progressive administrative measures of Lord Bentinck gave a fillip to the growth of Indian journalism. Bang Dutt (in Bengali), with the effort of Dwarkanath Tagore, Prasanna Kumar Tagore and Raja Ram Mohan Roy, was founded in 1830.

In Bombay, the Jam-e-Jamshed (in Gujarati) was started in 1831 by P.M.Motiwala. RastGoftar and Akhbar-e-Saudagar was founded.

With the enactment of the Indian Council Act of 1861, both Indian and non-Indian Press expanded. The Times of India which supported the policy of the British Government in India was founded in Bombay in 1861. The Pioneer which supported the landowning and mercantile interests was in Allahabad in 1865. The Madras Mail which represented the interests of the European commercial community was founded in 1868. The Statesman which criticised the government as well as the Indian nationalist groups was founded in Calcutta in 1875. The Civil and Military Gazette which was distinctly an organ of British conservative opinion was founded in Lahore in 1878.

The nationalist press such as The Amrit Bazar Patrika, The Bengali, The Tribune of Lahore, The Hindu, Bangbasi, Basumati, The Kesari, Young India and many others were started during this period. Though the newspaper press was steadily expanding in India, the rate of its growth was slow. The primary reasons were mass illiteracy, great poverty, and repressive Press laws.

Since the Press was a powerful weapon in the development of Indian nationalism and the nationalist movements, it was subjected to restrictions by the British Government which was reluctant to satisfy the aspirations and grant of the demands of Indian nationalism. The very fact that the British government had to enact a series of Press Acts proved the decisive role played by the Press in the development of the nationalist movement.

The history of the Indian Press was the history of the increasing diminution of its liberty, in spite of minor vicissitudes. The history of Indian nationalism proves that the freedom of the Press in India suffered a proportional curtailment.

From the early period a number Indian nationalist leaders fought for the freedom of Press. In 1799, Lord Wellesley appointed an official censor entrusted with the duty of passing all matter for publication and framed drastic rules to punish those who infringed them. Lord Hastings repealed those restrictions in 1818. In 1878, the Vernacular Press Act was enacted. This Act restricted the freedom the vernacular Press. The Vernacular Press Act was repealed in 1882 by Lord Ripon.

Till 1908, the Indian Press enjoyed considerable freedom. However, due to the phenomenal growth of the nationalist movement, the Newspaper Act was passed in 1908 and the Indian Press Act in 1910. The Indian Press enjoyed relative freedom till 1930. However, the Press Law of 1932 and Foreign Relations Act of 1932 diminished the freedom of the Indian Press.

Role of the Press in the national movement: The Press was a powerful factor in building and developing Indian nationalism and nationalist movement, social, cultural, political and economic.

The national movement, on its political side, was possible because of the facility of political education and propaganda provided by the Press. It was a weapon, in the hands of the nationalist groups, to popularise among the people their respective political programmes, policies, and methods of struggle, and to form organisations with a broad popular basis.

With the Press, all India conferences of nationalist organisations could not have been prepared and held and big political movements organised and directed.

Since the Press was a powerful weapon of the nationalist struggles, the Indian nationalists staunchly fought for its freedom throughout the Indian nationalist movement.

The Press alone made possible exchanged of views among different social groups of different parts of the country. The establishment and extension of the Press in India brought about a closer and intellectual contact between the Indian people. It also made possible the daily and extensive discussions of programmes of inter-provincial and national collaboration in sphere of social, political and cultural. National committees were appointed to implement the programmes adopted at these conferences throughout the country. This led to the building of an increasingly rich, complex, social and cultural, national existence.

The Press also helped the growth of provincial literatures and cultures, which were provincial in form and national in content.

The Press was an effective weapons in the hands of social reform groups to expose social evils such as caste fetters, child marriage, ban on remarriage of widows, social, legal and other inequalities from which women suffered and others. It also helped them to organise propaganda against such inhuman institutions as untouchability. It became a weapon in their hands to proclaim to the masses, principles, programmes, and methods of democratic reconstruction of the Indian society.

Further, the Press also brought to the Indian people, knowledge of the happenings in the international world. It became a weapon to constrict solidarity ties between the progressive forces of different countries.Such was the role of the Press in the building up of an increasingly strong national sentiment and consciousness among the Indian people, in the development and consolidation of their growing nationalist movement, in the creation of national and provincial literatures and cultures, and in the forging of bonds of fraternity with other progressive peoples and classes in the outer worlds.

Q8. 'New communication technologies have a marked social impact.' Do you agree with the statement? Substantiate your answer.

Ans. Refer to Chapter-3, Q.No.-14 and Q.No.-15

Q9. Critically analyse the potential of television as a medium of education in the present media scenario, with suitable examples.

Ans. Refer to Chapter-4, Q.No.-12

Q10. Write short notes on any two of the following:

(a) Press Council of India

Ans. Refer to Chapter-5, Q.No.-18

(b) Song and Drama Division

Ans. Refer to Chapter-4, Q.No.-8

(c) Censorship

Ans. Refer to Chapter-3, Q.No.-2 (a)

(d) Soap Operas

Ans. Refer to Chapter-3, Q.No.-7

(e) Audience as Markets

Ans. Refer to Chapter-2, Q.No.-13

❑❑❑

Introduction to Journalism and Mass Communication: JMC-001

June, 2018

Note: At tempt any five questions. All questions carry equal marks.

Q1. What is communication? Explain at least five functions of communication, with suitable examples.

Ans. Refer to Chapter-1, Q.No.-1 and Q.No.-2

Q2. Compare the characteristics of print media and television media. Which, according to you, is more powerful?

Ans. Refer to Chapter-1, Q.No.-5

Q3. What are the Normative theories of mass media? Explain the relevance of the theories in the perspective of contemporary media scenario.

Ans. Refer to Chapter-1, Q.No.-20

Q4. What is survey method? Explain its strengths and limitations with suitable examples.

Ans. Refer to Chapter-1, Q.No.-24

Q5. Discuss the factors which can be used to enhance the effectiveness of media messages, with relevant examples.

Ans. Refer to Chapter-2, Q.No.-17

Q6. Discuss the organisational structure of a media organisation of your choice. Explain the role and responsibilities of the editorial department.

Ans. Refer to Chapter-4, Q.No.-2

Q7. You are reporting at the site of an accident. What ethical dilemma are you likely to face and how will you deal with it?

Ans. As far as essential and honorable careers go, journalism ranks high on the list. Many who enter the field aren't driven by fame and fortune – life as a reporter isn't as glamorous as the Oscar-winning Spotlight would have you believe. Instead, journalists tend to have a passion for promoting truth, awareness, accountability, and engagement within their communities and the world at large. That said, the field of journalism is only as noble as its individual outlets and practitioners. For that reason, establishing and maintaining a personal and professional code of ethics is essential for journalists. Without one, it will be harder to identify and respond to both the red lines and grey areas you might face in your career. As you work toward your journalism degree, think about these five important ethical considerations and how you would approach them as a reporter, editor, or producer.

(1) Protecting Sources: To a journalist, sources are sacred. Ethical reporters will go to great lengths to cultivate and protect sources for the sake of preserving their access and integrity. Some journalists have even risked jail time rather than identify a source such as a government whistleblower or corporate leak. There may be times as a journalist that you have to weigh the promise of anonymity against other factors, including the newsworthiness and credibility of your story or even questions about the source's own motives and reliability.

(2) Protecting Victims: Another basic rule you'll encounter in newsrooms is that certain victims of crimes are not identified by name – particularly when the victim is a child who may have been sexually abused. There are cases, however, when these rules are bent or broken. What if the accuser is a public figure? What if the abuse is incidental to a larger story such as the recovery of a kidnapping victim? You may face these kinds of dilemmas when a victim's right to privacy confronts the news value in play.

(3) Privacy vs. News Value: This kind of dilemma isn't limited to situations like those above. In general, public figures like government officials and celebrities enjoy a lesser degree of privacy than average citizens. How do you know when a matter is too private to report on? What if an ordinary citizen is involved in a genuinely newsworthy story, but reporting on it may require the disclosure of compromising information? Journalists and editors often work together to balance an obligation to accurately report the news while also doing no harm.

(4) Conflicts of Interest: One of the pillars of journalism ethics is impartiality. News stories should be reported fairly, objectively, and without undisclosed conflicts of interest that could influence the reporter's coverage. What if you're assigned to a story about someone you have an existing personal relationship with, whether it's positive or negative? How should a newsroom cover alleged misconduct by a major advertiser? What if the publisher's ownership structure encompasses other newsworthy individuals or companies that you ought to report on? Should a reporter participate directly in an event that he or she is going to write about later? These are all questions you are likely to face if you pursue a career as a journalist.

(5) Audience as Customer: With some exceptions, journalism today is a business first and a profession second. Like any other business, the rules of demand apply. A news outlet's audience is usually its customer base too, so how much of an obligation does an outlet have to produce the kind of stories people want as opposed to news the public needs? At what point does running popular stories undermine a news organization's commitment to meaningful reporting? A publication or broadcast outlet is only as strong as its audience, but reporters also have to remember that journalism plays a unique role in society that most other businesses do not – and act accordingly. These are just a few of the ethical dilemmas you could encounter in your career in the field of journalism. What's key is understanding where the ethical boundaries lie and how to stay on the right side of them, even when it might be easier not to. Doing otherwise ultimately can harm not only your career, but also the profession itself.

Q8. Discuss the features of a news agency. How is its operation different from that of a newspaper?

Ans. Refer to Chapter-4, Q.No.-3

Q9. Critically examine the role and relevance of folk media in today's context, with suitable examples.

Ans. Refer to Chapter-3, Q.No.-9 and Q.No.-11

Q10. Write short notes on any two of the following:

(a) Reach and Access of Mass Media

Ans. Refer to Chapter-1, Q.No.-28

(b) Shannon and Weaver Model of Communication

Ans. Refer to Chapter-1, Q.No.-9

(c) Audience as Market

Ans. Refer to Chapter-2, Q.No.-13

(d) Second Press Commission

Ans. Refer to Chapter-5, Q.No.-19

(e) Films Division

Ans. Refer to Chapter-4, Q.No.-6

Introduction to Journalism and Mass Communication: JMC-001

December, 2018

Note: Attempt any five questions. All questions carry equal marks.

Q1. Among the various models of communication, which according to you is more applicable in the contemporary media scenario? Discuss with examples.

Ans. Refer to Chapter-1, Q.No.-8, Q.No.-9, Q.No.-10, Q.No.-11, Q.No.-12, Q.No.-13 and Q.No.-14

Q2. Discuss the `gatekeeping' role of mass media with suitable examples from India.

Ans. Refer to Chapter-1, Q.No.-14

Q3. "The concept of audiences has changed in the recent times." Do you agree with the statement? Substantiate your answer.

Ans. Refer to Chapter-2, Q.No.-12

Q4. Critically examine the role of films in raising social awareness, with examples.

Ans. Refer to Chapter-2, Q.No.-9

Q5. Compare and contrast the characteristics of radio and television media.

Ans. Refer to Chapter-2, Q.No.-7 and Q.No.-8

Q6. What are the challenges being faced by educational media in the present time? In your opinion, how can these be addressed?

Ans. some new challenges were identified as well.

Challenge 1: professional development. Key among all challenges is the lack of adequate, ongoing professional development for teachers who are required to integrate new technologies into their classrooms yet who are unprepared or unable to understand new technologies.

"All too often, when schools mandate the use of a specific technology, teachers are left without the tools (and often skills) to effectively integrate the new capabilities into their teaching methods," according to the report. "The results are that the new investments are underutilized, not used at all, or used in a way that mimics an old process rather than innovating new processes that may be more engaging for students."

Challenge 2: resistance to change. Resistance to technology comes in many forms, but one of the key resistance challenges identified in the report is "comfort with the status quo." According to the researchers, teachers and school leaders often see technological experimentation as outside the scope of their job descriptions.

Challenge 3: MOOCs and other new models for schooling. New in this year's report, new models for teaching and learning are providing "unprecedented competition to traditional models of schooling." In particular, the MOOC (massive open online course) — probably the hottest topic in higher education right now — was identified as being "at the forefront" of discussions about new modes of delivering K-12 education.

"K-12 institutions are latecomers to distance education in most cases, but competition from specialized charter schools and for-profit providers has called attention to the needs of today's students, especially those at risk," according to the report.

Challenge 4: delivering informal learning. Related to challenge 3, rigid lecture-and-test models of learning are failing to challenge students to experiment and engage in informal learning. But, according to the report, opportunities for such informal learning can be found in non-traditional classroom models, such as flipped classrooms, which allow for a blending of formal and informal learning.

Challenge 5: failures of personalized learning. According to the report, there's a gap between the vision of delivering personalized, differentiated instruction and the technologies available to make this possible. So while K-12 teachers seem to see the need for personalized learning, they aren't being given the tools they need to accomplish it, or adequate tools simply don't exist.

Challenge 6: failure to use technology to deliver effective formative assessments. The report noted: "Assessment is an important driver for educational practice and change, and over the last years we have seen a welcome rise in the use of formative assessment in educational practice. However, there is still an assessment gap in how changes in curricula and new skill demands are implemented in education; schools do not always make necessary adjustments in assessment practices as a consequence of these changes. Simple applications of digital media tools, like webcams that allow non-disruptive peer observation, offer considerable promise in giving teachers timely feedback they can use."

Q7. Discuss the contribution of the Indian Press in India's Independence Movement.

Ans. Refer to Dec-2017, Q.No.-7

Q8. Describe the roles and responsibilities of a journalist in a private television channel.

Ans. Refer to Chapter-5, Q.No.-14

Q9. Describe the important features of new communication technologies and their contribution to mass media.

Ans. Refer to Chapter-4, Q.No.-14

Q10. Write short notes on any two of the following:

(a) Content Analysis

Ans. Refer to Chapter-1, Q.No.-23

(b) Cultivation Theory

Ans. Refer to Chapter-1, Q.No.-20

(c) Osgood's Model of Communication

Ans. Refer to Chapter-1, Q.No.-11

(d) Joshi Committee

Ans. Refer to Chapter-3, Q.No.-7

(e) Vernacular Press Act

Ans. Refer to Chapter-3, Q.No.-3

It's possible to go on,
no matter how impossible it seems.
-Nicholas Sparks

Introduction to Journalism and Mass Communication: JMC-001

June, 2019

Note: Attempt any five questions. All questions carry equal marks.

Q1. "Communication regulates and shapes all human behaviour." Discuss various functions of communication in the light of above statement.

Ans. Refer to Chapter-1, Q.No.-2

Q2. Analyse the role of different components of communication in the process of communication with the help of a model of your choice.

Ans. Refer to Chapter-1, Q.No.-8, Q.No.-9, Q.No.-10, Q.No.-11, Q.No.-12, Q.No.-13 and Q.No.-14

Q3. "Print media serve the information needs of audience better than television." Do you agree with the statement? Substantiate your answer.

Ans. Refer to Chapter-2, Q.No.-4

Q4. Describe the nature and characteristics of effective communication with suitable examples.

Ans. Nature of Effective Communication:

(1) Two-way process: Communication is a two-way process of understanding between two or more persons – sender and receiver. A person cannot communicate with himself.

(2) Continuous process: Exchange of ideas and opinion amongst people is an ongoing process in business and non-business organisations. Continuous interaction promotes understanding and exchange of information relevant for decision-making.

(3) Dynamic process: Communication between sender and receiver takes different forms and medium depending upon their moods and behaviour. It is, thus, a dynamic process that keeps changing in different situations.

(4) Pervasive: Communication is a pervasive activity. It takes place at all levels (top, middle, low) in all functional areas (production, finance, personnel, sales) of a business organisation.

(5) Two people: A minimum of two persons — sender and receiver — must be present for communication to take place. It may be between superiors, subordinates and peer group, intra or inter se.

(6) Exchange: Communication involves exchange of ideas and opinions. People interact and develop understanding for each other.

(7) Means of unifying organisational activities: Communication unifies internal organisational environment with its external environment. It also integrates the human and physical resources and converts them into organisational output.

(8) Verbal and non-verbal: Though words are active carriers of information, gestures can sometimes be more powerful than words. Facial expressions, sounds, signs and symbols are the non-verbal forms of communication.

(9) Mutual understanding: Communication is effective when sender and receiver develop mutual understanding of the subject. Messages conveyed should be understood by the receiver in the desired sense.

(10) Goal-oriented: Communication is goal-oriented. Unless the receiver and sender know the purpose they intend to achieve through communication, it has little practical utility.

(11) Foundation of management: Though communication is a directing function, it is important for other managerial functions also. Designing plans and organisation structures, motivating people to accomplish goals and controlling organisational activities; all require communication amongst managers at various levels.

(12) A means, not an end: Communication is not an end. Effective communication is a means towards achieving the end, that is, goal accomplishment. It smoothens managerial operations by facilitating planning, organising, staffing, directing and controlling functions.

(13) Human activity: Since communication makes accomplishment of organisational goals possible, it is essential that people understand and like each other. If people do not understand each others' viewpoint, there cannot be effective communication.

(14) Inter-disciplinary: Communication is the art of how communicators use knowledge of different fields of study like anthropology, psychology and sociology. Making best use of these disciplines makes communication effective. It is, thus, an inter-disciplinary area of management.

Now, Refer to Chapter-1, Q.No.-3

Q5. Describe the main features of a News Agency. Explain how the functioning of a news agency differs from newspapers organisation.

Ans. Refer to Chapter-4, Q.No.-3

Q6. "Journalist acts as a harbinger of social change. Critically examine the role and responsibilities of journalists citing suitable examples.

Ans. Refer to Chapter-5, Q.No.-14

Q7. Critically analyse the role and functions of any two of the following:

(a) Press Council of India

Ans. Refer to Chapter-5, Q.No.-18

(b) Press Information Bureau

Ans. Refer to Chapter-4, Q.No.-6

(c) Central Board of Film Certification

Ans. Refer to Chapter-4, Q.No.-6

Q8. Trace the growth and development of a Hindi or regional language newspaper of your choice.

Ans. Refer to Chapter-5, Q.No.-6

Q9. Define media ethics. Discuss the need and importance of media ethics in the present context with suitable examples.

Ans. Refer to Chapter-5, Q.No.-15

Q10. Write short notes on any two of the following:

(a) Content Analysis

Ans. Refer to Chapter-1, Q.No.-23

(b) Mass Society

Ans. Refer to Chapter-2, Q.No.-11

(c) Joshi Committee

Ans. Refer to Chapter-3, Q.No.-7

(d) Documentary Films

Ans. Refer to Chapter-4, Q.No.-9

Introduction to Journalism and Mass Communication: JMC-001

December, 2019

Note: Attempt any five questions. All questions carry equal marks.

Q1. Define communication research and discuss its scope and applications in the Indian context.

Ans. Communication research is concerned with identifying, exploring, and measuring the factors that surround communication, in any form and regarding any topic. Often from a theory-driven perspective, but increasingly with empirically-grounded methods.

Now, Refer to Chapter-1, Q.No.-22 and Q.No.-25

Q2. Among the normative theories of mass media, which according to you is more relevant in the Indian context. Substantiate your answer.

Ans. Refer to Chapter-1, Q.No.-20

Q3. Discuss the new trends in Print media with suitable examples.

Ans. Refer to Chapter-2, Q.No.-4

Q4. "The commercialisation of media has led to a situation where audiences are treated as markets. Do you agree with the statement? Give reasons for your answer with examples.

Ans. Refer to Chapter-2, Q.No.-13

Q5. Write a detailed note on any one of the following:

(a) Origin and development of radio in India.

Ans. Refer to Chapter-3, Q.No.-6

(b) Indian Film Industry.

Ans. Refer to Chapter-4, Q.No.-9

Q6. Discuss the role of Folk media in communicating modern themes citing suitable examples.

Ans. Refer to Chapter-3, Q.No.-11

Q7. Discuss the main characteristics and features of the new communication technologies.

Ans. Main characteristics:

- **Immateriality:** they carry out the process of creating essentially immaterial information, which can be transposed with transparency and instantaneously to distant places.
- **Interactivity:** the tics make possible the exchange of information between a user and a computer, and it is precisely this interaction that allows to adapt the resources used to the requirements and characteristics of said user.
- **Interconnection: it** has to do with the creation of new possibilities, starting from the link between two technologies. An example of interconnection is telematics, which results from the union between information technology and communication technologies, and has given rise to new tools such as the famous e-mail or *e-mail.*
- **Instantaneity:** this feature refers to the ability of Communication Technologies to transmit information over long distances and in a very fast manner.
- **Digitization:** information is represented in a unique universal format, which allows sounds, texts, images, etc., to be transmitted through the same means.
- **Wide scope that covers the cultural, economic, educational fields, among others:** Communication Technologies have not only generated a considerable impact in a single area or in a specific group of individuals, but have also expanded and penetrated important areas such as the economy , education, medicine, among others, all this at a global level.
- **Greater influence on processes than on products:** Communication Technologies not only give individuals the possibility of accessing a large amount of information to build knowledge from it, but also allows them to do so through association with other connected users to network. Individuals have a greater role in the creation of knowledge collectively.
- **Innovation:** the development of tics has been characterized by generating a need for innovation, especially with regard to the social field, giving rise to the creation of new means to enhance communications.
- **Examples of CT**

Television
Radio
The landline and mobile phone
MP3 players
Memory cards
Portable digital versatile discs (DVD)
Global positioning system (GPS) devices
Computers:

- **Diversity:** information and communication technologies do not fulfill a single purpose, on the contrary, they are quite useful for the execution of more than one function. In this way, they can be used to carry out communication between people, as well as for the creation of new information.
- **Tendency to automation:** the development of tools for the automatic management of information in a large number of social and professional activities is discussed.

Features

- **They facilitate long distance communication.** There are fewer and fewer barriers that hinder the interaction between each other, since information and communication technologies have made it possible to exchange messages remotely and instantaneously.
- **They provide access to abundant and varied information.** we can be aware of what happens in any part of the world, in addition to having information from different sources but that revolves around the same topic.

They allow the development of activities or operations through the network, as is the case of popular *e-commerce* or electronic commerce, which has greatly facilitated the lives of its users and every day continues adding more and more of them. In this way, our need to move and leave the physical space in which we find ourselves to obtain a product have considerably decreased. Like e-commerce, other similar terms have also been developed, such as e-business (e-business), e-health (e-health), e-government (e-government), e-learning (e-learning), e- work (teleworking), and the already well-known e-mail (e-mail), all thanks to the impact generated by the application of ICT in the different sectors of society and the global economy.

- **They give rise to the creation of new jobs** in the area of telecommunications (teleworking), and have made possible the emergence of new professions such as: software engineer, multimedia designer and web designer, network engineer, network technician, computer teacher, teleworker, etc.
- **Information and Communication Technologies favor the promotion of business and business activity**, through the combination of the internet and marketing.

Q8. Critically analyse the role and functions of any two of the following in detail:

(a) Central Board of Film Certification

Ans. Refer to Chapter-4, Q.No.-6

(b) Films Division

Ans. Refer to Chapter-4, Q.No.-6

(c) Directorate of Film Festivals

Ans. Refer to Chapter-4, Q.No.-6

Q9. Describe the challenges being faced by magazines with suitable examples.

Ans. The Indian Media and Entertainment sector will cross the $40 billion mark by 2021 flourishing at the compounded annual growth rate. The industry is going through a great transformation with the increasing importance of digital media. The process of economic liberalization has taken another significant step by opening up the print media sector. The Government also announced the customs duty exemption on newsprint.

Despite having these growth symbols, the magazine industry in India is going through a tough phase. The increased penetration and adoption of the Internet in the country is the main problem. Now, people are consuming news and stories on the web and mobile. Presently, India has 49,000 publications, but when it comes to revenue it is just $1.1 billion.

The major challenges of the Magazines Industry:

Reduced Revenue: In this modern-day publisher's revenues are going down as readers are increasingly going for free content within the pages of the magazine. With print circulation also on the declines and ad blockers on the growth in digital magazines, it prevents any earning coming into magazine companies.

Online Competition: The increasing online competition is becoming an unsolved puzzle for the print industry. Online articles can be posted any minute at any time and reach readers quickly. It causes a serious problem for magazines to be able to keep up with all the latest articles and data and be able to get their story out first to their readers.

Regional languages: The Indian print industry is highly fragmented due to various local languages. As per the data, the regional language publications own 46% of the market share, Hindi language publications cover 44% and the remaining 10% is served by English publications. The English language magazines are limited to metros and urban centers though the growth is increasing to smaller cities as the education and income levels rise among the middle class.

Quality in Print Content: Increasing demand for high-quality print content and magazines is introducing another issue for the print industry. They need to deliver the quality people want, to avoid losing market share to other mediums. Besides, they also need to explore and offer their content on the websites and mobile platforms to present multiple options to their subscribers to read content from anywhere and at any time. In the limited earning scenario, it is becoming a tough nut to crack for publication houses.

Additional Problems: Apart from the above, reduction of paid circulation sales, dependency on advertising revenue, and consolidation of distributors, ad agencies, retailers and suppliers that leaves a small amount of room for price negotiations are some other primary issues in the magazine industry in India.

Q10. Write short notes on any two:

(a) Individual Difference Theory

Ans. Refer to Chapter-1, Q.No.-18

(b) Survey Research

Ans. Refer to Chapter-1, Q.No.-23

(c) Creative Ad message

Ans. Refer to Chapter-2, Q.No.-20

(d) Second Press Commission

Ans. Refer to Chapter-5, Q.No.-19

❑❑❑

Feedback is the breakfast of Champions.

Ken Blanchard

You can Help other students.
"Inform any error or mistake in this book."

We and Universe
will reward you for Your Kind act.

Email at : feedback@gullybaba.com
or
WhatsApp on 9350849407

Wondering who is Gullybaba?

© Gullybaba is a combination of two significant words '**Gully**' & '**Baba**'. The word 'Gully' comes from the ancient game played in Rural India–**Tip cat.** In Hindi, we call it **Gully Danda** (गुल्ली डंडा) which is a great **symbol of Focus & Fitness.**

The word 'Baba' stands for **Respect & Honour**. And these are the fundamental parameters for achieving success. **Focus & Fitness** are required to help one go a long way in life. This is all about achieving excellence in education and giving respect & honour to everyone, and thus, the name 'Gullybaba'.

To know more about why name GullyBaba visit: **GullyBaba.com/why-name-gullybaba.html**

NOTES

NOTES

www.ingramcontent.com/pod-product-compliance
Ingram Content Group UK Ltd.
Pitfield, Milton Keynes, MK11 3LW, UK
UKHW021707190726
13853UKWH00001B/451

9 789381 970782